PlayStation

Top

YACHT RACES

OF THE WORLD

PRIMAGAZ
PRIMAGAZ
PRIMAGAZ
PRIMAGAZ
L'ENERGIE D'ALLER PLUS LOIN

Top YACHT RACES OF THE WORLD

Foreword by PETE GOSS

SUE & ANTHONY STEWARD

CB
CONTEMPORARY BOOKS

DEDICATION

For our sons: Shackleton and Selbourne, and in loving memory of Morgan.

This edition first published in 2001
by Contemporary Books, a division of
NTC/Contemporary Publishing Group, Inc.
4255 West Touhy Avenue
Lincolnwood (Chicago), Illinois 60712-1975
U.S.A.

ISBN 0-8092-9321-8

Library of Congress Catalog Card Number: on file
Published in conjunction with New Holland Publishers (UK) Ltd.

DESIGNER **PETER BOSMAN**
PUBLISHER AND EDITOR **MARIÉLLE RENSSEN**
ILLUSTRATOR **STEVEN FELMORE**
CARTOGRAPHER **JOHN LOUBSER**
PICTURE RESEARCHER **CARMEN WATTS**
CONSULTANTS **JEFF TOGHILL (AUSTRALIA)**
JOYCE TALBOT (NEW ZEALAND)
DONALD REID (UK)

Reproduction by
HIRT & CARTER (PTY) LTD, CAPE TOWN

Printed and bound in Singapore by
TIEN WAH PRESS (PTE) LTD

2 4 6 8 10 9 7 5 3 1

Half title page CREWMAN OPERATING 'COFFEEGRINDER' WINCH ONBOARD A WHITBREAD 60 BOAT.

Title page LAURENT BOURGNON'S TRIMARAN *PRIMAGAZ* FLYING ON TWO HULLS.

These pages THE US TEAM, WINNERS OF THE 1997 ADMIRAL'S CUP, ON *FLASH GORDON*.

Pages 6–7 JOSH HALL'S *GARTMORE* UNDERGOING SEA TRIALS FOR THE 1998 AROUND ALONE RACE.

MUMM
CHAMPAGNE
20 U.S.A.

CONTENTS

PRADA
PRADA

FOREWORD

by Pete Goss

YACHT RACING IS ABOUT PERSONAL CHALLENGE – whether as part of a team or as an individual – sailors pitting themselves, physically and mentally, against the natural elements which can, and do, constantly test them in unexpected ways. It is also about placing their confidence in the craft that will take them into the heart of the challenge.

I have personally experienced the indescribable thrill and powerful emotions of sailing a good race, or confronting a crisis at sea, described eloquently in the stirring human dramas throughout this book. The Vendée Globe round the world race gave me great insight into the rigorous preparation that is required for the race, and the focus and single-minded determination demanded of the solo sailor. Equally, crewed races such as the British Steel Challenge emphasized for me that one cannot underestimate the role of team spirit, both in terms of sharing difficult situations while at the mercy of wind and water, and the hardships of living at such close quarters with fellow sailors under testing conditions.

And, of course, I speak from personal experience of the agony one undergoes when an ambitious project is faced with overcoming a huge and unanticipated hurdle before moving on again – the well-publicized incident of 28 March 2000, when the port hull of my 36.5m (120ft) catamaran *Team Philips* cracked and tore off during sea trials, in preparation for the Jules Verne Trophy. After two years of intense planning and construction, our dream was shattered. Again, it highlights the tenuous thread that binds sailor and craft – as crewmate Paul Larsen aptly summed it up, 'Your future hangs on a couple of strands of carbon' – and underscores the testing by the elements of body and mind. We can, however, console ourselves that this didn't occur deep in the Southern Ocean, where the icy waters could have proved fatal to the boat's team. So, in the words of fellow crew member Mike Calvin, 'The dream is not dead. Merely on hold.'

The fact remains that, despite the dramas that play themselves out on the world's oceans, the thrill of challenge will continue to draw brave individuals, prepared to push themselves to the limit. And though – in the spirit of fairness and the need to give every sailor an equal chance – the introduction of handicapping has balanced the smaller boat wins with the line honours victories of the big, hi-tech yachts (backed by enormous budgets), most of the races in this book were originally established for 'first home' wins. The handicap concept works – but the excitement of an event such as the forthcoming The Race, which has a 'no limits' ruling, encourages daring that stretches the imagination: emotions that are admirably captured in the fusing of text and superb photographs in this beautiful book.

Opposite *PRADA LUNA ROSSA* LEADS THE PACK IN THE QUARTERFINALS OF THE 1999 LOUIS VUITTON CUP, THE CHALLENGER ELIMINATION SERIES IN THE RUN-UP TO THE AMERICA'S CUP COMPRISING THREE ROUND ROBIN ELIMINATION SERIES, A SEMI-FINAL SERIES AND A FINAL MATCH.

This page PETE GOSS AND HIS GIANT WAVE-PIERCING CATAMARAN, *TEAM PHILIPS* (THE WORLD'S LARGEST), WHICH BEARS TWO WISHBONE RIGS.

AN INTRODUCTION TO YACHTING FIRSTS

THE LIST OF 'FIRSTS' IN SAILING is a Who's Who of yachting history. Portuguese adventurer Ferdinand Magellan was the first to lead an expedition, under the Spanish flag, which, as far back as 1519, successfully circumnavigated the world (the trip was completed in 1522). He set off with a fleet of five ships manned by 240 sailors. Magellan was killed in the Philippines whilst attempting to convert the native Filipinos to Christianity, and only 17 of his crew survived the voyage to return on the *Vittoria*. Englishman Sir Francis Drake was the first sailing commander to complete a circumnavigation in his own ship, *Golden Hind*, from 1577 to 1580.

In 1895 Joshua Slocum, Canadian-born but later a naturalized American, initiated the concept of solo adventure at sea. Slocum left Boston on his self-restored boat *Spray*, an 11m-long (36.5ft) sloop. After three years of erratic navigation and 46,000 nautical miles (85,100km), Slocum arrived in Newport (Rhode Island, USA), having completed the first around-the-world solo trip on a sailboat.

Then in 1942 an Argentinian farmer, Vito Dumas, became the first person to circumnavigate the globe via the Southern Ocean on his 9m (31ft) ketch, *Lehg II*.

From 1955–59, the tiny 6m (20ft) *Trekka* manned by lone UK sailor John Guzzwell sailed her way into the records by achieving the first British solo circumnavigation – and being the smallest yacht to do so.

American teenager Robin Lee Graham set off on his yacht *Dove* in 1965, at the age of 16, finishing five years later to become the youngest round the world sailor, at the age of 21 years and two months. A year later, Briton Sir Francis Chichester achieved a round the world trip on *Gipsy Moth III* in only nine months, with a sole stop in Sydney, Australia. This incredible feat inspired the very first race around the world, the Golden Globe challenge, sponsored by UK-based *The Sunday Times*, who put up a prize of £5000. The aim was to achieve the fastest nonstop, single-handed voyage around the world, sailing from anywhere in the UK on any day before 31 October 1968. Nine yachts took up the challenge, all at different times, but only one person was successful in completing the circumnavigation – Briton Robin Knox-Johnston, on his 10m (33ft) ketch, *Suhaili*. The 30-year-old Royal Navy reservist finished the race in 313 days, after having covered 30,123 nautical miles (55,727km). His was the longest time spent solo at sea.

Controversy surrounds the issue of who holds the record of being the first person to sail alone around the world nonstop. Although Knox-Johnston officially won the race, it has been claimed that Frenchman Bernard Moitessier crossed his own outward path on his 11m (36.5ft) ketch *Joshua* prior to Knox-Johnston's title claim. While Knox-Johnston did sail around the globe, starting and ending in the port of Falmouth at the southwestern tip of England, Moitessier left Plymouth (further east of Falmouth) and headed south. It was 145 days later that he recrossed his path some 700 miles (1295km) west of Cape Town before deciding to continue to cross the Indian Ocean (and carry on with his circumnavigation) a second time.

Top NATURALIZED AMERICAN JOSHUA SLOCUM IS THE FIRST PERSON TO HAVE CIRCUMNAVIGATED THE WORLD, SINGLEHANDEDLY, ON A YACHT – WHICH HE ACHIEVED IN THREE YEARS.

Left IN 1967, SIR FRANCIS CHICHESTER REDUCED SLOCUM'S THREE-YEAR RECORD OF A SOLO ROUND-THE-WORLD TRIP TO ONLY NINE MONTHS, ALTHOUGH IT INCLUDED ONE STOPOVER.

This 'recrossing of the outer path' has led to the controversial issue of what exactly constitutes a circumnavigation.

Ironically, Briton Nigel Tetley, who was also a participant in the Golden Globe on his yacht *Victress*, crossed his own outward path only 2 hours 35 minutes after Knox-Johnston sailed into his home port. Tetley was never granted recognition of his feat as his boat broke up and sank before he reached port. He had been involved in a psychological race against fellow British contender Donald Crowhurst, who had been feeding him with fictitious positionings, causing Tetley to push his boat beyond limitations. Crowhurst's trimaran was later found adrift; his diary supplied evidence that he had never followed the course he'd led race authorities and fellow contenders to believe. His body was never found.

During the 1970s, great strides were made in the marine industry: technical improvements in yacht construction, marine forecasts, and the fact that sailors were able to better equip themselves for long-distance sailing. In 1971, Briton Chay Blyth succeeded in his 292-day nonstop round the world trip, sailing from east to west against prevailing winds and currents, and around the three Capes (South America's Cape Horn, South Africa's Cape of Good Hope and Australia's Cape Leeuwin). He also was credited with having sailed the largest monohull (his 18m/59ft ketch *British Steel*) around the world.

In 1973, Frenchman Alain Colas completed his round the world trip on his 21m (69ft) multihull *Manureva*, in a record time of 169 days with only one stopover in Sydney.

After then, attempts to beat the time record were numerous, and the records fell. In 1985, US sailor Dodge Morgan reduced the record for a round the world, nonstop trip to 150 days. Frenchman Philippe Monet, on a trimaran called *Kriter*, needed only 129 days to pulverize the time record for a Brest to Brest trip, alone and with a few technical stopovers.

In 1993 South African Anthony Steward (co-author of this title) was the first person to sail around the world alone, in an open boat, while in 1984 Australian Serge Testa sailed around the world in the smallest yacht ever, *Acrohc Australis* – it was 4m (13ft 1in) long.

The fastest solo circumnavigation record presently held is that of Frenchman Christophe Auguin, which he achieved in the last Vendée Globe Challenge in 105 days 20 hours 31 minutes 23 seconds. The as yet unbroken record for the fastest crewed circumnavigation was set by the latest holder of the Jules Verne Trophy, French skipper Olivier de Kersauson, which he accomplished on his 27m (90ft) trimaran *Sport-Elec* in 71 days 14 hours 18 minutes.

In terms of 'firsts' achieved by women in global sailing, New Zealander Naomi James, at the age of 28, was the first woman to circumnavigate the world single-handed (in 272 days), stopovers included; it was Australian Kay Cottee who in 1988 accomplished the feat nonstop, on her yacht *First Lady*, in 189 days.

FORMALIZATION OF GLOBAL RACES

Because Knox-Johnston was a member of the Royal Naval Sailing Association (RNSA), his win on *Suhaili* in 1969 created a stir amongst its members, and the RNSA's Rear Admiral Otto Steiner was inspired to challenge the members to a race around the world with fully crewed yachts. When his suggestion was met with enthusiasm, he formed a race committee, sought financial backing and in 1973 the Whitbread Round The World Race was created.

It was not until the advent in 1982 of the BOC Around Alone that a new solo race designed for monohulls was formally established. The BOC Around Alone went on to inspire the creation of the Vendée Globe (alone, nonstop, around the world), which led to the Jules Verne Trophy, and thereafter, in the year 2000, The Race – the no-limits, fastest dash around the world.

Top left SIR CHAY BLYTH, THE FIRST MAN TO CIRCUMNAVIGATE THE WORLD THE 'WRONG WAY ROUND' IN 1971, AT THE HELM OF *UNITED FRIENDLY* IN THE 1981/82 WHITBREAD RACE.

Top centre THE PIONEERING SPIRIT OF THE EARLY SAILORS LED TO MODERN SINGLE-HANDED ROUND THE WORLD RACES ON TODAY'S SLEEK RACING MACHINES, SUCH AS CHRISTOPHE AUGUIN'S *GÉODIS*.

Top right KNOX-JOHNSTON, WHO SAILED HIS WAY INTO THE HISTORY BOOKS ON THE FIRST NONSTOP, SOLO CIRCUMNAVIGATION ON HIS YACHT *SUHAILI*, WITH ITS TEAK HULL, IRON KEEL AND PINE MAST.

UNRAVELLING HANDICAPS

It is because of a complex handicapping system – that maximizes fairness of competition but confounds the spectator – that mixed regattas have generated very little public appeal and stoked the fires of debate surrounding the controversy of yacht handicapping.

Match racing and One Design racing, on the other hand, have been enormously successful. Simple to follow, the first boat across the line takes the laurels. This may be the reason why so many of the races covered in this book are limited by yacht design. For one, sponsors are happiest when their investment attracts media attention; for another, the public are only interested in what they understand. The French, particularly, are masters at this art and as a nation are excited more by yachting than almost any other sport. A major reason is that their regattas are easy to follow: the Tour de France is a race of Mumm 30 One Designs competing against one another, and the winner is always the one at the front of the fleet.

Confusion can still reign, however. In the Cape to Rio, for example, the winner of the 1996 race was the smallest boat in the fleet and finished eight days behind the first boat to cross the line! Over the years, because of the variety of yacht designs worldwide, and the enduring competitive spirit that prevails in the sport, a handicapping system has been devised to allow all of these yachts to compete against each other and have as fair a chance of winning as any other.

A PHRF (Performance Handicap Rating Factor) handicapping system assumes that every boat is in absolute top racing condition; this includes a clean and smooth hull undersurface as well as a suit of competitive sails. A rating is given to each yacht, and it is against this rating that the yacht races, until obvious performance improvements have been made to the boat, which would then necessitate a revised rating.

For greater clarification, the rating system can be simpified as follows:

Boat A (a big, sleek racing machine) has a rating of 1.5, whilst Boat B (the small family cruising yacht) in the same race has a rating of 0.7. Boat A finishes the race in 10 hours, and Boat B takes 20 hours. Their race time is multiplied by their rating as follows:

Boat A: 10 hrs x 1.5 = 15 hrs (corrected time)

Boat B: 20 hrs x 0.7 = 14 hrs (corrected time)

Therefore the handicap winner is Boat B. The real time taken, i.e. 10 hours and 20 hours, is known as the elapsed time.

Every region has its own handicapping committee, and many have their own handicapping system – which has always frustrated performance handicap racers worldwide. There are grey areas within which changes can be made to the boat, and depending on the opinion of the current handicap committee, these are allowable; but it is possible that a year later, with the advent of a new committee, such changes could be penalized. However, a successful handicapping system does mean that it is possible for the smallest yacht in the race to win overall, assuming that their actual performance was superior to that of any other boat in the fleet. This means that their tactics, sail trim and crew work outranked their competitors.

It is a compromise. A serious racer will often sail a boat fitting into a specific Class category, ensuring that there are no deviations from the rules, and therefore pitting his skills fairly against his competitors. But then he may be drawn by the challenge of initiating new trends, for example, the Mini-Transats, which fall into a Low Limits Class. This stipulates that yachts being pitted against one another must be of equal size, but each has the opportunity to initiate radical changes to enhance the yacht's performance. It is thanks to the resulting maverick yacht designs that water ballast and canting keels have become racing phenomena in the single-handed sailing marathons.

Another form of handicapping is the International Measurement System (IMS) where a formula derived from a set of measurements pertaining to a yacht determines its handicap. Sail area, the boat's waterline length, type of keel, and weight are among the criteria used to calculate the IMS rating.

AN UNCOMMON CHALLENGE IN A BOAT NAMED *CHALLENGER*

Cape Town-based South African sailor, Anthony Steward, in 1993 was the world's first person – and still the only one today – to complete a journey around the globe, alone, in an open boat.

Steward's craft *NCS Challenger* was a TLC, designed as a day sailer by fellow South African Dudley Dix. It was only 5.8m (19ft) long and had no cabin, therefore no shelter, to protect him from the sun or the sea. Its open transom (boat stern) was designed as a self-draining cockpit, allowing water to drain from the decks. Provisions, clothing and his solar-powered VHF radio were stored in watertight storage lockers built around the cockpit.

During the course of his epic journey, Steward was capsized more times than he can remember, knocked down and spat out of the wake of an enormous ship just outside the Panama Canal (which crosses the isthmus that joins North and South America, separating the Caribbean Sea and the Pacific Ocean), dismasted off the Pacific island of Samoa, and shipwrecked for nine days on the Seychelles' Ile de Cerf.

His planned route was to cross the South Atlantic, sailing north to the Caribbean, through Panama to the Pacific Ocean, and finally crossing the Indian Ocean to get back to his starting point at the tip of Africa. After setting out, he reached St Helena (a volcanic island in the southeast Atlantic roughly at the same latitude as the southern border of Angola) after 18

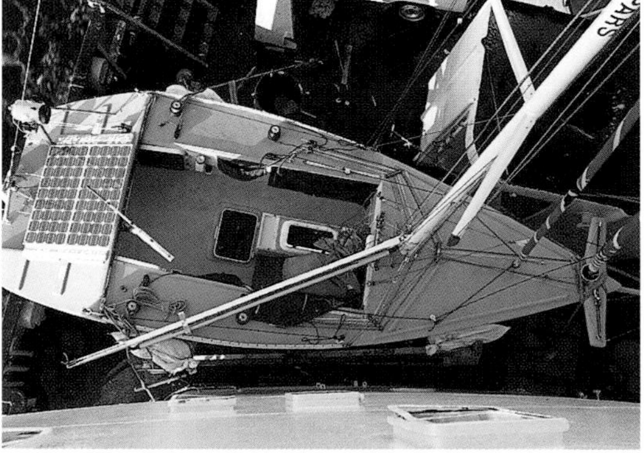

Above A VIEW OF CO-AUTHOR ANTHONY STEWARD'S OCEAN HOME FOR EIGHT AND A HALF MONTHS. HIS LIVING AREA WAS NO BIGGER THAN A DOUBLE BED – AND THAT MINUS THE COMFORTS!

days. He was barely able to walk after the cramped conditions of his boat. However, the islanders nurtured him, and it was their encouragement – and the absence of any airport – that set Steward on his way north to the Caribbean.

The longest leg of Steward's adventure was a 30-day stint in the Pacific Ocean. After being dismasted off Samoa, northeast of the Fiji islands, he erected a jury, or makeshift, rig and pressed on to Brisbane, halfway up Australia's east coast, to catch up on maintenance work and sit out the cyclone season.

Once he had taken his boat through the Barrier Reef, round Australia's northern tip, and set off across the Indian Ocean from Darwin to meet his own wedding date, he was again capsized and dismasted. His freshwater supplies were spoiled by salt water and he was forced to physically helm the boat for four days with no break, the yacht surfing down enormous waves headed for Madagascar. In a state of sheer exhaustion he spotted the palm-fringed island of Cerf, but an enormous reef protected the island from the breaking waves of the Indian Ocean. Unable to navigate his broken boat around the island, his only hope was to surf his way over the coral reef. As the little boat thundered down onto the coral, the rudder and keel were torn away and Steward found himself bobbing in the quiet, serene waters of the inner reef – reputed to be one of the world's largest breeding grounds for the Tiger Shark! His bloodied hands attracted a swarm of sharks as he swam

toward the island, and he was forced to fend them off with a marlin spike. Finally reaching the beach, he quenched his thirst on the milk from a coconut and slept from exhaustion.

When he awoke, Steward set about looking for help, but the island was deserted, one of many little uninhabited islands in the outer ring of the Seychelles group. He was fortunate to find the ruins of the home belonging to a former island resident on the leeward side of the island, and he set up camp where he lived off coconuts and pawpaws. The EPIRB (Emergency Position Indicating Radio Beacon) from his boat was corroded, but he pulled apart his radio and managed to get a signal going. He was not to know that no-one would receive his signal.

It was only nine days later that a small fishing vessel sought shelter on the leeward side of the island so that the crew could effect repairs to their storm-damaged boat. The crew, catching sight of Steward's white distress flare, wrote it off as cloud; the young captain Frank Bebe was not convinced, however. He set off for the island in a dinghy, but when he saw a 'mad white man dancing on the beach', he sent for backup. Four crewmen boarded another dinghy, and armed with fishing knives they made their wary approach. They were convinced that the stranded hull was merely the tender to Steward's bigger yacht, so the shipwrecked sailor – desperate – climbed aboard the dinghy, refusing to budge. The fishermen were forced to take him aboard their boat, where he was able to make radio contact with his seriously anxious family members. He made it home on Air Seychelles with only 20 days to spare before his impending wedding. . .

His boat was taken back to South Africa for considerable repairs, after which the Mediterranean Shipping Company took him to his outer path just before the island so he could continue with his voyage (the last leg comprised the eastern coast of Southern Africa and the rounding of Cape Agulhas to finally dock in Cape Town). Steward went on to complete his voyage, sailing alongside Killer Whales in the Mozambique Channel between Madagascar and the Mozambican coast and navigating along the hazardous South African coastline. With no cooking facilities on board, he survived on raw fish and a tight ration of tinned stores. His feat took him a total of 260 days, although the actual trip took nearly two years, with the required time off between each leg to recover.

Above *NCS CHALLENGER* HAS HER SAILS REEFED RIGHT IN DURING BAD WEATHER; SHE ENDURED COUNTLESS SQUALLS, INNUMERABLE CAPSIZES, AND WAS KNOCKED DOWN BY A SHIP NEAR PANAMA.

Above ALREADY THREE-QUARTERS OF THE WAY AROUND THE WORLD, STEWARD APPROACHES THE COMORES IN THE INDIAN OCEAN SHORTLY AFTER RESUMING THE TRIP FOLLOWING HIS SHIPWRECK.

Above and top STEWARD WAS EXPOSED TO ALL WEATHER CONDITIONS EN ROUTE (ABOVE); HIS BOAT IS DWARFED BY THE WELCOMING FLEET (TOP) AS HE FINALLY SAILS INTO CAPE TOWN.

EVOLUTION OF YACHT DESIGN

ONE WOULD EXPECT that the sole objective of a racing yacht designer is to achieve the greatest speed. However, because of the various handicapping systems that exist worldwide – and the fact that the first over the finish line is not necessarily the winner – the trick is to design a boat that wins the race overall. It is the boat that most effectively utilizes any advantages offered within the handicap rules, and thus thwarts the accepted standards, fooling people into believing that the boat is not actually as fast as it really is – thereby getting a more favourable rating under which to race.

Innovative ideas in yacht design have a limited life span as, over the years, racing innovations have become outlawed by handicapping rules which are continuously changed and updated, edging out the radical designs that can give a boat an 'unfair' advantage.

The biggest innovation in yacht design was the move away from heavy yachts that could plough through big seas, and were thus perceived as the safest option, to what were called 'light displacement' boats – yachts so light that they would slide over the big swells and their speed would sail them out of danger. The huge, heavy keels were traded in for high aspect keels (deeper and narrower, offering more stability with less weight).

Hollander Ricus van de Stadt gained a huge advantage with his design of a trim tab on the keel of his yacht, *Zeevalk*, but was penalized by handicap rules, to give every yacht an equal chance of winning. The trim tab was so heavily penalized, though, that it soon fell out of favour.

Two years later, van de Stadt changed the perception that light displacement was a foolhardy design concept with his *Stormvogel,* which also had two masts and greatly increased sail area but remained a remarkably seaworthy craft.

Great strides made in the improvement of yachting equipment enabled designers like Frenchman Guy Ribadeau Dumas to take up the same concept of more sail area equalling greater speed but to reduce the amount of crew required. His *Crédit Agricole* was designed specially for the BOC, a single-handed round the world race – she in fact set the standard for what would become a new level of international yacht racing: a professional approach and a very large budget. She was also very lightweight – considered to be extreme for her time (although she is fairly moderate against current standards).

With the IOR (International Offshore Rules) handicapping method increasingly prejudicing the progress of modern yacht design, it eventually fell out of favour and a new method of handicapping was introduced – the International Measurement System (IMS), initially to attract advancements to the sport. But being a handicapping system, its objectives were also to ensure fair competition between boats from all yachting spheres – and so the cycle of inhibiting design innovations began again.

A master at designing around International Offshore Rules was New Zealander Bruce Farr. He was already 'cleaning up' on the yacht racing circuit with his extremely fast designs, but each one was hampered by the continually changing rules. He reacted by taking a complete break from yacht racing and focusing instead on cruising yachts; with his Farr 38, the very qualities that fell into contention under IOR rules found favour in the new IMS handicapping system.

The rules, however, tended to create a type-casting process; by designing to gain maximum advantage within the rules, architects found the common loopholes, which resulted in one ideal winning formula producing similar-looking boats. Californian Bill Lee was one yacht designer who broke away from the handicap type-casting. He created boats which have become known as California Sleds (see also page 83) – his response to the prestige offered by the Barn Door trophy for Transpac line honours winners. Bill Lee's *Merlin* went on to win three times.

Above DESIGNER JEAN-MARIE FINOT HAS DOMINATED THE FIELD OF SINGLE-HANDED SAILING WITH HIS YACHTS, WHICH HAVE ACHIEVED VICTORIES IN THREE AROUND ALONE AND TWO VENDÉE GLOBE RACES.

Top FRENCHMAN PHILIPPE JEANTOT ABOARD HIS YACHT *CRÉDIT AGRICOLE*, WHICH WAS TO SET THE STANDARD FOR WHAT HAS BECOME TODAY'S OPEN 60 CLASS, SINGLE-HANDED BOAT.

Above RENOWNED NEW ZEALAND BOAT ARCHITECT, BRUCE FARR, WAS INSTRUMENTAL IN FOREGOING MEASUREMENT RATINGS IN HIS INNOVATIVE APPROACH TO THE ONE DESIGN CLASS.

ZEEVALK

1967

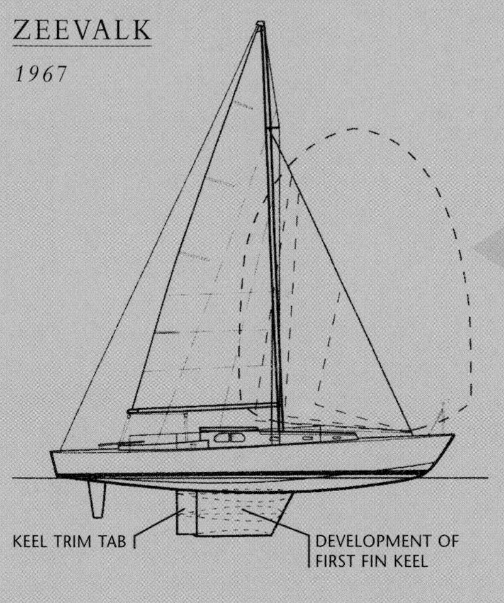

Designed by: Ricus van de Stadt

Van de Stadt's design featured a trim tab on the keel, which operated the same way as the flaps on an aeroplane wing – it served to give the keel an extra lift, enabling the boat to sail very close to the wind.

STORMVOGEL

1969

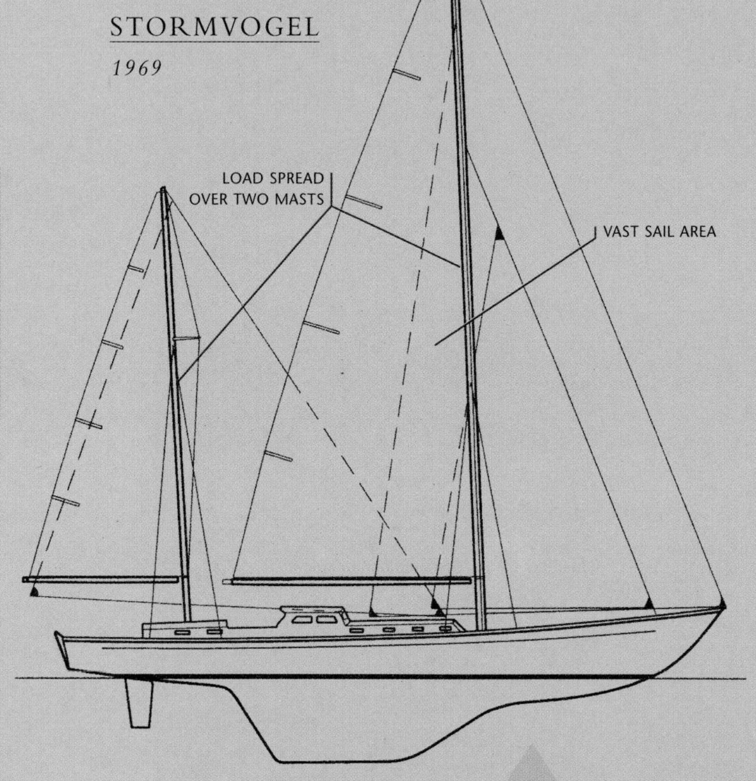

Designed by: Ricus van de Stadt

Spread over two masts, *Stormvogel's* vast sail area enabled greater speeds but also ensured safety by not placing too much load on a single rig. She required massive crews, but was considered one of the more seaworthy racing passage-makers of her time.

FARR 38

1983

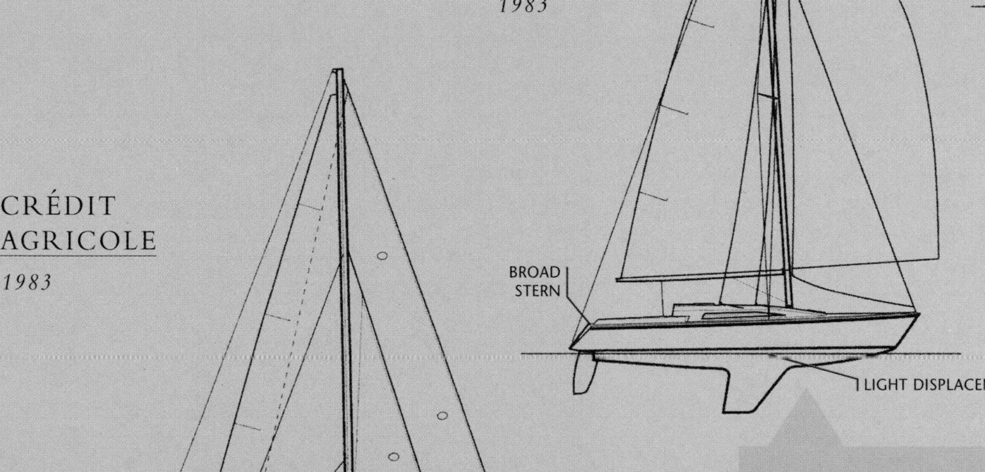

Designed by: Bruce Farr

Frustrated by handicap rules, Farr turned to the design of cruising boats. The Farr 38 was designed as a fast, light displacement cruiser. It had a broad stern, was seaworthy and yet very easy to handle.

CRÉDIT AGRICOLE

1983

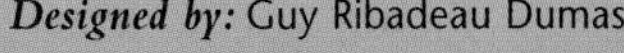

Designed by: Guy Ribadeau Dumas

Due to vastly improved sail fabrics and advancements in mast building, masts could handle enormous loading. Dumas took advantage of a greater sail area for increased speed, and his use of roller furler systems enabled a sole crewman to reduce the sail area; winches, too, were much more powerful.

MERLIN

1985

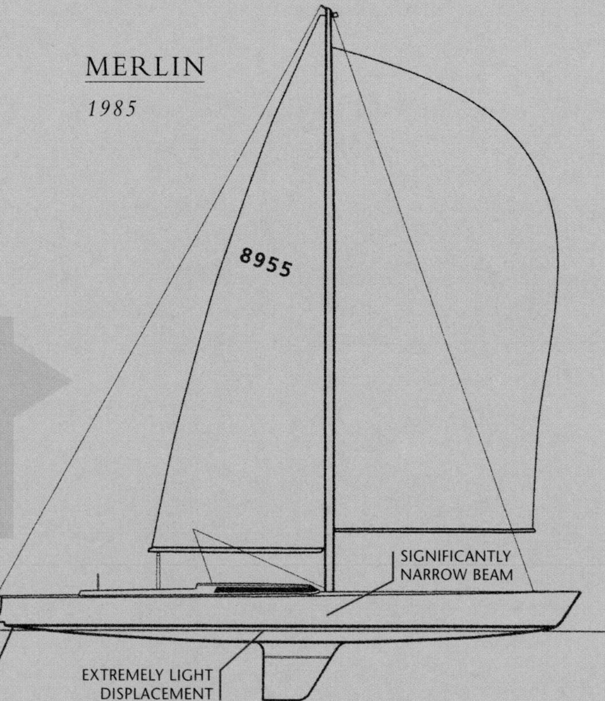

Designed by: Bill Lee

Lee created his California Sleds purely for speed rather than for handicap rule advantage. The Sleds are designed to a 'box rule' – they have to conform to set limits that apply only to size.

SCALE

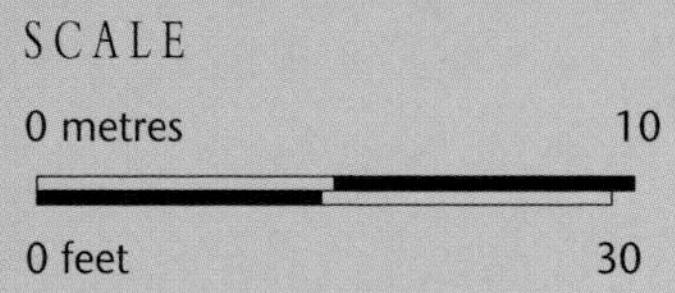

OFFSHORE

CLASSICS

FASTNET

Although there are many different kinds of offshore events in various parts of the world today, the original three 'Classics', which are all about the same length (just over 600 nautical miles, or 1110km), have remained: these are the Newport–Bermuda (from Rhode Island, USA, to the Bermuda islands, a self-governing British colony), the Sydney–Hobart (from the New South Wales capital on Australia's east coast to the capital of the island of Tasmania, in the south) and the Fastnet (from Cowes on the Isle of Wight to the Fastnet Rock and back to Plymouth, in southwestern England).

Inspired by the Newport to Bermuda Race which was established by American sailors in 1923 and 1924, some sailing enthusiasts in the UK sought out a course which could be considered an equivalent race. After a heated debate about the wisdom of a 'public ocean race' in their more northern waters, the initial Fastnet course – starting off Ryde on the Isle of Wight and ending at Plymouth near the southwestern tip of England – was decided upon.

Seven British cruising yachts lined up on 15 August 1925 for what turned out to be a light weather race. It was won by *Jolie Brise*, in six days. After the event, at a dinner in Plymouth, the competitors decided to form the Ocean Racing Club, with the object of holding one 600-nautical-mile race every year.

During the first years, several of the races had to contend with severe westerly gales. As a result, the race earned a name for rough weather (partly because the early yachts made slow progress beating to windward). In contrast to some of the other races that were notable at the time (these were often comfortable reaches along continental coasts), the Fastnet Race was named 'the Grand National of ocean racing' – because of its variety and unpredictability – by Alf Loomis, a great US yachting writer, and a participant of the race between the two World Wars.

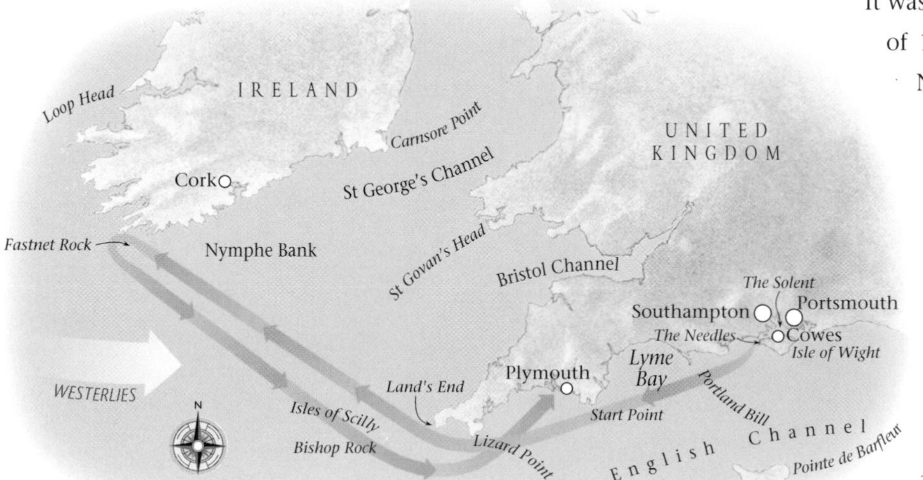

It was held every year until 1931, but since 1933 (with the exception of 1941 to 1945), it has been run on alternate years, while the Newport–Bermuda Race is held on each even year. In 1931 the organizing club became the Royal Ocean Racing Club (RORC), and by that time was expanding into other offshore races of lesser distances around the British coasts as well as to France, Spain, Denmark, and others.

The major expansion in Fastnet participation occurred from 1947 onwards. Numbers of entries from many countries, especially the USA, France, the Netherlands, and Germany increased, and in 1949 the total number of participants rose to 29, with 58 in 1959, 185 in 1969 and finally, in 1979, a total of 303 participants. The latter was the greatest number ever; today it averages at about 250 entrants.

Previous pages AT THE START OF THE 1990 SYDNEY–HOBART RACE IN THE CAPITAL OF THE AUSTRALIAN STATE OF NEW SOUTH WALES, THE FLEET, FETCHING TO SYDNEY HEADS, USES TO BEST ADVANTAGE A 60-DEGREE WIND DIRECTION TO THE SAIL.

Top *VIPER* ROUNDING THE INFAMOUS FASTNET LIGHTHOUSE DURING THE COURSE OF A FASTNET EVENT.

Opposite UK YACHT *SKANDIA*, SKIPPERED BY SWEDISH SAILOR LUDDE INGVALL, IN THE FASTNET RACE OF 1999.

COMPAQ
MAXI ONE 04
SOUTHAMPTON
Skandia
Adecco

INTRODUCTION OF THE ADMIRAL'S CUP

Traditionally the focal point of yachting in the UK, the nine-day Cowes Week regatta was first held way back in 1826 and offered the substantial prize of a 45kg (100 lb) gold cup. Long associated with royalty, the regatta in its early days enjoyed patronage from William IV, and even today, the royal touch is extended by Prince Philip, husband of Queen Elizabeth II, who frequently participates in the nine-day event.

A turn of events occurred after a number of first-class US boats invariably arrived to participate in Cowes Week as well as the Fastnet. In 1957, some senior private members of the RORC (one of them was Captain John Illingworth who was also responsible for the creation of the Sydney–Hobart Classic race) decided not to limit the gold Admiral's Cup (see page 139) to UK competitors but to offer it also to the US teams; the recipient would be the three-boat team (that is, the three yacht size-categories permitted per nation-team) who won a combination of four races: two inshore races – the Britannia Cup and the New York Yacht Club Cup – together with the Channel Race (a 225-mile/416km triangle) and the Fastnet Race.

In 1959, the right to compete for the Admiral's Cup was opened to other nations and the RORC took charge of organizing the competition. The increasing numbers for this contest thus helped to swell the international nature of the Fastnet fleet. An interesting aspect of the contest was that no yacht leading in the Admiral's Cup was safe when the concluding event was the Fastnet Race. This sometimes brutal offshore race was so heavily weighted in terms of points that a team could go from 'zeros to heroes' (or vice versa) as a result of a minor shift in the breeze.

Above THE FRENCH TEAM OF *CORUM* (IN THE FOREGROUND, RIGHT), AT THE START OF THE FASTNET RACE IN 1991, PULLED OFF A TRIUMPHANT FINISH AFTER LAGGING FOURTH IN POINTS AT THE START.

Opposite top A SPECTACULAR BIRD'S EYE VIEW OF THE SOLENT DURING COWES WEEK IN 1993 AS THE FASTNET FLEET BREAKS OUT FROM THE CROWDS OF SPECTATOR BOATS AND RACING FLEETS.

Opposite centre *JAMESON WHISKEY* MANNED BY AN IRISH CREW TACKS AWAY FROM THE FLEET EARLY ON IN THE 1997 FASTNET RACE. IN THE FOREGROUND IS THE AMERICAN TEAM ON *FLASH GORDON* .

The ease with which fortunes changed is typified in the 1991 Fastnet Race, when the Italians entered with a 9-point advantage over the British and 10 points over the Americans. The French, who were 20 points behind at the start, sailed a brilliant race and leap-frogged all three teams, becoming the all-round winner.

In 1999 the Admiral's Cup was rescheduled to take place two weeks prior to Cowes Week, allowing the inshore racing to be run in the Solent (a strait in the English Channel between the UK coast and the Isle of Wight), and giving the crews time to recover from the intense physical sailing at the same time enabling them to enjoy the festivities of Cowes Week. The Fastnet Race remained a part of the Cowes events (it is scheduled at the end of the week), while a new medium-distance race, the Wolf Rock, was created for the Admiral's Cup.

Today, the 600-nautical-mile (1110km) Fastnet Race starts at Cowes on the Isle of Wight off England's south coast. The fleet heads westwards out of the Solent, passing through Hurst Narrows and leaving the white, chalk rocks of the Needles to port (they do so quickly, as the race begins on a west-going tide). The crews then set themselves about the task of navigating for the best speed along the south coast of England. This is a succession of headlands, each with its own tidal strategy. First comes Portland Bill, just 50 miles (93km) from Cowes, where the boats confront a notorious tidal race. This negotiated, the race heads across Lyme Bay and past Start Point, then there's the great coastal indent in which Plymouth and Falmouth lie, before the low craggy sight of the Lizard, the southernmost tip of England.

The weather is sometimes such that a 'wild card' decision is made to take an alternative offshore route towards the Channel Islands, off the northwest coast of France, which brings better wind, and thus advantage in the race. It is an event driven by pressure, with tension and excitement when the fleet splits to gain advantage.

Right A CONTENDER BEATS PAST 'THE NEEDLES' IN 1993. THE INCREDIBLY STRONG TIDES IN THESE WATERS MAKE THIS ONE OF THE TRICKIEST PLACES TO SAIL ALONG THE SOUTH COAST OF ENGLAND.

From the Lizard, the course turns northwest to the last mark on the English coast – the Runnelstone. This is close to Land's End, where winter gales have long battered the coastline, leaving rugged scars. Runnelstone to Fastnet Rock is about 30 hours' sailing for a middle-of-the-fleet boat. No land is sighted until the famous rock itself appears, 10 nautical miles (18.5km) off the southwestern tip of Ireland. Once around this landmark, the yacht crews discover how they have fared against each other and the race almost begins again. They head back on a southeasterly course for Bishop Rock, in the Isles of Scilly – a further 160 miles (296km). From here, it is still 100 nautical miles (185km) to the finish at Plymouth, with plenty of scope for fast-altering weather, failing winds, and tactical success or disappointment.

Above *BRAVA Q8* OF ITALY, PART OF THE WINNING TEAM IN THE ADMIRAL'S CUP EVENT OF 1995, AT THE FINISH IN PLYMOUTH OF THE SUBSEQUENTLY HELD FASTNET RACE. THE LONG-DISTANCE RACE WAS WON BY LUDDE INGVALL ON *MORNING GLORY*.

Left *TOSHIBA,* A WHITBREAD MAXI, ROUNDING FASTNET ROCK DURING THE 1997 FASTNET RACE. *MORNING GLORY*, SKIPPERED BY HASSO PLATTNER, CAME IN AS THE WINNER.

THE 1979 FASTNET RACE

This race is responsible for the worst maritime tragedy of its kind in the UK. In the contest of 1979, 303 yachts and some 3000 sailors set out on 11 August, sailing into the worst summer storm in 30 years. They were not to know that 194 yachts would retire from the race, 24 would be abandoned and 15 lives would be lost.

The race started in light-to-moderate WNW winds which increased in strength and reversed in direction as a rapidly deepening depression moved across the Fastnet area over the next two days. It had taken shape over the north of the USA and worked its way southeast across the states of New York and New England, wreaking havoc along the way. Yachts dragged anchor and drifted ashore, roofs blew off houses, trees were blown over, a woman was killed by a falling branch. By the time the start gun had fired for the Fastnet Race, the depression had left the American continent and was crossing the Atlantic at 80kph (50mph).

The Met office had received scanty reports from a few ships in the Atlantic Ocean, but by the time they came to realize that danger was heading their way, it was too late to put out the warning at standard forecast times when all competitors generally listened in (the standard reports that go out four times a day on BBC Radio 4). So, although warnings were immediately issued with other news flashes, the majority of the fleet was already way out to sea and experiencing the beginning of the storm by the time the Force 10 (storm conditions) warning was put out on the weather forecast. A Force 10 wind, according to the Beaufort Scale, results in:

Above MAXI CLASS WINNER *BOOMERANG*, CARRYING AN AMERICAN CREW AND GEORGE COUMANTAROS AS SKIPPER, EASILY BROKE *NIRVANA*'S 1985 COURSE RECORD IN THE 1999 FASTNET.

Left OPEN 60 TRIMARANS *KINGFISHER*, *FUJICOLOR* AND *BROCÉLIANDE* (IN THE FOREGROUND, LEFT TO RIGHT) DURING THE FASTNET EVENT OF 1999. IT WAS WON BY *FUJICOLOR* (SKIPPERED BY LOÏC PEYRON).

Very high waves with long overhanging crests. The resulting foam in great patches is blown in dense white streaks along the direction of the wind. On the whole, the surface of the sea takes on a white appearance. The tumbling of the sea becomes heavy and shock-like. Visibility affected.

What this 'official definition' does not describe is how a yacht is carried higher and higher as the wave builds up, then careens straight down the face of the wave – if she is lucky; more often than not she finds herself suspended at the very top of the crest and is poured backwards into the trough behind the wave. The Beaufort Scale also fails to describe what happens to the yacht when she stalls at the bottom of a wave, and the next wave thrashes down on her, knocking her over like a small cork. And it does not elaborate on the unbelievable power of the water, which has the force of a solid wall, ripping apart everything in its path.

Many very experienced competitors in the 1979 race said the wind strength was not unusual; it was the sea conditions, however, that were the most dangerous they had ever encountered. The seas became massive, and by the time the fleet started turning back, the waves were 'the size of a block of flats, but three times wider'. [Nick Ward, crew member aboard *Grimalkin*]

Within hours the Land's End Coastguard Station had a major disaster on its hands. Mayday calls jammed the airwaves from every part of the 180-nautical-mile (333km) stretch of water between Land's End and the Fastnet Rock. Airbases at Kinloss and Culdrose had been alerted, and helicopters and Nimrods were standing by for a dawn take-off. Every available lifeboat from the south coast of Ireland had already been called out.

Of the entrants, 112 yachts were knocked horizontal, while 77 experienced substantially more than a knockdown – some underwent total inversions – or 360-degree rolls. At dawn the next morning, more than 70 yachtsmen were airlifted to safety within the first few hours of daylight. Nineteen of the 24 yachts abandoned were recovered; five sank.

Along with Sir Edward Heath, former prime minister of the UK, celebrities caught up in the tragedy included US billionaire and television mogul Ted Turner – founder of Cable News Network (CNN) – who emerged from the drama to win the event on his 18.5m (61ft) *Tenacious*. 'Sure we were scared,' he recalls. 'Everybody was scared. It was rough as hell.'

Above SISKA REEFING DOWN IN THE EARLY STAGES OF THE INFAMOUS 1979 FASTNET – WHICH WAS WON BY TED TURNER ON *TENACIOUS*, THE ONLY BOAT TO FINISH THE RACE.

THE PERSONAL TRAGEDIES

Fourteen crew members survived when they took to the life rafts from their sinking yachts, but on one particular raft, seven lives were lost; ironically, their yacht was later found afloat.

Of another crew, six lost their lives after they were swept overboard despite five of them wearing harnesses and being clipped-in on the boat: two of the harnesses failed, two sailors were washed out of their harnesses, and one who was clipped onto the guard rails was washed away when the rails subsequently parted.

Matthew Sheahan, a 17-year-old, was crewing aboard his father's yacht, *Grimalkin*, when his father, David, drowned. He said afterwards:

'During the long, terrifying night, each crew member had frequently been towed behind the boat after she had righted herself following the numerous knockdowns and pitchpoles. Accelerating down the face of waves behind a surfing boat under bare poles, being towed by your safety harness and not knowing – not even caring which way up you are – is a simple way to go! No time to panic, no time to shout out. You are totally at the mercy of the elements – and you know it. Nothing you do or say in these moments will make the slightest difference.'

Above A LONE CREW MEMBER ON BRITISH BOAT *CAMARGUE* WAITS TO BE RESCUED FROM ROUGH SEAS DURING THE DISASTER-FILLED FASTNET EVENT IN THE HISTORIC YEAR, 1979.

Above IT WAS AS A RESULT OF THE TIRELESS EFFORTS OF THE ROYAL NAVY, AMONGST OTHERS, THAT 70 YACHTSMEN WERE AIRLIFTED TO SAFETY IN THE AFTERMATH OF 1979'S GALE FORCE WINDS.

Opposite MAXI ONE DESIGN ENTRANTS IN 1999: *HENRY LLOYD* SKIPPERED BY SWEDE GUNNAR KRANTZ (RIGHT), GUIDO MAISTO'S ITALIAN TEAM (CENTRE), AND JULES MAZAR'S FRENCH TEAM (LEFT).

David Sheahan was swept away, unconcious, after the crew had cut his harness in an attempt to untangle him from the guard rails and pull him back on board after a particularly violent capsize. Another crew member, Gerry Winks, was so badly injured during the same capsize that he later died on the boat from his injuries.

Sheahan, owner and skipper of the boat, was a meticulous planner and, perhaps because of his lack of offshore experience, he had taken extra care in preparing the boat for the race. Despite *Grimalkin* being unusually well-equipped with safety gear, she was one of the hardest hit in the fleet.

The Fastnet Race has been the most decisive event in the Admiral's Cup series (although today it is run separately from the Cup series), and is widely regarded as one of the most challenging events in the racing world because the weather can be truly atrocious and the Solent is famous for its swirling tides and shoals. Although rules on equipment and procedures play a role, the spirit of ocean racing lies in the self-reliance of the crew on each yacht – this is the attraction of, and satisfaction in, the race. And it is the Fastnet, rather than any other, that typifies the essence of offshore racing.

FRA
Mini
Disc
SONY
339
Mini
Disc
SONY
9
323
Mini
Disc
SONY
Mini
Disc
SONY
X-Yachting
SONY
Sun

TOUR DE FRANCE À LA VOILE

Tour de France immediately conjures up images of the famous cycle race and its pack of long-distance cyclists rather than sailing. However, in 1978, a sailing event was added to the Tour de France – less-publicized than the cycle tour but, nevertheless, it has attracted some of the world's best skippers. The yachting event runs concurrently with the cycling, and the concept for both is the same: to tour France – country or coastline – in a competitive spirit.

The concept originated with Bernard Decré, manager in 1977 of the publishing house, Editions Maritimes et d'Outre Mer. He aspired to create a race that was fun as well as serious, and that offered a medley of courses against which the sailors could pit their skills. Against all odds, he managed to pull together enough sponsorship from various French city councils to finance 20 boats for the first race.

The sailing event takes place along France's three coasts – the English Channel, the Atlantic Ocean and the Mediterranean Sea – every summer, over a period of approximately three to four weeks. Raced by a fleet of identically classed yachts, the race includes offshore and coastal races, and windward-leeward courses. This combination enhanced the reputation of the Tour de France à la Voile in foreign countries, which led to the French Yachting Federation (FFV) selecting the event as the French International Offshore Championship in 1999.

Since the first Tour de France à la Voile in 1978, more than 15,000 people have sailed at least two legs of the race. The course and stopovers have varied slightly over the years, but generally it starts in the English Channel and finishes after approximately three weeks in the Mediterranean. The route of the 1999 Tour de France à la Voile totalled about 1150 nautical miles (2130km) and included 11 point-to-point legs. These are:

- Scheveningen (Netherlands) to Oostende (Belgium)
- Oostende to Dieppe (English Channel)
- Dieppe to Granville (English Channel)
- Granville to Saint Quay-Portrieux (English Channel)
- Saint Quay-Portrieux to Brest (Atlantic Ocean)
- Brest to Pornichet (Atlantic)
- Pornichet to La Rochelle (Atlantic)
- La Rochelle to Saint Cyprien (overland)
- Saint Cyprien to La Grande Motte (Mediterranean Sea)
- La Grande Motte to Bandol (Mediterranean)
- Bandol to Le Lavandou (Mediterranean)
- Le Lavandou to St Raphaël (Mediterranean)

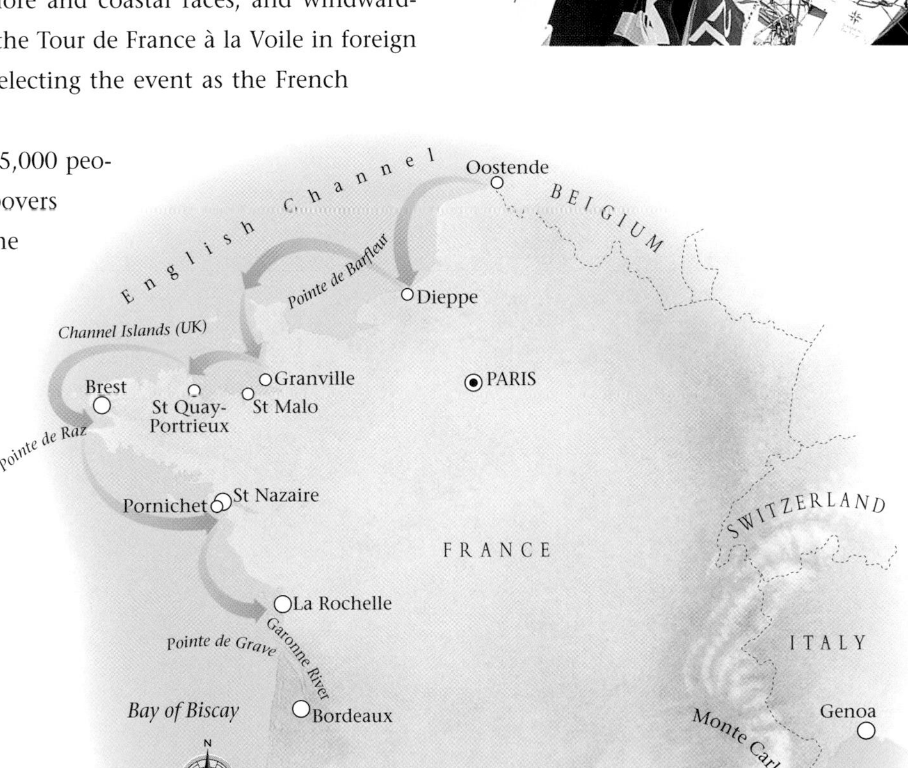

Opposite RACE ENTRANTS ON THE SCHEVENINGEN–OOSTENDE LEG OF THE TOUR DE FRANCE À LA VOILE IN 1999. EACH BOAT TRIES TO COVER THE BOAT IN FRONT IN AN EFFORT TO COLLAPSE ITS SPINNAKER AND SLOW IT DOWN; THE BOATS ARE ON A TIGHT REACH.

Above BOATS MOORED IN LORIENT, FRANCE, DURING THE TOUR DE FRANCE OF 1996. THE RACE CREATES A FESTIVAL EN ROUTE FOR SPECTATORS OF THE RACE, WITH A TRAVELLING OFFICIAL 'RACE VILLAGE, WHICH IS ASSEMBLED AT NIGHT TO ENSURE THE LEAST DISRUPTION TO THE PUBLIC.

A year after the initial Tour De France à la Voile, Bernard Decré introduced the First 30 with the idea of regulating a One Design racing fleet. He chartered the boats out to competitors, opening up opportunities for aspirant skippers.

With the growing success of the race, in 1981 he was able to buy 25 Jeanneau One Design boats. The prestige of the event had grown to such an extent that winning it was seen almost as a rite of passage into the world of professional

Left SOUTH AFRICAN ENTRY *FOORD & MEINJTIES* AHEAD OF *ÉCOLE CENTRALE* (FOREGROUND), BEATING INTO A 30-KNOT WESTERLY WIND IN THE NORTH SEA ON THE SCHEVENINGEN–OOSTENDE LEG IN 1999.

yacht racing. The winner of the event was given the title, Skipper Elf Aquitaine, and was permitted to sail one of the boats for the subsequent sailing season – a great opportunity to launch his or her career as a professional sailor.

In 1989, Bernard Decré handed over the event, which at that point was in financial trouble, to the French Yachting Federation, who took on management responsibility together with the national Offshore Yacht Club.

1999 heralded the introduction of the Mumm 30, the One Design that would take the race into the new millennium. According to boat designer, New Zealander Bruce Farr, 'The design goal in creating [this class] was a state-of-the-art One Design keelboat that would be fast and exciting, yet uncomplicated and economical. We set about the design of the Mumm 30 with a "clean sheet of paper" in that there are no rating-rule-driven compromises in performance.'

Opposite top CÔTES *D'ARMOR*, A JEANNEAU ONE DESIGN (THREE OF WHICH WERE BADLY DAMAGED BY STRONG WINDS), CO-SKIPPERED BY JEAN-CHARLES SCALE AND ERIC BASSET IN 1998.

Above RACE LEADER *KATEIE*, SKIPPERED BY LUC DE WULF OF BELGIUM, CARRIES THE RED SPINNAKER IN THE SAME WAY THE LEADING CYCLIST OF THE FRENCH CYCLE RACE WEARS THE YELLOW JERSEY.

Top THE BELGIUM TEAM ON *KATEIE*, UNDER SPINNAKER OFF ST MATHIEU DEWULF LIGHTHOUSE AT WESTERGAARD DURING THE 1999 RACE. THE BOAT CAME IN ULTIMATELY AS RACE WINNER.

BUDGETING FOR THE RACE

Private entry fee	FF30,150
Charter of a Mumm 30 (fee charged in 1999 by K Yachting for 5 weeks with training sails)	FF67,416
New sails (mainsail, 3 new jibs)	FF55,000
Transportation of yacht	FF11,000
Extra technical fittings	FF10,000
Rental of a van	FF18,500
Rental of a camper	FF12,000
Petrol/diesel and tolls	FF12,000
Crew's food supply	FF20,000
Crew's transportation	FF18,500
Hotel (1 twin bedroom for 21 days)	FF 6,500
Different advertising markings (hull, flag, vehicles)	FF10,000
Unforeseen items	FF10,000
TOTAL BUDGET	FF281,066 (VAT included)

Although the Tour de France yacht race is a high-level regatta, and some of the best Whitbread, Admiral's Cup and America's Cup crews have taken part in the race, it remains open to crew members of all levels.

An added attraction is the specific Amateur subdivision that was established for nonprofessional teams, as well as a Students ranking, which has contributed to steadily increasing student participation in both yachting and watersports in general.

President of the actively involved Class Association, Farr is thrilled with the success of the class. He is quoted as saying:

'The Mumm 30 has amazed competitors on the race course with its speed in all conditions, but the real test is when sailors actually take the helm. The boat has balance and superb control both upwind and down. It accelerates like a dinghy, but feels like a big boat going upwind in a breeze. The cockpit is a marvel of comfort and efficiency, from innovative folding footracks to the internal sail controls. Everything is easily at hand, functional and smooth. This sailing machine will be easy for less experienced crews to handle, and will never stop rewarding the most experienced sailor.'

Intentionally designed to be the most versatile downwind boat, each feature and detail of the Mumm 30 was aimed at maximizing 'fun' sailing. There is a maximum crew weight limit of 525kg (1158 lb) and a crew number of five, six or seven individuals. Boat entrants for the race usually represent towns, geopolitical districts, regions or countries; and boat names, sponsors.

Left HAVING COMPLETED FIVE LEGS OF THE 1998 TOUR DE FRANCE RACE, BOATS CROSS THE MORBIHAN GULF OFF SOUTH BRITTANY, FRANCE, DURING THE BREST–PORNICHET LEG.

The race is characterized by the mobile Official Village (actually composed of three separate villages), which commandeers each stopover and ensures a carnival atmosphere in each town. To minimize disruption, the Village is assembled and disassembled at night. Within its 6000m^2 (54,600ft^2) area, it accommodates organizing bodies, sponsors, crew promoters, and cocktail venues. It is a place where all race participants meet each other before and after racing – for a quiet drink or to join some of the wild parties. The public also has access to the Village and can participate in the promotional road shows put on by the different event sponsors. About 50,000 people visit the Official Village at each stopover.

Above SUNSET DURING THE TOUR DE FRANCE À LA VOILE IN 1999. A RACE LEG CAN CONTINUE INTO THE EVENING IF WINDS ARE LIGHT, EXTENDING THE LEG BY AS MUCH AS SIX TO EIGHT HOURS.

Left CONTENDERS APPROACHING THE START LINE IN THE RACE OF 1999. ALL 31 ENTRIES STARTED TOGETHER, WITH BOATS JOSTLING FOR POSITION, CREATING A SHOW FOR THE SPECTATORS.

SYDNEY–HOBART

The Sydney–Hobart Yacht Race was created in 1945 by Captain John Illingworth of the UK, who was instrumental in ocean yacht racing taking root in Australia. An annual Classic event, it was organized then (as it still is today) by the Cruising Yacht Club of Australia, which had been formed a year earlier. Despite the club's name, it quickly became the leading exponent of ocean racing in Australia, at that time a somewhat unusual sport in the rest of the world. The Sydney–Hobart race instantly captured the imagination of the Australian public, and it was not long before it developed into an international yachting Classic, attracting competitors from around the world.

The race, which covers 630 nautical miles (1167km), starts in Sydney Harbour, with the yachts tacking out through the Heads (the turning mark) and then heading south along Australia's east coast. If conditions are ideal, north to northeasterly winds drive the boats down to the far south coast of New South Wales, where they enter the Bass Strait (separating the island state of Tasmania from the Australian mainland). Here, there are often southerly or southwesterly winds blowing up through the Strait, which tend to slow up the boats. The finish takes place in the Derwent River, in the southeast of Tasmania, at Constitution Dock, off the capital Hobart's historic Battery Point.

The annual event starts traditionally on Boxing Day, 26 December. The present race record, at 1 day 19 hours 48 minutes 2 seconds, was set in 1999 by the Australian–Danish yacht *Nokia* which surpassed *Morning Glory*'s 1996 elapsed time by over 18 hours.

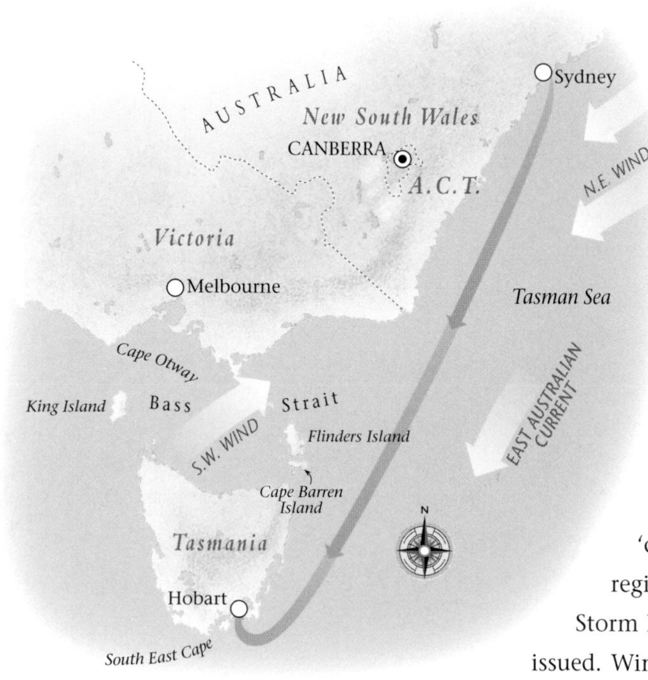

1998: A BLACK YEAR FOR SYDNEY

Although this event is not generally characterized by major personal tragedies, the 1998 yacht race was an utter catastrophe. Six yachtsmen died and seven yachts were abandoned by their crews when a severe storm hit the 115-boat fleet in Bass Strait on December 27/28. Of the seven yachts, five subsequently sank. In the end, only 44 boats finished the 630-nautical-mile course.

Because of the severity of the casualties, the Cruising Yacht Club of Australia established the Review Committee in the wake of the event. Extracts from its final report confirm the seriousness of the storm that was brewing around the southeasternmost reaches of Australia. It records that the Bureau of Meteorology had issued a gale warning for the southern New South Wales coast four hours before the start of the race, and about one hour into the race this had been upgraded to a storm warning. The Storm Force winds and heavy seas experienced by the struggling yachtsmen were the result of a 'complex low pressure system which developed and rapidly intensified in the Bass Strait region overnight Saturday 26 December and during Sunday 27 December'. It appears that Storm Force winds developed over the race area 18 to 21 hours after the first storm warning was issued. Winds from the west and southwest were reported at up to 78 knots, with breaking seas of

Top FOR SPECTATORS THE MOST DRAMATIC ASPECT OF YACHT RACING, AND THE ONE THAT AFFORDS THE MOST VISUAL PLEASURE, IS THE FLEET SAILING UNDER SPINNAKER. HERE, THE FLEET OF THE 1994 SYDNEY–HOBART RACE SPORTS ITS GLORIOUS COLOURS.

Opposite *NOKIA*, A VOLVO 60 CLASS YACHT, LEADS THE FLEET DOWN THE TASMAN COAST TO WIN THE 1999 SYDNEY–HOBART IN RECORD TIME.

DEN
2001
NOKIA
P&O Nedlloyd

Above AMERICAN-CREWED YACHT *SAYONARA* LEADING THE FLEET OUT OF SYDNEY HARBOUR IN THE 1998 TELSTAR-SPONSORED RACE.

10m (33ft) in height southeast of Gabo Island, off the southeastern tip of mainland Australia.

Some race competitors confirmed experiencing thunder and lightning, and extremely poor visibility. Instrument readings supplied by *Young Endeavour*, the Royal Australian Navy's race relay ship, and by ESSO Australia Limited, Kingfish B Platform (in the Bass Strait), point towards high winds averaging 54 to 56 knots (storm-warning mean wind-speeds are estimated at 45–55 knots); however, reports received from the yachts themselves indicated that maximum mean winds actually experienced were between 55 and 60 knots, with frequent gusts up to 75 knots. Measured against Bureau storm-warning forecasts of wave heights from 4–7m (13–23ft), readings from the yachts indicate that waves of 5–8m (16–26ft), with some individual waves of 15m (49ft), occurred.

The storm initiated the biggest search and rescue operation in the history of this ocean classic, with a total of 55 yachtsmen being rescued, 50 of them by helicopter. Involved in the heroic operations were the police air wing, the Australian Maritime Safety Authority (AMSA), the Royal Australian Navy (RAN), and the Royal Australian Air Force (RAAF).

Extracts from the official press releases issued during the race paint a sad scenario:

'Owner/skipper Bruce Guy and his friend and crew Phil Skeggs died aboard Business Post Naiad, *Guy's Farr 40 [designer, New Zealander Bruce Farr] after it was rolled twice in the huge seas. Guy is reported to have suffered a fatal heart attack, Skeggs drowned after being unable to detach his safety line as the*

Above AUSTRALIAN ENTRANT *WILD THING* IN THE 1998 RACE. THE LINE HONOURS WINNER WAS *AFR MIDNIGHT RAMBLER.*

Above *NOKIA,* FORMER SWEDISH WHITBREAD MAXI *THE CARD,* BATTLING AGAINST 70-KNOT WINDS DURING THE 1998 RACE.

Above *STAND ASIDE* LYING DISMASTED IN HEAVY SEAS IN 1998 AFTER BEING KNOCKED DOWN ABOUT 50NM (92KM) OFF THE COAST.

boat rolled a second time. The search continued unsuccessfully for British yachtsman Glyn Charles who was washed overboard on Sunday night from the 43-footer Sword of Orion. *Charles represented Great Britain as skipper of the Star Class yacht at the Atlanta Olympics and sailed four times in the Admiral's Cup.'*

Equally unfortunate was the team from Australia's *Winston Churchill* – skipper Richard Winning, Paul Lumpton, Michael Rynon and Bruce Gould aboard one life raft, and John 'Steamer' Stanley and John Gibson on a second raft (although three other crew members, Jim Lawler, Mike Bannister and John Dean, had been washed out of the raft earlier that day). Almost 24 hours after having to abandon their sinking timber cutter, the four crew members of the first raft were located some 65 miles (120km) east of Gabo Island, and were subsequently winched to safety. Later, the second life raft was sighted by an RAAF Orion during a flare search, and that evening, a Navy helicopter launched from the frigate HMAS *Newcastle* was able to airlift two more *Winston Churchill* crew members.

Another successful airlift was described in the press release as follows:

'. . .the Victorian yacht Kungarra *was rolled over in huge seas some 19 nautical miles [35km] south of Gabo Island. The man, John Campbell, an American, was in the water around 40 minutes and was suffering from hypothermia when he was winched to safety by Senior Constable Barry Barclay, who dropped into 6-metre [20ft] swells to secure Campbell in a difficult rescue operation. The Victorian Police Air Wing helicopter used an infrared night vision system to locate Campbell.'*

The first boat to cross the finish line was the 28m (93ft) Maxi, *Sayonara*, with a US crew on board. It was a double for owner Larry Ellison, who had taken line honours in 1995 with the same boat, a Bruce Farr design. As she crossed the finishing line to the resounding boom from an Army cannon, *Sayonara* was more than three hours ahead of the Australian Maxi, *Brindabella*.

Top *WINSTON CHURCHILL* SKIPPERED BY RICHARD WINNING IN 1998 SANK WITHIN 20 MINUTES. THREE CREW MEMBERS WERE LOST.

Centre WINNING YACHT *SAYONARA* (OWNED BY NEW ZEALANDER LARRY ELLISON) SAILED INTO HOBART TO A MUTED WELCOME IN 1998.

Above THE MASS START OF THE 1997 SYDNEY–HOBART RACE, WITH THE FLEET TACKING TOWARDS THE SYDNEY HEADS.

1999: A RECORD FALLS

This year, the main contest for line honours among the big boats was, for the most part, between the Maxis *Brindabella* (the race favourite) and *Wild Thing*, and the 18m (60ft) Volvo round-the-world racer, *Nokia*. It was *Wild Thing*, skippered by Grant Wharington, that took the initial lead out of Sydney Harbour. Two hours later, she was closely tailed by *Brindabella* (skippered by George Snow), *Marchioness* and *Nokia*. Strong northerly winds were a boon to the fleet, fuelling strong predictions that race records would be smashed. By the time the leading yachts were in the vicinity of Flinders Island (off Tasmania), *Nokia* was maintaining a strong lead position, with *Brindabella* hard on her tail and *Wild Thing* closer inshore.

Co-skippers Michael Spies and Stefan Myralf succeeded in taking *Nokia* first across the line, which she did by knocking 18.5 hours off *Morning Glory*'s race record. Her win did not go uncontested, however. Both *Brindabella* and *Wild Thing* voiced their protest – with the former lodging a formal complaint – concerning the fact that *Nokia* had had an unfair advantage after receiving permission to use water ballast. She also appeared to have had more than her crew limit on board. The protest was later overruled, however, by the International Jury.

Left *BRINDABELLA*, AUSTRALIA'S MOST RENOWNED MAXI, TOOK SECOND PLACE ACROSS THE LINE IN THE SYDNEY– HOBART RACE OF 1998. THE YACHT CROSSED THE LINE FIRST IN SYDNEY–HOBART EVENTS IN 1991, AND AGAIN IN 1997.

Above THE INDENTED SHORELINE OF SYDNEY HARBOUR OFFERS A GREAT NUMBER OF VANTAGE POINTS FOR CROWDS TO WATCH THE START OF THE ANNUAL RACE.

Rima
Rima
HARKEN
O
V
R
P

NEWPORT–BERMUDA

The Newport–Bermuda Race is the premier ocean racing event on the US East Coast for IMS (International Measurement System) sailing yachts. Sponsored jointly by the Cruising Club of America (CCA) and the Royal Bermuda Yacht Club (RBYC), it is a biennial event (held on even years), and attracts yachts and their crews from all over the world.

The 635-nautical-mile (1176km) race starts in Newport, Rhode Island, at the mouth of Narragansett Bay and finishes at St David's Head, on the northeastern tip of Bermuda (a UK dependency) in the west Atlantic Ocean. The route crosses the Gulf Stream – an unpredictable, meandering ocean current in the Atlantic which flows up towards Europe from the Gulf of Mexico – and separates temperate from tropical waters, continental weather from mid-Atlantic conditions and, in the Newport–Bermuda race, the 'men from the boys'!

The presently held record for elapsed time is just over 57 hours, set in 1996 by George Coumantaros on *Boomerang* – an average speed of just over 11 knots; compare this with *Tenacious*, under Ted Turner's (of CNN fame) command, which in 1978 was first to finish – in 105 hours.

The ocean course for the Newport–Bermuda Race is one of the most interesting and challenging anywhere, and depending on weather conditions, the race can be won by any contender – large or small. Once the race has started, it is divided into three general parts, each requiring its own strategies and posing its own problems.

Between Newport and the Gulf Stream Sailing in cold water and often in fog, navigators must first select their point of entry into the Gulf Stream. The warm eddies north of the Stream, which rotate in a clockwise direction, need to be approached in such a way as to allow the yachts to take advantage of the favourable side – that is, by manoeuvring into the clockwise rotation. The speed of the current in the eddies can reach three knots and the eddies themselves can extend 60–100 miles (111–185km) in diameter. These days, the availability of satellite photos and their interpretation gives navigators a pretty good idea of the Gulf Stream's course and its major eddies.

Crossing the Stream Depending on the configuration of the Stream (there is no typical configuration), the navigator needs to cross the generally north-east-flowing current in the most efficient manner. The current has an average strength of up to four knots. Due to the extreme temperature difference between the Gulf Stream and the slope water to the north (the Atlantic waters into which the Gulf Stream penetrates), it is not unusual to have thunder squall activity in the Stream. The racers often find light winds punctuated by powerful, fast-moving cells of wind and lightning. The Stream itself is often quite lumpy as current and wind interact. There are many theories about how to cross it

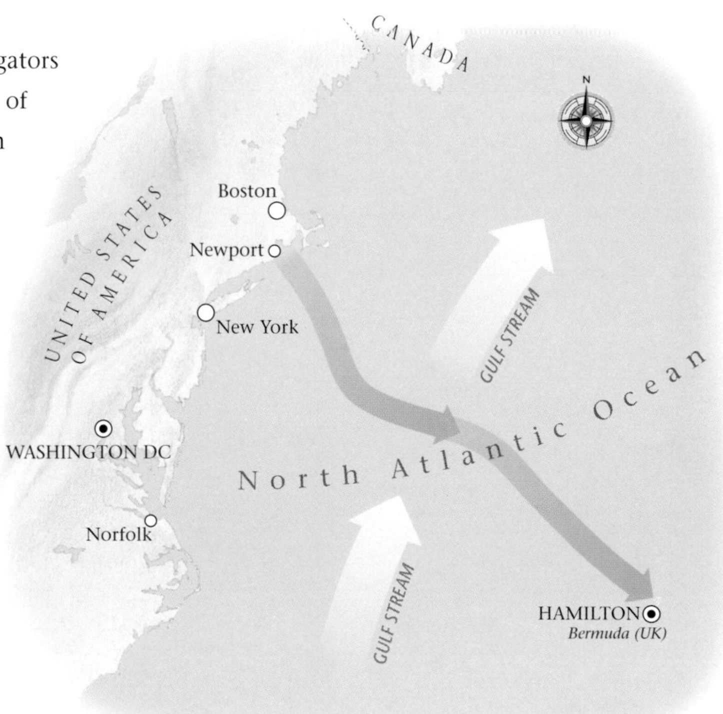

Opposite THE FARR 60 MAXI *RIMA*, OWNED BY ISAM KABBAMI AND CARRYING AN AMERICAN CREW ON BOARD, FINISHED FOURTH IN HER CLASS IN THE 1998 NEWPORT–BERMUDA RACE. SHE ACHIEVED AN ELAPSED TIME OF 100 HOURS 32 MINUTES 42 SECONDS.

Top A CREWMAN ON BOARD *RIMA* CRANKS AN ENORMOUS WINCH IN THE YACHT'S COCKPIT TO TRIM THE SAILS.

– correlating closely with the number of boats participating in the race each year!

Happy Valley to the Finish To the south of the Gulf Stream, the 300 miles (555km) or so to Bermuda are generally most pleasant. The racers travel in warm waters, and the winds are warmer and blowing generally from the southwest. Bets are made on when the island will be sighted, and there is the anticipation of completing the race – and the after-parties to come!

Bermuda is guarded on its north and northeast sides by a barrier reef that is not to be ignored. In the old days, the anticipation of meeting these reefs made the landfall more dramatic, often because of the fact that yachts had been sailing a track of dead reckoning (calculating their position by direction and the distance travelled), not having sighted the celestial horizon for several days. However, modern satellite navigation systems have made the task easier for

Left SAILING CLOSE TO THE WIND ON A BEAT IN MODERATE AIRS, CREW WEIGHT ON *ARIEL* IS MAXIMIZED AS MEMBERS GATHER ON THE RAIL AT THE START OF THE 1998 NEWPORT–BERMUDA RACE.

Above YACHTS, DECKED OUT IN COLOURFUL FLAGS, LIE AT THEIR MOORINGS AT THE YACHT CLUB HARBOUR IN NEWPORT, EMBODYING THE FESTIVE SPIRIT OF THE BIENNIAL REGATTA.

Opposite *ALEXIA* EXPERIENCES A GLORIOUS SPINNAKER RUN AS THE WIND PUSHES HER TO VICTORY IN THE MAXI CLASS IN 1998. SHE FINISHED THE RACE IN 90 HOURS 56 MINUTES 16 SECONDS.

GBR
7070T
GBR
7070
ALEXIA

51047
USA
21733
USA
43520
USA
43551
USA
50910
50910
U. S. COAST

navigators, and yachts skirt the reef to round the Northeast Breaker Buoy, and the natural features known as Kitchen Shoals and the Spit, on the way to the finish line at St David's Head, in the northeast of St George's Island, Bermuda.

1996: A RECORD-BREAKING YEAR

The Newport–Bermuda Race is not for the timid or inexperienced. It is a test of a crew's seamanship and a yacht's seaworthiness. The list of past winners reads like a Who's Who of ocean racing yachts, testifying to the race's need for seasoned sailors supported by their prestigious craft.

In the race of 1996 – the 40th biennial event – over 145 yachts with more than 1200 crew members finished in Bermuda. A frontal weather system bringing southwest winds followed by lingering calms split up the fleet, which set off on 21 June, into two groups: the bigger boats experienced a record-breaking fast race while the rest of the fleet drifted along windlessly – but finished nevertheless.

New York City investment broker George Coumantaros, on his new 24m (78ft) yacht *Boomerang*, set a new record of 57 hours 31 minutes 50 seconds, beating the 14-year-old record by almost five hours. He achieved this as a result of the following strategies: confronted at the start with the unfavourable side of a warm eddy (the northwards-sweeping arm of the clockwise-moving current), he first set his state-of-the-art IMS Maxi on a westerly course, then turned southeast into the Gulf Stream to optimize her crossing angle. She held to the west of the rhumb line (that is, the fixed compass bearing) in the face of forecasted southwest winds, taking advantage of the favourable side of the cold eddy (lying to the south of the Gulf Stream, and moving anticlockwise; Coumantaros maximized the southeast-flowing arm of the current). The wind, in fact, was more westerly, at about 20 knots, so the Maxi had a power reach for 250 miles (463km) and her skipper cranked up the pace when he was absolutely sure the winds would hold to Bermuda's islands.

Boomerang managed to stay ahead of a front, pushing down from the north, which overtook smaller boats and brought with it confused weather of up to 40-knot squalls, then periods of no wind (several boats sat becalmed for a day – with Bermuda clearly in sight!).

Boomerang averaged 11 knots for the race, achieving top speeds of around 18 knots. By the end of the event, four yachts had broken the previous line honours record of just over 62 hours, set by *Nirvana* in 1982.

Top left AN EXHAUSTED CREW MEMBER TAKES ADVANTAGE OF A NAP AMIDST THE RELATIVE COMFORT OF THE SAIL BAGS, AS VIGILANCE IS REQUIRED DURING THE COURSE OF THE FOLLOWING TWO TO THREE DAYS TO SUCCESSFULLY NEGOTIATE THE GULF STREAM.

Left WITH THE SAILS PERFECTLY SET, THE START OF THE 1998 RACE SAW CLOSE RACING BETWEEN THE CONTENDERS; MAKING USE OF THE WIND APPROACHING FROM THE FRONT, AND SLIGHTLY TO THE RIGHT, THE BOATS ARE ON A STARBOARD TACK.

Opposite THE CLASS 5 FLEET GET OFF TO A MAGNIFICENT START IN THE 1998 NEWPORT–BERMUDA RACE WHILE THE US COAST GUARD MONITORS THE YACHTS' PROGRESS ACROSS NARRANGANSETT BAY.

Top right A BUSTLE OF ACTIVITY ONBOARD *RIMA* AS THE AMERICAN CREW PUT THEMSELVES TO THE TASK OF ENSURING THEIR MAXI STAYS AHEAD OF THE FOLLOWING FLEET.

Above CLASS WINNER (1998) *BLUE YANKEE*, A FARR 47 DESIGN. TWO STEERING WHEELS ALLOW THE HELMSMAN TO STEER FROM THE BEST VANTAGE POINT AND MAXIMIZE HIS BODY WEIGHT.

CHICAGO–MACKINAC

'I hereby publicly retract anything and everything I have ever said about inland sailing.'
— *America's Cup veteran, Ted Turner*

The Chicago–Mackinac is the world's oldest freshwater yacht race. Officially known as the Chicago Yacht Club Race to Mackinac (pronounced 'mackinaw'), it was founded in 1898, and suspended only during the war years in order for participants to serve in the armed forces. Evolving over more than 100 years – from the first competition between five boats to a fleet of over 300 – and facing constantly unpredictable weather, changing rules and new technology, the race is a favourite fixture. Its popularity has been reinforced by author Donald F Prather, who in 1932 published his book entitled *There Will Always be a Mackinac Race*.

From Chicago at the southern end of Lake Michigan, the third largest of the Great Lakes and covering an area of 57,504km^2 (22,336 sq miles), the race course travels the lake's length. At its centre, 80 nautical miles (148km) separate the shores of Wisconsin from those of Michigan. Its greatest depth is 269m (882ft). The race route passes the Sleeping Bear's hump (a great mountain of white sand which juts out into the lake towards the Manitous), navigates through the Manitou Islands, passing Pyramid Point, Grand Traverse Light, South and North Fox islands, Grays Reef, Beaver Island, Skilligalee, the treacherous reef of Waugoshance, and finally rounds White Shoal Light. This is located 25 nautical miles (46km) from the finish line stretching between Round Island Lighthouse and the weather bureau tower on Mackinac Island. The island, lying in the north of Lake Michigan in the Straits of Mackinac (a channel between the upper and lower peninsulas of Michigan State), is wooded and attains a length of 5km (3 miles).

The race was created by yacht owners who spent summers on Lake Michigan sailing to Mackinac Island, where many of them had summer homes. They would frequently get to brag about their fast passages, and this eventually led to a challenge and counter-challenge until, in 1897, an official race was suggested. It was duly scheduled for the following summer – a formal challenge to see just who was the fastest. This first race in 1898 had five participants, and the winning boat, *Vanenna*, completed the 333-nautical-mile (616km) passage in 51 hours. The race became a permanent annual fixture on the Chicago Yacht Club calendar in 1904, and proper race instructions were established; in 1906 a trophy was

Top THE CLASS START FOR THE 1996 CHICAGO-MACKINAC RACE; CLASS STARTS ARE STAGGERED 30 MINUTES APART. THE COURSE FOR THE RACE RUNS THE FULL LENGTH OF LAKE MICHIGAN, ONE OF NORTH AMERICA'S FIVE GREAT LAKES, A DISTANCE OF 333 NAUTICAL MILES, OR 616KM.

Opposite LOOKING DOWN ON THE CREW OF THE US YACHT *SORCERER* FROM THE MACKINAC BRIDGE AS THEY BUSY THEMSELVES WITH A SPINNAKER PEEL – CHANGING TO A LIGHTER SAILCLOTH IN LIGHT AIRS – DURING THE RACE OF 1995.

CHOATE 48
SORCERER
CHICAGO

purchased and awarded to the overall winner. The official start line of the race was established 1.5 nautical miles (3km) east of Chicago's Monroe Harbour and the lighthouse on Round Island, off Mackinac Island, was decreed the finish mark. The first woman to participate in the Chicago–Mackinac Race was Miss Evelyn Wright, in 1905. She is appreciatively described in historical records as 'a pretty, dainty little woman, with soft brown hair that curls in the wet lake breezes and wistful brown eyes'.

Today, the 'Mac' has evolved to a fleet of 300 boats and approximately 3000 sailors in 13 divisions. The start is a half-hourly staggered affair, with the slowest boats starting first.

Top THE TIGHT FLEET START OF THE 1996 RACE – WITH SUCH CONGESTION AT THE START LINE, THE SKIPPER RELIES ON THE BOWMAN TO MAKE THE TACTICAL DECISIONS.

The organizing committee believes that much of the race's success can be credited to a consistent record of inviting only well-qualified participants up to the maximum allowable entry limit (set at 300). Consequently, and as standard procedure, the first invitations are sent to those participants who successfully completed the previous race. Invitations for the remaining openings are then issued to qualified written requests, with priority given to those who can document that they have sailed their yacht in previous 'Macs' or have experienced crews who have participated in the race. These criteria for limited and well-qualified entries have ensured that the core fleet of Mac sailors are 'old-timers'

Left YACHTS MOORED AT THE CHICAGO YACHT CLUB IN MONROE HARBOUR. THE CLUB ESTABLISHED BY EIGHT SAILORS IN 1869 COMPRISED AN OLD WOODEN SHACK AND A 5.5M (18FT) CATAMARAN.

– regulars who sail the race every year, 'goats' (those who have sailed in at least 25 Mac races) and aspiring 'goats' – building camaraderie and fun rivalry, thus enhancing the tradition.

On the island of Mackinac the horse is king – no motorized vehicles are allowed (except for emergency vehicles), including motorcycles. Thus the sailors joke about the informal race directions: 'Go to the top of the lake, turn right, and keep going until you smell the manure.'

The village gives one the feeling of stepping back into the past – there are almost as many fudge shops as there are horses – and in summer the island teems with tourists. The small, deep, crescent-shaped harbour is surrounded by brilliant-white cottages and hotels, and the Mackinac Island Yacht Club is situated across the main street from the dock.

Above *WINDQUEST*, SKIPPERED BY RICHARD DE VOS, PASSES UNDERNEATH THE MACKINAC BRIDGE NEAR THE FINISH OF THE 1994 RACE; *WINDQUEST* WON THE MACKINAC CUP THAT YEAR.

Top left MISTY CONDITIONS FOR THE RACE OF 1997 – WEATHER OFTEN EXPERIENCED ON THE INLAND LAKES. DURING THAT PARTICULAR YEAR, WINDLESS CALMS ENSURED A SLOW START TO THE RACE.

Above A YACHT SETS ITS SPINNAKER AND MAINSAIL TO MAXIMIZE THE LIGHT AIRS – IN 1997, GENTLE BREEZES RESULTED IN THE FLEET NOT HAVING DISPERSED BY DAY TWO OF THE RACE.

A RACE WITH A WINDY REPUTATION

The 'Year of the Gale' was attributed to 1911, which had 'weather varying from an eight-mile-an-hour breeze to a slashing eighty-mile-an-hour hurricane'. George Ade from the *Chicago Tribune* sailed aboard *Polaris* and filed the following report on the infamous race:

'The Polaris *adjusted itself, standing on one edge and scudding like mad, while we sat on the roof wide-eyed and a little bewildered. Then came the rain. Also an occasional hogshead of greenwater. We would come down from the roof to meet the water and after we had met it we would find ourselves up on the roof again. The wind howled and shrieked and whooped. It grappled with the* Polaris *and tried to tear it to pieces. We went plowing through huge waves capped with tatters of foam and occasionally landed with a sinking splash into a trough, but we always shook ourselves and emerged dripping. As dusk came on and the fury was abated, we clung to the rail and had all the delirious sensations of trying to ride a submarine bronco.'*

It was during this race that a record of 31 hours 14 minutes 30 seconds was set by the schooner *Amorita* (owned and skippered by D L Baum) despite a wasted four hours in the last 30 miles (56km) which the crew spent tending to a broken bowsprit shroud. Amazingly, this record was unbroken right up until 1987.

Now the giant racer fought and pitched
and slammed into the run!
Her loyal crew sat dry-eyed, tense, full
knowing her race was done!
For three men now at her tiller-bar scarce
held her on the sea.
On the starboard bow loom'd Fisher's Reef,
and a murderous surf alea!
And now wild surge becomes a dirge,
chanting a last refrain,
As the gaunt white throat of the faithful
boat is turned to sea again.
To sea she strained! Here safety lay, away
from the treacherous shore.
For surging wave but formed her grave,
'twas land killed Vencedor!

FROM *'THE WRECK OF THE VENCEDOR'*
BY MAURICE BEAM

In the same race, the yacht *Vencedor* (see panel opposite) landed on the rocks off Fisherman Island. Her crew were all rescued, but the boat was utterly wrecked.

The 'Year of the Big Blow' was the name given to the Chicago–Mackinac race of 1937: only eight of the 42 starters finished. The wind built up to 97kph (60mph) and the seas were running 6–9m (20–30ft) high with a frequency occurring only on Canada's Great Lakes.

In 1968 the Island Goats Sailing Society was created for those sailors who had sailed in at least 25 Mac races. Membership is considered a serious honour and the choice of a name for the society was aptly explained by Percy Wilson in the Chicago Yacht Club magazine, May 1968:

'Well, goats inhabit many islands, and usually those who qualify have reached that stage in life where the name seems to fit, and no-one will deny that after three or four days aboard a Mackinac racer in July, most sailors smell like one.'

The race of 1970 gave birth to the quip, 'A funny thing happened on the way to Mackinac: eighty-eight boats didn't make it'. With winds pegged at over 60 knots, there were over a dozen broken masts, assorted broken gear, ripped sails, a number of crew injuries and plenty of fatigue and seasickness.

The 76-year-old speed record held by *Amorita* since 1911 was finally broken in 1987, by more than six hours, by *Pied Piper*, a 21m (68ft) Santa Cruz 70 skippered by Dick Jennings. In spite of this, two years later the very same boat set the slowest winning time in the history of the race – an elapsed time of more than 62 hours! Jennings went on to win the Mackinac in 1999.

Opposite top ERRATIC WINDS HERE TYPIFY THOSE THAT ALTERNATED BETWEEN A BREEZE AND A LASHING GALE IN THE STORM OF 1911, WHICH SAW THE SAD END OF THE *VENCEDOR*.

Above left RACE ENTRY *LEADING EDGE* PASSES MACKINAC'S COASTAL GUARD VESSEL, DECKED OUT IN INTERNATIONAL FLAGS IN CELEBRATION OF THE 1998 RACE FESTIVITIES.

Left WITH THE TALL, GLASS-ENCASED SKYSCRAPERS OF DOWNTOWN CHICAGO RISING AGAINST THE SKYLINE, YACHTS MUSCLE INTO THE WATERS TO GET THE BEST SPOT AT THE RACE START.

COASTAL CLASSIC

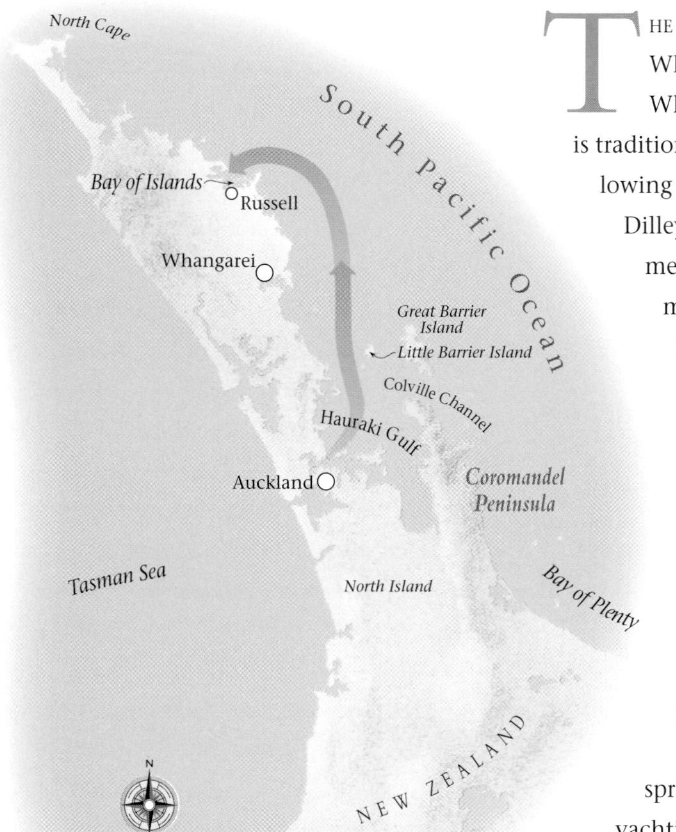

THE COASTAL CLASSIC is New Zealand's premier fleet yacht race, and runs from Devonport Wharf, on the north mouth of Waitemata Harbour in Auckland, northwards to Russell Wharf in the Bay of Islands. It is held every year over the last weekend of October, which is traditionally a national holiday weekend, as New Zealanders celebrate Labour Day on the following Monday. The Coastal Classic has its origins in a 'drag race' – conceptualized by Roger Dilley, and inspired by the powerboat races of 1921 – in which yachts were timed over a measured course (Auckland to Russell). The first race was organized in 1982 by the commodore of the NZ Multihull Yacht Club, Duncan Stuart, with the assistance of Devonport Yacht Club. Of the 12 entries, Stuart's trimaran *Krisis* set the record of 18 hours; it was upheld for four years. Today the race is a major event, with one cruising, five keeler, and two multihull divisions, attracting over 200 entries annually.

At 125.5 nautical miles (232km), the race is not long enough to be considered a major offshore event, but it does allow many lighter and faster multihulls and coastal racers to qualify and enter within the safety category rules. For the skippers and crews of these boats, this coastal race offers great adventure without the costs of complying with international offshore regulations, although compliance with coastal safety specifications (YNZ category three) must be strictly adhered to, and all yachts are required to provide inspection certificates prior to entering.

Labour Weekend is traditionally celebrated as the first weekend of New Zealand's spring/summer season, with a mass exodus to beaches and holiday locations. Many yachties regard the Coastal Classic as the first race of the season – a chance for crews to 'blow out' their winter blues on their yachts. At this time of year the Northland coast generally still has an equinoctial weather pattern, with either the prevailing northeasterly or southwesterly blowing at anything up to 40 knots, and often acting quite unpredictably. The sailors hope for a 20- to 25-knot southwesterly to give them a fast spinnaker run up the coast, in a flat-sea condition.

RIGOURS OF THE RACE

The race traditionally starts on Friday morning of the holiday weekend, with a spectacular mass fleet start in Auckland's Waitemata Harbour. In recent years there have been over 200 yachts starting simultaneously, leading to exciting and, at times, extremely close prestart and start-line manoeuvring, even when that line is stretched almost right across the harbour.

The fleet then sets sail up the Northland coast, which is renowned for its picturesque and sheltered sailing and cruising grounds within the Hauraki Gulf. The course is almost due north past the closer Gulf islands of Tiritiri-Matangi and Kawau, and then upon rounding Cape Rodney, the yachts head out of the

Left THE RECORD – A TIME OF 7 HOURS 20 MINUTES 51 SECONDS – SET IN 1996 BY *SPLIT ENZ*, A CATAMARAN DESIGNED BY NEW ZEALANDER RON GIVEN AND JOINTLY OWNED BY JASON SAGER, RUDI DEKKER AND JOHN HUGHES, WAS STILL THE COASTAL CLASSIC RECORD IN THE YEAR 2000.

Opposite *KICK*, OWNED AND SKIPPERED BY IAN HARVEY, CAME SECOND ON LINE IN DIVISION TWO (*AFTERBURNER* TOOK LINE HONOURS) IN THE COASTAL CLASSIC RACE OF 1998. SHE CAME IN JUST UNDER 8.5 HOURS AFTER THE LINE HONOURS WINNER.

49
8349
8349
8349
KICK

Hauraki Gulf, clear of the shelter of the Barrier Islands and Coromandel Peninsula, and are then at the mercy of the South Pacific Ocean. It is at this stage that a major tactical decision needs to be made: whether to race inside or outside the Hen and Chickens group of islands, which straddles the direct course about 30 miles (56km) to the north. The islands rise sheer out of very deep water, and have reefs, rocks and other obstacles between them, preventing the setting of a course through the middle of the group. There is invariably a Pacific swell crashing on the 100–150m-high (330–490ft) cliffs, making approach hazardous in the extreme.

The course outside, or east, of the Hen and Chickens, although slightly longer than the inside, westerly, course, is very much the favoured route if the breeze is backing from either the northeast or the southwest. Yachts taking the inside course head north-northwest for about 20 nautical miles (37km) from Cape Rodney to the western tip of the Hen Island, and then veer north again to clear Tutukaka Head on the main coast. This is the last real sheltering place on the northern coast until the yachts are well into the Bay of Islands.

The coastline north of Tutukaka is littered with reefs, rocks, small islands and hazards, and is not a place for the faint-hearted, especially those sailing close inshore through the night to achieve the best rhumb-line course (the fixed compass bearing the boat was following). On the other hand, yachts which have elected to take the outside course (usually only a few) head north from Cape Rodney up to the back of the Hen and Chickens, then turn a few degrees to the northwest for the run to Cape Brett. At this

Below *ACES HIGH*, DESIGNED AND SKIPPERED BY IAN VICKERS, TOOK LINE AND HANDICAP HONOURS IN THE PHRF CATEGORY IN THE 1999 COASTAL CLASSIC WITH A TIME OF JUST UNDER 14 HOURS.

Right THE FLEET AT THE START OF THE 1999 COASTAL CLASSIC WITH, IN THE FOREGROUND, *FUTURE PERFECT* (LEFT), *KIWI* (RIGHT) AND *SURE THING* (PARTLY OBSCURED). *FUTURE PERFECT* TOOK LINE HONOURS.

stage they are perhaps 20 nautical miles out to sea and can be out of sight of all land. This is clear sailing with no obstacles or hazards except for the Poor Knights Islands and rocks, which are several miles further to seaward of the rhumb line course.

In ideal conditions, this can be some of the most exhilarating yacht racing anywhere, surfing long 5–6m (16–20ft) Pacific swells, with spinnaker and staysail tightly sheeted on a blasting broad reach, for over 120 nautical miles from Auckland all the way to Cape Brett at the southern entrance to the Bay of Islands.

Just off the Cape to the east lies Piercy Island; the gap between the two is a natural short cut for racing yachts entering the Bay of Islands from the south. Feared and respected – with good reason – by all New Zealand mariners, the tide from the Bay of Islands empties out through this 200m-wide (60ft) channel between huge sheer cliffs at a very fast rate, and the Pacific swells (or in a northeasterly cyclonic weather system, huge seas) build against the outgoing tide and the vertical rock walls. It is not unusual to experience steep, breaking 10–12m (33–39ft) seas at Cape Brett. Much higher waves have been recorded here, sometimes breaking 40 and 50m (130 and 165ft) up the cliffs.

Sailors rounding 'The Brett' in the early hours of the morning for the final run in to the Bay of Islands can find this daunting. Inside the gap, conditions are often likened to being inside a washing machine – in the past, heavy displacement 15m (50ft) and 18m (60ft) yachts have been known to get tossed around like corks in the completely confused seas.

From Cape Brett it is a relatively short run in through the Bay of Islands and to the final destination, Russell. During this last challenge, yachts usually tack the last 25-odd nautical miles (46km) with no lighthouses on many of the islands, dozens of rocks, obstacles and hazards in the yacht's course, and often a dying breeze in the early hours of the morning.

Above THE START OF THE 1996 COASTAL CLASSIC: *PRIMO*, ONE OF THE LEADING BOATS, WON DIVISION ONE BOTH ON LINE AND HANDICAP, SETTING A NEW RACE RECORD FOR KEELERS.

Above WITH SPINNAKERS UNFURLED, THE THIRD START GETS UNDER WAY IN 1998. THE LEADING YACHT, *BLONDIE*, A YOUNG 88 OWNED BY TREVOR CANUTE, WAS SKIPPERED BY HIS SON CRAIG CANUTE.

Above BOATS PARTICIPATING IN THE COASTAL CLASSIC ON A REACH THROUGH RANGITOTO CHANNEL. THE SUBURBS OF COASTAL AUCKLAND SERVE AS A BACKDROP TO THE ACTION.

SOME MEMORABLE RACE YEARS

The first Coastal Classic held in 1982 certainly triumphed in its role to (unofficially) set up the challenge between multihulls and keelboats. Thereafter, the annual race has seen some surprises. The inaugural record of 18 hours was fixed by New Zealander Duncan Stuart and his trimaran *Krisis*. The first keelboat (which came in third overall) was *Hawkeye*, 2 hours 25 minutes short of the record elapsed time. In 1985, two yachts took up the challenge against each other. What piqued everyone's interest was their difference in size. David Barker on his self-designed 17m (56ft) catamaran *Sundreamer* was roundly overtaken early on by the smaller narrow-hulled, wide-beamed 12m (40ft) catamaran *Split Enz* and its triumphant crew of Rudi Dekker, Jason Sager and Neil Strong. *Split Enz* set a new course record of 17 hours 6 minutes 48 seconds. *Sundreamer* came in fifth on line.

The Coastal Classic of 1988 was characterized by 'dream' weather conditions, allowing the massive, high-tech multihull *Afterburner*, which had already set a new record the previous year,

Above THE START OF THE 1999 COASTAL CLASSIC: IN THE FOREGROUND ARE *LOVEA'LUCK* (SKIPPER PETER LORY), *GEORGIA* (SKIPPER JAMES FARMER) AND *HYDROFLOW* (RON BRITTAIN).

Opposite top THE CATAMARAN *SPLIT ENZ*, DESIGNED BY NEW ZEALANDER RON GIVEN, IS THE CURRENT RECORD HOLDER SINCE 1996. *SPLIT ENZ* ALSO SET NEW RECORDS IN 1985 AND 1993.

Opposite centre THE 15M LONG, 9M WIDE (50FT/30FT) MULTIHULL *AFTERBURNER* WAS DESIGNED BY MALCOLM TENNANT. ALASTAIR RUSSELL IS BOTH OWNER AND SKIPPER.

to shave 3 hours 19 minutes 5 seconds off her own record. Southwesterly winds that reached 20–25 knots between Whangarei Head and Cape Brett had *Afterburner* achieving a top speed of 25 knots, and averaging 20.5 knots for the duration of the race. Generally, most yachts didn't even have to hoist a headsail. *Afterburner*'s crew were tested once, however, between Cape Rodney and Sail Rock when the wind dropped, forcing them to make 13 sail changes in one and a half hours! They still managed to achieve their new race time of 9 hours 20 minutes 50 seconds.

In complete contrast was the race of 1989. Constant, stormy 25–30-knot head winds throughout the race forced 91 out of 155 contenders to retire (this time around, *Afterburner* completed her race in a very different time – 21 hours 39 minutes 51 seconds).

One catamaran, *Chesapeake*, with owners Robert and Alison Gunn on board, flipped over in a powerful gust of wind which also underwent a 90-degree change in direction, catching them unprepared. Not having time to release the mainsheet, the boat 'turned turtle' (hull-up) while Alison was below deck. However, she managed to emerge within 20 minutes, and the crew was rescued by a keelboat.

The 1996 race saw the fastest times ever experienced in the Coastal Classic. It was also the largest fleet to date, with 250 entries. Strong easterly winds caused many pullouts – mainly due to sea sickness – but for the 200-plus competitors who successfully made it to Russell, it was the ride of their life. All the records in all divisions were smashed, and still stand today. *Spit Enz* set the line honours time, and *Primo* holds the record for the first keeler in.

What started as a dream light southwesterly in 1997 eventually increased to a 30-plus-knot wind – with 11 casualties, among them two dismastings, a boat holed and a multihull capsized.

Notwithstanding such incidents, the Coastal Classic has an enviable safety record – no lives have ever been lost in the race.

Right THE CREW OF *AFTERBURNER* AFTER A CAPSIZE IN 1997. HER MAST WAS REMOVED, STRAPPED TO HER SIDE, AND SHE HAD TO BE TOWED IN TO AUCKLAND, WHERE SHE WAS RIGHTED BY CRANE.

KH-81
KH-818

SAN FERNANDO

THE YACHTING FRATERNITY OF HONG KONG, which functions as a Special Administration Region of China since the much publicized handover by the British in July 1997, represents the legacy left by Hong Kong's heyday of colonial capitalism. Today, local yachtsmen continue to enjoy first-class racing and scenically beautiful cruises around the former colony's many islands. In fact, the sailing grounds have expanded as a result of races to destinations along the China coast, including Hainan Island, lying 400 nautical miles (740km) southwest of Hong Kong. Such events enjoy the support of the Chinese Yachting Association, thus improving the relations between Hong Kong and the burgeoning sport on coastal China.

The magnificent Royal Hong Kong Yacht Club (RHKYC), at the centre of yacht race organization in Hong Kong, is today the setting for the San Fernando Race. Considered one of Asia's Classic offshore races, its original home was the port of San Fernando, on the island of Luzon in the Philippines.

Held over Easter (March/April), it has been recognized as the most important offshore event, and is sanctioned and supported by the UK's Royal Ocean Racing Club. No other institution better mirrors those colonial days and the RORC's long history of yachting and rowing than the RHKYC. The club is set on what was once an island – and the address of Kellett Island is still in use, even though the surrounding waters have long since disappeared under ongoing land reclamation. The departing expatriates are being replaced by affluent Chinese members, some of whom are taking a prominent place on the international yacht-racing scene (the club still maintains a staff of 240 to satisfy the desires of its 4000 members).

The first San Fernando Race was held in 1975. It attracted only six yachts, and started from San Fernando once the fleet had cruised down to the Philippine islands from Hong Kong. Since that first race, the start line has been in Hong Kong, and the race has subsequently become a popular biennial event. Competitors cross the South China Sea, sailing southeast to Luzon – a distance of 500 nautical miles (926km). As there are no intermediate ports en route, yachts venture further offshore than the Sydney–Hobart Race. While primarily catering for Hong Kong-based sailors, the race has attracted an international yachting cast, including entrants from Japan, the Philippines, Singapore, Australia, the UK and the USA. Perhaps the most famous yacht from the UK to sign up for the race was *Rothmans*, helmed by Lawrie Smith. *Rothmans* set a line honours record – which has not yet been surpassed – in 1987 of 2 days 2 hours 2 minutes, although this feat was somewhat eclipsed by a handicap victory by the local yacht *Bimblegumbie*. In 1999, Frank Pong of Hong Kong just failed to break the line honours record on his new 24m (80ft) Sled *Jelik*; he was thwarted by light winds within sight of San Fernando.

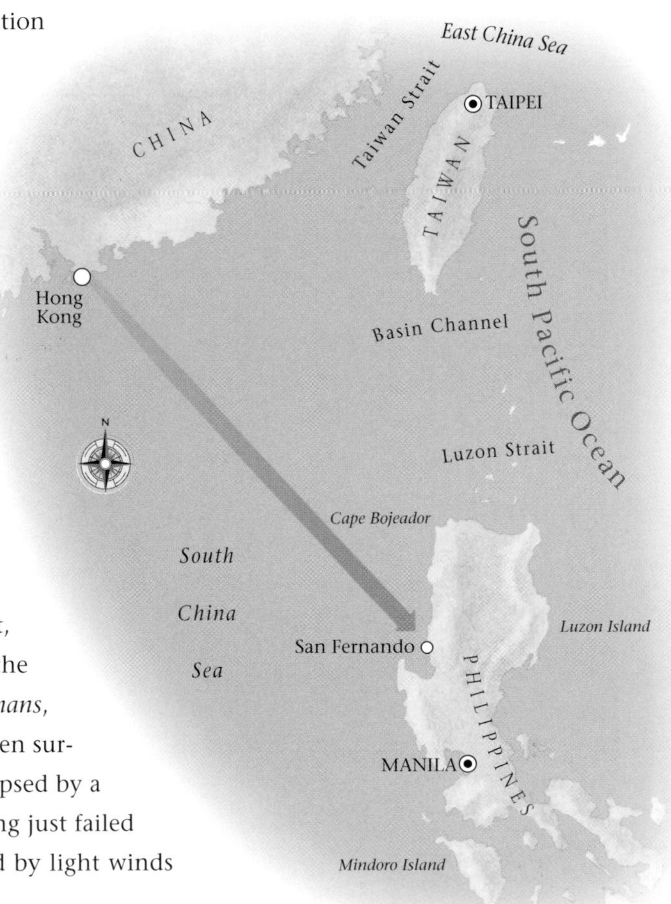

Opposite *BIMBLEGUMBIE*, HERE AT THE START OF THE 1989 SAN FERNANDO RACE, IS AN ED DUBOIS DESIGN, OWNED BY AUSTRALIAN KEITH JACOBS.
Top ONCE THE YACHTS HAVE COMPLETED THEIR RACE TO SAN FERNANDO, THEY LIE AT ANCHOR JUST OFFSHORE IN THE SOUTH CHINA SEA. LOCALS LAUNCH THEIR COLOURFUL *BANCAS* (BEACHED HERE IN THE FOREGROUND) TO SERVE THEM EXCELLENT BEER FROM THE ISLANDS.

Left DWARFING THE REST OF THE FLEET, THE MAXI RACER *ROTHMANS* (FOREGROUND, LEFT), SKIPPERED BY AMERICAN LAWRIE SMITH, IN 1987 SET THE RECORD WHICH IS STILL CURRENT.

Hong Kong is normally under the influence of the northeast monsoon during March/April. Competitors can face brisk winds and challenging seas for the first couple of days. The malevolent character of the South China Sea gradually wears off as the yachts approach the Philippine coast of northern Luzon, where the crews gladly cast off foul-weather gear in favour of T-shirts and sunscreen. Long spinnaker reaches accompanied by balmy breezes and starlit skies make helming a magical experience, especially when steering by a low moon. This is 'champagne sailing' at its best.

San Fernando, on the coast of Lingayen Gulf in La Union province, is about 225km (140 miles) north of Manila, the nation's congested capital in southwest Luzon, and is about as different from the capital as one can get. The finish line is set at the southern end of a reef, which protects the resort area of Bauang; it is manned by a yacht which will have preceded the fleet setting off from Hong Kong. Inside the reef, yachts at anchor attract the attention of the local *banca* drivers who ply the thirsty yachtsmen with local beer. *Bancas*, the Philippine solution to coastal transport, are craft – inevitably painted in bright, garish colours – comprising a narrow plywood hull supported on either side by bamboo outriggers. They are powered by Briggs & Stratton air-cooled petrol engines and are capable of speeds in excess of 20 knots.

And there are always anxiously eager takers for the beer that they sell, as it is both excellent and very cheap.

Once the race is over, the party begins. Most skippers insist on keeping their boats 'dry' during the race, reserving the drinking of alcohol for the finish. The rustic waterfront resorts on the palm-fringed sea form a natural party environment. The high point of the festivities is the traditional Cabana bash when most crews put on a unique song-and-dance act usually involving stories of the misfortunes and foul-ups suffered during the race. Such is the generally risqué nature of the revelry, the unspoken rule is that stories are never repeated back in the Main Bar of the Royal Hong Kong Yacht Club!

A unique aspect of the race and after-party is the financial support subsequently given to a children's orphanage in San Fernando, which has benefited enormously through the generosity of the competitors.

Race Chairman Vic Locke felt that they had been treated well over the years in San Fernando and that they should put something back into the community. He is recorded as saying, 'A lot of people see the hedonistic side of yachting and I feel this charity and the support it's getting shows the real face – and heart – of the yachtsmen and women who take part in the San Fernando race.' In 1995, HK$140,000 was raised at a function attended by 140 yachtsmen, and it went towards the building of a new dormitory.

A few days after each race finish, most yachts head back to Hong Kong, leaving behind a few fortunate skippers who have the time to cruise the scenic local waters, where good rum costs US$1 for a litre (almost 2 pints) and fishermen supply the freshest of catches. Leisure-seeking sailors can explore the beautiful waters around the limestone isles of the Linguyen Gulf, known as the Hundred Islands, or venture to the little-visited islands like Mindanao (in the past, visitors stayed away because of political instability). El Nido, a small town on the island of Palawan in the eastern Philippines, is particularly beautiful with its sharp cliff drops and jagged heights surrounded by turquoise seas.

Right DURING THE 1989 SAN FERNANDO, *L'AVENTURA*, A STEVEN JONES OYSTER, RACES NECK AND NECK WITH *SWEET CAROLINE*, OWNED BY AUSTRALIAN STEVE ELLIS, A HONG KONG-BASED PUBLISHER.

Opposite *WINDSEEKER*, OUT FRONT ON A FAVOURABLE STARBOARD TACK AT THE START OF THE SAN FERNANDO RACE OF 1989. THANKS TO ENTHUSIASTIC OWNER JOHN BLAY, SHE IS A MUCH-SAILED YACHT.

1198
KH
1195
Windseeker
RHKYC

OCEAN

CLASSICS

ROUTE DU RHUM

The Route du Rhum (deriving from the 'rum-making' heritage of the French West Indies) is a 3700-nautical-mile (6852km), single-handed race from Saint Malo, the top commercial port on the north coast of Brittany, France, to Point-à-Pitre, a city-port on Guadeloupe's Grande-Terre island in the French West Indies. The race takes some 10–15 days to complete. Created by Frenchman Michel Etevenon, it was first held in 1978, and it takes place every four years. Etevenon's intention was that the event be driven by total freedom (it is open to all yachts), but over the years it has become a duel between multihulls. What the Route du Rhum did do was to introduce an era of 'show' sailing that gave rise to the creation of new boats.

In November, the month in which the yachts set off on the race, the North Atlantic is swept by a stream of depressions (the Westerlies) which form over the USA and then move towards Europe. It is therefore always highly probable that the competitors will encounter very bad weather during the first part of the race. At this time, the trade winds are well established in the south and blow from the north-east, and it is these carrying winds that enable the boats to quickly make progress towards the finishing line. The dilemma with which sailors are confronted is whether to first pass north of these depression systems and then take advantage of the carrying winds, or whether to pass south (therefore sailing into westerly head winds), with the ultimate aim to also gain the advantages of the trade winds to the south as quickly as possible. This optimization of one's route is up to each boat's routers, or weather forecasters, who talk to the racing crew and help them, via their onboard PC, to make the best choice using simulation programmes which integrate the weather patterns into five-day forecasts.

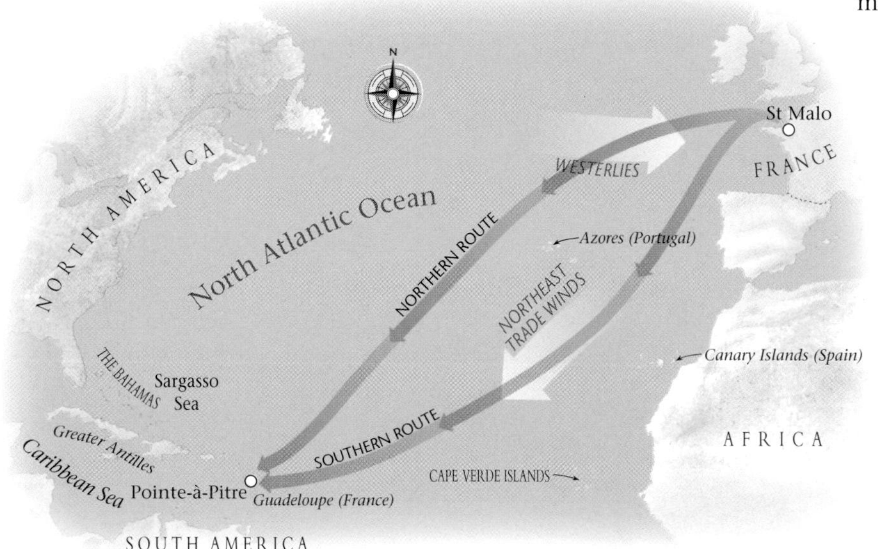

A HISTORIC FINISH IN 1978

At the finish of the first Route du Rhum race, at Pointe-à-Pitre, only 98 seconds separated the winning boat from the second after 23 days of racing – almost impossible to believe. Of the 38 racers at the starting line, 12 boats did not cross the finish.

Weather conditions were very difficult right from the start and several favourites had had to abandon the race already in the first few days. Others, including Philippe Poupon on *Pen Duick III* (formerly Frenchman Eric Tabarly's boat), were forced to stop over in the Azores, islands lying off the coast of Portugal. In the lead, Olivier de Kersauson, on *Kriter IV*, chose to look for better conditions much more to the south, after which Michel Malinovsky took over the

Previous pages ROY DISNEY'S *PYEWACKET II* IN SAN DIEGO IN 1999; IN THE SAME YEAR, DISNEY WON THE TRANSPAC RACE ON *PYEWACKET III*.

Top SKIPPER MIKE BIRCH, WINNER OF THE 1978 ROUTE DU RHUM, NEAR THE FINISH ON HIS BOAT *OLYMPUS*; HE PIPPED CANADIAN MICHEL MALINOVSKY TO THE POST BY 98 SECONDS. A SERIOUS RACE CONTENDER, BIRCH CAME IN THIRD IN 1982, FOURTH IN 1986 AND FOURTH IN 1990.

Opposite *CACOLAC D'AQUITAINE* SKIPPERED BY YVES PARLIER DURING THE ROUTE DU RHUM IN 1994. CLAUDE BISTOQUET, WHO WAS IN THIRD PLACE EARLIER ON IN THE RACE ON *TWINSEA DÉFI GUADELOUPE*, OVERTURNED TWO DAYS FROM THE FINISH LINE, RELINQUISHING HIS POSITION TO PARLIER.

CACOLAC
d'Aquitaine
LA ROUTE DU CACAO
ARCACHON
CACOLAC
d'Aquitaine

Left FRANCIS JOYON ON *BANQUE POPULAIRE* CAME IN 10TH IN THE 1990 ROUTE DU RHUM RACE. MODIFICATIONS MADE TO THE TRIMARAN IN 1997 AND 1998 INCLUDED A PIVOTING WING MAST TO INCREASE THE ACTIVE SAIL SURFACE AREA WHEN THE BOAT HEELS.

lead in the north on *Kriter V*. Because the boats were not equipped with Argos positioning systems (see page 79) in this first race, it was anyone's guess as to who would win. When Malinovsky reached the Guadeloupan coasts, the odds were placed on him. But it was Canadian Mike Birch, who had not been in radio contact for several days, who took everyone by surprise. (Two years previously he had finished third in the Ostar [see page 69] – a single-handed transatlantic race – on the trimaran *Third Turtle* behind Tabarly and Alain Colas.) Taking advantage of the high speed of his small yellow multihull *Olympus*, Birch passed Malinovsky a few nautical miles from the finishing line, crossing it as the winner, with only a 98-second lead (in a time of 23 days). This kind of close finish had never been seen in the history of offshore racing.

Alain Colas left the starting line of the Route du Rhum on the old trimaran *Manureva*, on which he had won the Ostar race six years previously. The famous sailor, emulator of Tabarly, ceased sending messages at 05:00 on the 17th November, while in the centre of an enormous depression. Saint-Lys radio sent his final call to his home. It described an apocalyptic situation: 'I'm in the centre of a typhoon, there's no more

Above LAURENT BOURGNON'S *PRIMAGAZ* AT ST MALO, FRANCE, IN THE ROUTE DU RHUM RACE OF 1994, FOR WHICH HE TOOK LINE HONOURS. BOURGNON WAS ALSO WINNER OF THE FASTNET IN 1997.

sky, there's no more sky!' Tragically, the marine search aircraft scoured the Atlantic Ocean thereafter without any success.

A REPUTATION FOR BAD WEATHER

In the 1996 Route du Rhum race, bad weather as usual decimated the fleet; only 15 out of the 33 boats at the start reached the finishing line. Many of the favourites were forced to withdraw: Eric Tabarly gave out the first SOS of his sailing career when one of the hulls on his trimaran *Côte d'Or* broke up. Loïc Peyron (brother of Bruno) set off a second time after a three-day delay when he was dismasted at the start. Sailing Mike Birch's former 15m (49ft) catamaran, he finished fifth at Point-à-Pitre after a superb recovery.

In the end it was Philippe Poupon who crossed the finishing line victorious, on the trimaran *Fleury Michon*, with more than two days' lead over Bruno Peyron. The latter gracefully paid tribute to Poupon, acknowledging that he had known 'how to attack, even with a fifty knots wind'.

Loïc Caradec, on his giant 26m (85ft) red-and-white catamaran, did not come back from that year's Route du Rhum. His last radio contact was on the 14th November: 'I'm being buffeted about in all directions. The boat, with no sails up, nearly overturned in a fifty-two-knot gust. It went on one hull. I had to hurry to the helm to straighten it up. The heeling alarm keeps going off.'

A signal from an Argos beacon in the hours that followed indicated a problem. French woman-sailor Florence Arthaud discovered the overturned boat the following day. Scuba divers explored the hulls two days later and found no trace of Caradec, who must have been carried off by the sea. The boat was fully intact, except for its mast which had been torn away.

Four years later, the race of 1990 stood up to its reputation of unfavourable weather. The competitors left under a well established west wind, which enabled them to clock up miles during the first few days, but they were greeted by three big depressions approaching the Azores. As in every year, many favourites were forced to pull out or to stop over in the Portugese archipelago to repair the damage.

On the third day Florence Arthaud took the lead, but was overtaken early in the beginning of the second week by Mike Birch and Philippe Poupon who had both chosen a more northern route; Arthaud had lost her routing system due

Top left 1994 ROUTE DU RHUM CONTENDER JEAN MAURÈL SUFFERED DAMAGE ON *HARRIS WILSON* TWO DAYS AFTER THE START OF THE RACE. HE EVENTUALLY CAME IN EIGHTH.

Above FRENCH SAILOR PHILIPPE POUPON SAILED *FLEURY MICHON* INTO NINTH PLACE IN THE ROUTE DU RHUM RACE OF 1982, INTO FIRST PLACE IN THE EVENT OF 1986 AND SECOND PLACE IN 1990.

Top right SWISS SAILOR THOMAS COVILLE'S *AQUITAINE INNOVATIONS* WAS THE FIRST MONOHULL TO ARRIVE AT POINTE-À-PITRE IN THE FRENCH WEST INDIES IN THE 1998 RACE.

to an electrical failure. Less than 48 hours before the finishing line, the race was a close contest between Laurent Bourgnon and Birch, Poupon and Arthaud. It was the trimaran *Pierre 1er*, skippered by Florence Arthaud, that took the laurels in a nail-biting finish, by only a few minutes.

Thirty-year-old Thomas Coville was the winner of the monohull division in the 1998 Route du Rhum. Having had only one month to prepare for the race, he resolved to sail with caution on his 18m (60ft) wing-masted yacht, *Aquitaine Innovations*, particularly since his mainsail was fairly old. For the first two-thirds of the race, his course imitated the traditional great circle to the north, after which he curved southwards. Coville took 18 days 7 hours 53 minutes 32 seconds to cover 3530 nautical miles, at an average speed of 8.02 knots. Laurent Bourgnon once again won the multihull division on *Primagaz,* in 12 days 8.75 hours.

Top left AN IMAGE OF *FUJICOLOR I* TAKEN FROM LAURENT BOURGNON'S *PRIMAGAZ* DURING THE 1994 ROUTE DU RHUM. *FUJICOLOR* WAS LATER DISMASTED AND UNABLE TO COMPLETE THE RACE.

Centre left A TRANQUIL MOMENT DURING THE 1998 ROUTE DU RHUM FOR RACE WINNER LAURENT BOURGNON. SECOND PLACE WENT TO PAUL VATINE, WHO WAS FOLLOWED BY YVES PARLIER.

Left ON BOARD *PRIMAGAZ,* A VIEW FROM THE COCKPIT OF THE MULTIHULL, LOOKING DOWN THE COMPANIONWAY INTO THE CABIN WHERE THE NAVIGATION STATION IS SITUATED.

Above FLORENCE ARTHAUD ON BOARD HER TRIMARAN *PIERRE 1ER,* WHICH KEPT SPECTATORS SPELLBOUND WHEN IT CAME IN FIRST BY ONLY MINUTES IN THE ROUTE DU RHUM RACE HELD IN 1990.

LAURENT BOURGNON

In 1994 France's quadrennial single-handed transatlantic Classic, the Route du Rhum, saw the course record being broken by three hours – despite half the fleet retiring before the halfway mark – by Laurent Bourgnon from Carnac, France, on his multihull *Primagaz*. His time for the 2900-mile (5370km) course was 14 days 6 hours 28 minutes 29 seconds.

Early on in his career, he completed what he describes as an 'extreme voyage', sailing from France to Guadeloupe in the Caribbean on a Hobie Cat. On that voyage he reached severe limits of fatigue, and has since spent many years working with the best doctors in sleep therapy. He is a great believer in polyphasic sleep – falling into a deep sleep immediately, but undertaken in multiple, short phases. He has trained himself, through self-hypnosis and meditation, to achieve this; he stayed awake for 10 days for the 1990 Route du Rhum race, with the aid of the drug Ephidrine (a stimulant), used by fighter pilots. 'This experience tells you that fatigue is all in the head and self-control is the key element,' maintains Bourgnon.

He receives an annual budget of US$1.1 to 1.5 million from his sponsor Primagaz, a budget that is modest compared to some but suits Bourgnon's simple organizational style.

He claims, 'What I dream of at night is not to finish first or in the first three in a race. I dream of preparing my boat well, of putting my energy into achieving the best results. Win or lose, that matters more than proving that I am a better racer than another skipper.'

Above BOURGNON ON *PRIMAGAZ* PULLS AHEAD OF *FUJICOLOR I* DURING THE 1994 ROUTE DU RHUM. PAUL VATINE, AT FIRST IN THE LEAD ON *HAUTE NORMANDIE* ON THE NORTHERN ROUTE, WAS BEATEN BY BOURGNON BY A THREE-HOUR LEAD, AFTER HE TOOK THE SOUTHERN ROUTE.

FRA 111
FRA 111
111
111
POSTAPHOTO

MINI-TRANSAT

THE MINI-TRANSAT IS A SINGLE-HANDED RACE that crosses the North Atlantic. Held every two years, it spans a month, and involves the racing of tiny yet extremely fast yachts (it is limited to 6.5m/21ft craft) through a variety of weather conditions. The Mini-Transat was created in 1977 by Briton Bob Salmon, the objective being a solo transatlantic race that was affordable. (At the time, events such as the OSTAR [*Observer* Single-handed Transatlantic Race] were being dominated by ever bigger yachts at ever greater cost.)

The yachts start in Concarneau, on the southern tip of the northwest arm of France, and sail to the Canary Islands, off northwest Africa, for leg one of the race; they continue on to Guadeloupe, in the Caribbean's French West Indies, for the second and final leg, covering approximately 4800 nautical miles (8890km). The fleet has to endure the unpredictable weather of the Bay of Biscay (lying between the French west coast and the north coast of Spain), while during the second leg, the boats seek the northeast trade winds of the North Atlantic, when route planning and weather forecasting play a vital part in the success of their performance in the competition.

The 55-strong entry for the first Mini-Transat, in 1977, was made up of representatives from six countries. The size of the fleet was remarkable considering that although the initial concept of the race was to make it relatively easy on the budget, boats can still cost upwards of US$100,000 to build and race for a year. The strong links between the 6.5m (21ft) Mini-Transat yachts (referred to as 'Minis' among yachtsmen) and their bigger Open 60 cousins (see page 108) of the Vendée Globe and BOC were clearly visible.

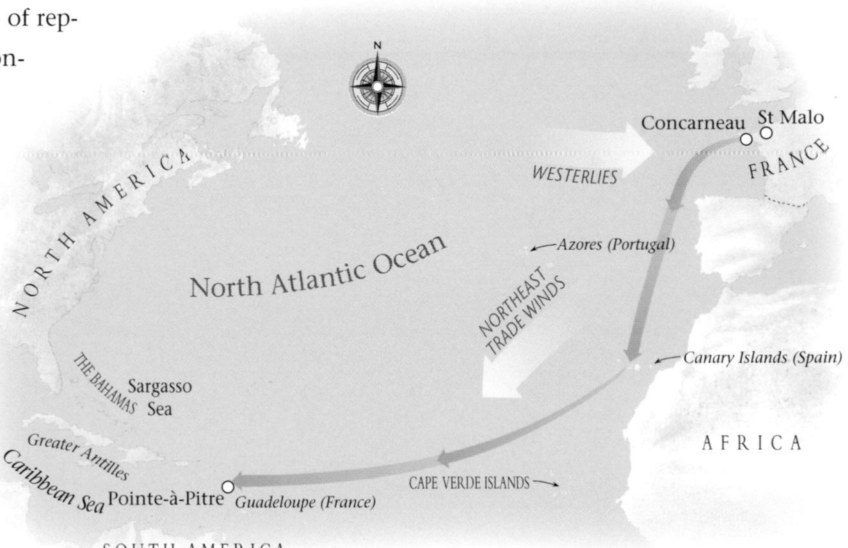

A RACE DETERMINED BY BOAT CLASS

The Open 6.5 Class – the boat class regulated for the race – is known as a 'Low Limits' Class. That is, the designers have only two limitations – overall size and materials used. The Mini Class represented a vitally important testing ground for new ideas. Some of the innovations, such as hingeing spinnaker poles, longitudinally adjustable keels and multiple bilge boards, at first appeared radical developments – as did twin rudders, water ballast and canting keels when they were first introduced. Today, as a result of the radical amendments and features introduced in response to the low design limits, some of the 6.5m (21ft) Minis actually match those sailed by the BOC and Vendée Globe contenders.

Active production lines exist for only two One Design classes: the Pogo and the outdated Cocoa designs. The basic features common to all are: an overall length of 6.5m (21ft), a 2m (6.5ft) draught and

Opposite THE YACHT *POSTAPHOTO* IN THE MINI-TRANSAT OF 1995. IT WAS SKIPPERED BY FRENCHMAN NICOLAS RAYNAUD, AND CAME IN SEVENTH OVERALL. THE RACE WAS WON BY YVAN BOURGNON, ON *OMAPI-SAINT BREVIN*.

Top SKIPPER LIONEL LEMONCHOIS ON *MÉCÉNAT CHIRURGIE CARDIAQUE* AT THE START OF THE 1999 MINI-TRANSAT IN CONCARNEAU; HE HAS SHEETED THE SAILS RIGHT IN AND IS SAILING CLOSE TO THE WIND ON A BEAT. LEMONCHOIS WAS PLACED 24TH IN THE RACE.

a mast length of 11m (36ft). The more modern Pogo is constructed from polyester-glass: the deck is of a balsa-polyester-and-glass sandwich; the rudders of polyester, glass and foam; and the ballast is lead. As a result of the few design restrictions for the Mini 6.5, rig and sail design is an area where much can be gained. Costs are controlled due to the regulated absence of Kevlar/spectra sails, and carbon rigs.

What is significant about the Mini-Transat is that a significant subclass of production-line boats participate in the race. In 1997, the first two Pogos were eight minutes apart after 4000 miles (7408km), and were in the top 10 overall. A 'kit boat' sells for as little as £13,000; for £22,000 the boat is ready to sail, with all the extra equipment required for a transatlantic race. Meanwhile, a professionally built prototype, on the water, costs in excess of £60,000.

As the Mini-Transat is an essential element of any Vendée Globe hopeful's CV, it has become an increasingly professional race. For the rule makers, this is proving more difficult – there is the 'spirit of the Mini' to consider, as conceived by Bob Salmon, versus the need to remain an Open Class in order to attract the best. Many of the boats that sailed in the first, 1977 race came off the production line or were home-built cruisers like the winner *Serpentaire*. The lack of suitable designs led some sailors to cut away the bow of their boat to qualify for the length limit.

The winner of the next race, held in 1979 – *American Express*, skippered by Norton Smith – was designed specifically to the class requirements, with 280 litres (62gal) of water ballast on each side of the hull. This generated the high-performance battle that has since so dominated the event; the race that followed in 1981 saw canting keels, which have become a typical Vendée Globe and BOC characteristic.

Today, the Mini-Transat attracts sponsorship and professional skippers, and is sailed in high-

Above THOMAS COVILLE ON *ZÜRICH INSURANCE* IN THE 1997 MINI-TRANSAT. AFTER PUSHING HIS BOAT TOO HARD, HE LOST VALUABLE TIME FOLLOWING A WIPEOUT IN WHICH HE LOST A SPINNAKER.

Above right SPARTAN LIVING CONDITIONS AND HI-TECH NAVIGATIONAL EQUIPMENT ARE INDICATIONS OF THE PRIORITIES IN MARK TURNER'S CABIN. HE CAME FIFTH IN 1997 ON *CARPHONE WAREHOUSE*.

Top LIONEL LEMONCHOIS ON HIS YACHT *MÉCENAT CHIRURGIE CARDIAQUE*, POWER REACHING WITH A REEFED MAINSAIL AND FLYING AN ASYMMETRICAL SPINNAKER OFF THE BOWSPRIT.

tech boats with correspondingly high budgets. The race itself is well organized with stiff entry qualifications that include the completion of a 500-nautical-mile (926km) passage, single-handed, prior to the race start. The event has wide media appeal throughout Europe, providing a first-class platform for name and product exposure through newspapers, magazines, radio and television (terrestrial and satellite).

What still remains special about the Mini-Transat race is that, despite the number of professional entrants, it is easy for amateurs to form part of the fleet: there are those undertaking their first major offshore race, those whose only aim is to get to the finish, and finally those who are there only to win, with the best boats, sponsorship, and a minimum of six months' solid preparation. It makes for a fascinating mix – and the sharing of the experience serves to

Right THE START OF THE 1997 MINI-TRANSAT. RACE WINNER SEBASTIEN MAGNEN COMPLETED THE RACE ON *KAREN LIQUID* IN AN ELAPSED TIME OF 24 DAYS 15 HOURS 11 MINUTES 16 SECONDS.

Top SEBASTIEN MAGNEN (HERE ON *KAREN LIQUID*) IMPROVED ON HIS 1997 TIME BY WINNING OVERALL IN 1999 ON *VOILE MAGAZINE JEANNEAU* IN JUST UNDER 24.5 DAYS, DESPITE A DAMAGED RIG.

break down any barriers or rivalry that potentially exists between the skippers.

The physical demands of the race, however, are strenuous. Gear failure and the need for constant maintenance are unavoidable. Although adrenaline and the will to win keeps entrants pushing their boats to the limit, often there comes a time when they have to reassess their priorities. Sleep is always a major consideration; a weary mind and exhausted body make for irrational decision-making. A postponed maintenance problem could develop into gear failure. Achieving the correct balance is critical. If too many problems develop, or if too much fatigue builds up, this often leads to broken equipment and a lot of down time. Swiss sailor Thomas Coville, the race favourite in 1997 while skippering *Zürich Insurance*, pushed too hard under a masthead spinnaker and destroyed it after a major wipeout. He lost valuable time which probably cost him the race overall.

Above ELLEN MACARTHUR ON *FINANCIAL DYNAMICS* IN THE 1997 RACE, IN WHICH SHE WAS PLACED 15TH OUT OF 51 ENTRIES. IN 1998 MACARTHUR WAS NAMED THE BT/YJA YACHTSWOMAN OF THE YEAR.

Thomas Coville also learnt the hard way about sleeping while sailing. Sailors estimate that it takes about 14 minutes for the average freighter to reach the boat they are on from its spot on the horizon, which in turn determines the amount of sleep that can be taken in one go. After trying to sneak in some rest, Coville woke up in a large shadow to find his spinnaker brushing against the bulb of a freighter. A crash gybe saved his boat – and probably his life – but unfortunately not his remaining spinnaker.

Without question, the most demanding aspect of racing a Mini-Transat yacht is gear

stacking and 'shifting'. With the boats being so light, the continuous shifting of weight is vital. The time taken to gybe or tack can be extended by almost 20 minutes if it includes the struggle to shift all the kit (20-litre/4gal water containers have to be moved to the high side of the craft, a strenuous task while the boat is continuously being thrown around).

Above right YACHTS GATHERING AT THE START OF THE 1997 RACE IN PREPARATION FOR THE FIRST LEG – STARTING IN CONCARNEAU, FRANCE, AND FINISHING IN LANZAROTE, IN THE CANARY ISLANDS.

On the upside, some of the latest autopilots make it possible to leave the helm with the boat in full sail, including the masthead spinnaker, and even with the boat surfing. Some very impressive runs of over 12-knot averages for 24 hours – not bad for a 6.5m (21ft) craft – have been recorded, the best by yachtsman Fred Seeten.

The 1997 race was the first in which the competitors were allowed to carry a GPS navigational system. Prior to that, navigation had been by sextant only (although not all competitors knew how to operate a sextant!); also, the rules were satisfied with lightweight plastic sextants not known for giving accurate sights. One 1997 competitor lost the use of his GPS as well as the back-up, and was forced to use his sextant. He did find land, but the wrong one! After a quick stop in Barbados, in the eastern Caribbean, he made it to Martinique, just inside the time limit.

Another tense moment of the race was when Eric Logais, in the mid-Atlantic, was sleeping below decks on his yacht and awoke to find the craft on its side after a broach. It continued turning till it rested upside down, and Logais realized that the keel had broken away. Swimming out from the airlock, the Frenchman then spent several hours diving back inside the boat to retrieve safety equipment and released an EPIRB (Emergency Position Indicating Radio Beacon). He was fortunate in that he was picked up within hours by a cruise ship.

The biggest difference between the Mini-Transat and the Vendée Globe races, apart from the boats, is that the only form of communication in the former is via VHF radio. There is no such luxury as Inmarsat C or satellite communication technology – simply line-of-sight radio contact. This means many days of silence – especially on the 2700-mile (5000km) second leg, when the fleet quickly disperses to chase favourable winds. There is no doubt that the single most unique element of the Mini-Transat is solitude. In 1997, for 20 of the 23 days of the second leg, some competitors had absolutely no communication with anyone. The only radio reception was Radio France, which occasionally broadcast details of the top three contenders.

Not knowing where they lie in the fleet plays havoc on the confidence of the competitors; they find making tactical decisions much more difficult. Certainly, mirror-like seas, being becalmed for 24 hours, total silence except for the 'flap, flap, flap' of the sails, and 2000 miles (3704km) still to go, is a psychological battle with solitude – epitomizing the challenge a solo voyage presents to the sailors who take it on.

OSAKA CUP

OSAKA IS A PORT SITUATED ON OSAKA BAY, an inlet of the Pacific Ocean at the south of Japan's Honshu island. The first maritime event ever held by this city was Osaka World Sail 1983. It was also the first of its kind in Asia. Ten tall ships (square-rigged sailing vessels) from seven countries paraded through Osaka Bay, followed by a stay in port – giving Osaka's citizens a chance to experience the elegant tall ships through tours of the vessels, one of a variety of events that were on offer. Following this festival, the possibility of holding a regular international maritime event was looked into, with the assistance of the Nippon Ocean Racing Club.

The first such international event, held in 1987, was the Melbourne–Osaka double-handed yacht race known as the Osaka Cup, which was timed to commemorate the 120th anniversary of the opening of the port at Osaka to foreign vessels. The city of Osaka scheduled the race to take place every four years, starting in Melbourne, the capital of Victoria State and situated on Port Phillip Bay, southeast Australia, in an effort to increase interest in maritime activities. Race rules stipulate that only two crew members are permitted aboard each boat (short-handed sailing). Because they race intensively for the duration of the entire event, it is an exhausting one, calling on tactical skills and physical endurance. Added to this are the interpersonal skills required to share the confines of a yacht with one person for an uninterrupted period of between 30 and 50 days – and nowhere to escape to! An objective of the Osaka Cup is to promote the development of technology and thereby create vessels that are suited to two-man crews on this difficult, long-distance passage, which is usually regarded as psychologically tougher than a single-handed race (the two crew members tend to push each other harder than one pushes oneself when alone on board).

Inspired by its quadrennial Osaka Cup race, in 1993 the city of Osaka constructed a three-masted training sailship, *Akogare*, to enable citizens to experience the feel of sailing on a tall ship. Since then, approximately 6000 people have participated in the sail training programme which develops leadership, teamwork and the spirit of cooperation that is the product of a crewman's life on board a tall ship.

A further event, the first Asian tall ships race, Sail Osaka 1997, organized with the cooperation of the UK-based International Sail Training Association, commemorated the 100th anniversary of the construction of Osaka's modern port. The race started in Hong Kong, on the Chinese coast, and sailed northwards to Japan, first stopping over in Okinawa, largest of the Ryuku coral islands at the southernmost extremity of Japan. The second stopover was Kagoshima, on the island of Kyushu, in south Japan, with the race finishing in Osaka, on Honshu Island. There were 15 tall ships among the 48 participating vessels from 17 countries. The 3400 sailors and trainees on board the vessels were warmly greeted in Osaka by more than 1.8 million spectators, making Sail Osaka '97 one of the biggest maritime events ever held in Asia.

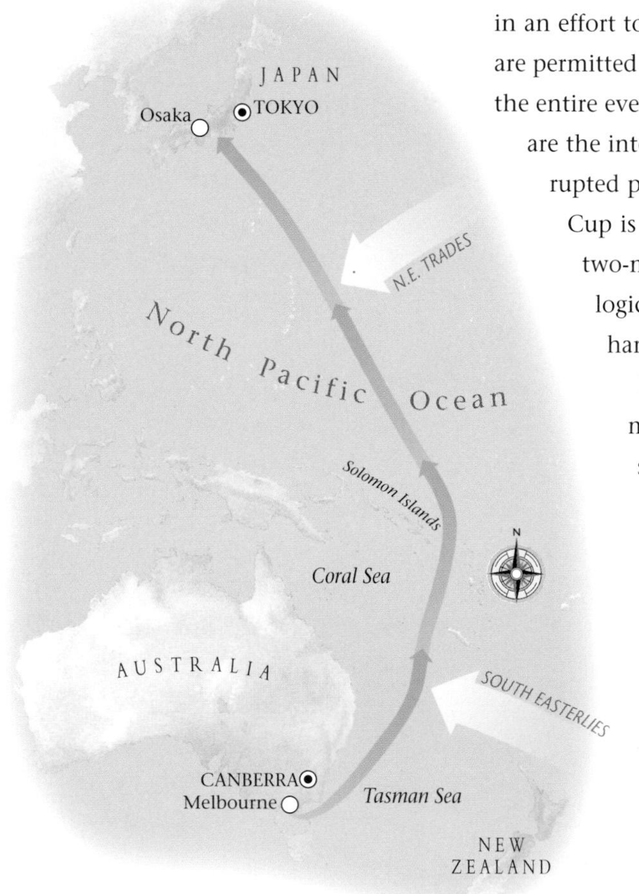

Top THE ROYAL SYDNEY YACHT SQUADRON'S WINNING ENTRY IN 1998, *SAYERNARA*, FINISHED IN 30 DAYS 3 HOURS 39 MINUTES 22 SECONDS.

Opposite THE START OF THE 1998 OSAKA CUP: THE BOATS FOLLOWING *SAYERNARA* WILL BE BLOCKING THE WIND COMING IN FROM BEHIND, SO AUSTRALIAN ROB DRURY AND NEW ZEALANDER JON SAYER HAVE TO MAINTAIN THEIR CONCENTRATION AND KEEP THEIR SPINNAKER FILLED.

R 1200
Coca-Cola
YAMAHA
16

Above UNDER THE WATCHFUL EYE OF TAILING SPECTATOR CRAFT, AN OSAKA CUP CONTENDER BEATS TO WINDWARD UNDER FULL SAIL IN FRUSTRATING LIGHT WIND CONDITIONS.

PROMOTING CULTURAL EXCHANGE

By virtue of the nature of the Melbourne–Osaka race, this event particularly has captured the fiercely competitive spirit so prevalent in the yachting fraternity. It is the first nonstop, double-handed yacht race in the world to cross the Pacific longitudinally, that is, from the Southern to the Northern Hemisphere, and has thus enjoyed enormous popularity and support. Boats travel a distance of 5500 nautical miles (10,186km) and move through the seasons backwards, experiencing autumn in Melbourne, summer at the equator, and spring in Osaka.

To add to spectator enjoyment, the race has two 'legs', although the first is a very short spectator race from Station Pier in Port Melbourne, across Port Phillip Bay, to Portsea Pier on the narrow peninsula at the mouth of the bay, complete with a big prize-giving that night. The media is very involved in the event, and the spectators are highly supportive.

The following day, the second leg sets off from Portsea Pier, and the yachts sail nonstop from here to Osaka. The course is full of difficulties, like the roaring Tasman Sea (between Australia and New Zealand), potential May storms in

Left DESPITE SUFFERING DAMAGE IN 1999, TONY WARREN AND ALISTAIR GREENWOOD MANAGED A CREDITABLE THIRD POSITION IN THE RACING DIVISION ON THEIR RELATIVELY OLD BOAT, *OUTRAGEOUS III.*

Right PETER DE LANGE AND LAURIE FORD IN THE WIDE COCKPIT OF OSAKA RACE ENTRY *SPIRIT OF DOWNUNDER*. THE BOAT FINISHED THE RACE AS WINNER OF THE RACING DIVISION IN 1999.

Japanese Pacific waters, heat in the equatorial doldrums (south of the Philippines), and countless jagged coral reefs.

The Osaka Cup is not about speed alone. Connecting the two cities of Japan and Australia, various cultural events contribute to the relation-building exercise between Melbourne and Osaka, and for two weeks prior to the actual race there are public Japanese cultural demonstrations in Melbourne, like Noh and Kyogen theatre (stylized classical drama), and Japanese drumming and harp recitals. The Australians correspondingly host their own Bush Night, and a sheep-shearing demonstration is just one of the activities on their agenda.

The event is massive in terms of strengthening relationships between the sister ports, and it is well supported by the media. Once the fleet reaches Osaka, there is a welcoming ceremony for the first boat to finish, a Welcome Festival for all those who finish, a Goodwill Yacht Race and barbecue, as well as a massive prize-giving and reception for the media and everyone involved in the race.

In yacht racing generally competitors race under a handicap system in an effort to accommodate many different types of yachts (see page 12); boats are therefore divided into classes that

Above ROBIN HEWITT AND SIMON DRYDEN, ON AUSTRALIAN ENTRY *YOKO*, WERE WINNERS OF THE CRUISING DIVISION (A TIME OF JUST OVER 33.5 DAYS) IN THE OSAKA CUP EVENT HELD IN 1999.

take account of factors such as overall length, displacement, and sail area. For the Osaka Cup, to ensure that the general spectator is able to understand the rules, the normally complicated method of handicapping has been simplified. One of the special characteristics of the race is the creation of a Cruising Division, which makes it possible for slower vessels to enter (they have a larger displacement and sail area in relation to the Racing Division). As a result, a variety of crews and vessels gather together for the race; the latest high-tech racing yachts aiming to win compete side by side with cruising yachts built to travel the world's seas. Overall length of the yachts ranges from 10–16m (33–52ft), therefore, within the Racing and Cruising divisions themselves, there are a further three divisions dependent on boat length: 10–12m (33–39ft, 12–14m (39–46ft), and 14–16m (46–52ft).

Safety criteria are strict: no-one under the age of 18 is eligible to enter, the boat must pass a stringent safety inspection and have completed, at the least, a nonstop voyage of 200 nautical miles (370km) in open seas. The participants themselves have to have completed a 500-nautical-mile (926km), nonstop ocean passage.

Of the handful of Melbourne–Osaka Races that have taken place to date, the yacht *Nakiri Daio* twice crossed the finishing line first (in 1987 and 1991), although with different skippers at the helm. Turbulent conditions characterized the Osaka race in 1999. New Zealand entry *Green Hornet* sank east of Sydney after encountering difficulties in 40–50-knot southwest winds, and only 12 of the 20-boat fleet finished the course. The current elapsed time record, set in 1995 by Grant Wharington and Scott Gilbert on *Wild Thing*, stands at 26 days 20 hours 47 minutes 6 seconds.

Below THE AUSTRALIAN YACHT *SAYERNARA*, A 13M (42.5FT) SLOOP, WAS DESIGNED BY JOHN SAVER AND IS CREWED BY ROB DRURY AND JON SAYER. IT TOOK LINE HONOURS IN 1999.

For long-distance communication, yachts use a SSB (single sideband) wireless radio operating on short-wave frequency. This method utilizes the short wave signal's ability to bounce off ion layers in the atmosphere, although due to atmospheric conditions, transmission success is dependent on time of day and frequency.

Communication via satellite has revolutionized modern-day human interaction. Satellites are able to continually circle the earth through the interplay of centrifugal force and the earth's gravitational pull. A 'stationary' satellite (appearing so as it orbits the earth above the equator at the same speed as the earth's rotation) rotates at an altitude of 36,000km (22,370 miles) – three times the diameter of the earth. Because stationary satellites remain in the same position in relation to the earth, transmissions from earth can be consistently picked up. However, because of the extreme distance from earth, a transmitter with a large output is necessary. It also takes time for the transmission to reach its destination, so during voice communication, there is a delay between conversations. As a result, satellites that orbit at low altitudes of 800–1100km (500–685 miles) have started to come into use.

Race organizers make use of the Argos satellite system to monitor the fleet and keep track of their positions. The Argos, installed on each yacht, has a transmitter that sends its position automatically, via satellite, on a predetermined schedule. The satellite, after receiving the signal from the ship's transmitter, stores the information until it is above the ground station, which then totals all the data and manages each participating yacht's position.

All yachtsmen rely on an EPIRB (Emergency Position Indicating Radio Beacon) in dire emergencies to pinpoint their position when it is too late to make any other form of contact. The EPIRB also transmits a signal (the identification code peculiar to that yacht) to a satellite when the switch is turned on in an emergency. The signal is then forwarded by the satellite to the ground station. The position of the transmission (the point of the accident) is calculated from the Doppler effect of the received signal. (The Doppler effect is when there is a change in frequency of a sound or light wave related to motion between the source and the observer.)

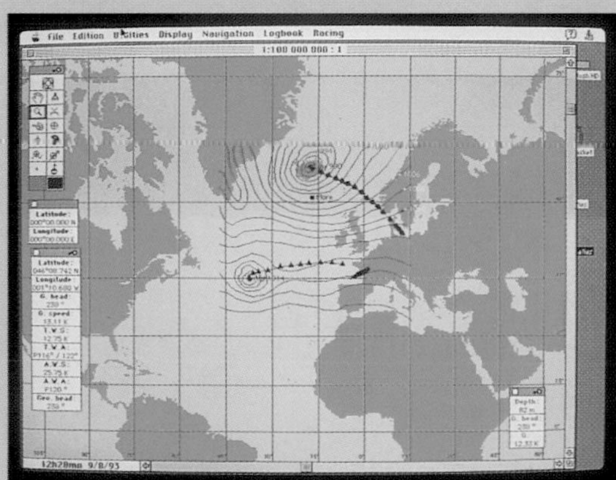

Top to bottom HAND-HELD EMERGENCY POSITION INDICATING RADIO BEACON (EPIRB); ONBOARD ELECTRONIC NAVIGATIONAL PROGRAMME; SATCOM B TRANSMITTER INSTALLED BELOW DECKS.

Advances in technology have also enabled two-way transmission (as in telephone communication) to be accomplished, separately, via satellite.

Inmarsat has been in use since 1982 as a satellite communication system for sea-going vessels. Communication across the entire globe is made possible by four stationary satellites – A, B, C, and M (to differentiate communication speed). Inmarsat Marine Mini M terminals come equipped with a small antenna that follows the satellite. The antenna is incorporated into a 27cm-diameter (10.5in) dome-shaped cover. The unit, including the phone set and power source, weighs 2.6kg (5.7 lb), much lighter than wireless radios up till now. Operation of the terminal is the same as using a telephone. Calls can be received from and sent to anywhere in the world.

Data transmission is also possible using a normal parallel cable connection to a computer and normal communication software. At 2400 bytes per second, the transmission speed cannot be considered fast, however it is possible, during a race, to send e-mail and pictures taken on board using a digital camera.

Iridium, an element found in platinum ores and having the atomic number of 77, is the name given to a communications system whose original plan was to have 77 low-orbit satellites. In actuality, the plan has been achieved with 66 satellites (six as backup). The satellites employed circle the earth in a north–south orbit at an altitude of 780km (485 miles), completing one orbit in 100 minutes. Due to their low altitude, the distance between satellites and the ground terminal is shorter, allowing for a small-sized terminal. The size and weight of the device is reminiscent of cellular phones about 10 years ago. This system also relays information between satellites. A satellite picks up the signal received from a terminal, this information is relayed to nearby satellites and finally sent back down to the ground station (this method of communication also reduces the number of ground stations required).

TRANSPACIFIC

THE IDEA TO ESTABLISH A YACHT RACE FROM SAN FRANCISCO, on the USA's west coast in the state of California, to Hawaii 's capital Honolulu, based on the island of Oahu, originated with local sailor H H Sinclair and Honolulu Yacht Club commodore, Clarence W Macfarlane. The proposal was first met with more criticism than enthusiasm by sailors who argued that the race itself was too long, and the return voyage too difficult. Not easily discouraged, Macfarlane and Sinclair enlisted support from other local yachtsmen, including Commodore T W Hobron of the Hawaii Yacht Club. Slowly, the idea for a transpacific race gained momentum.

By 1906 a conglomerate of Hawaiian bodies put forward a US$500 cup to become the permanent property of the Transpacific Race winner. Hawaiian King Kalakaua, well known for his enjoyment of deep-sea sailing, was named chairman of the race committee. The first race was scheduled for 5 May 1906, starting at 15:00 from San Francisco's Meggs Wharf – but still the yachtsmen were slow to enter. Macfarlane decided to put an end to the race apathy by himself proving that the return trip was achievable, so on 6 April 1906 he set sail – against the wind – on his boat *Lurline* to San Francisco. He had extracted promises from about 30 Californian yachtsmen and crews of the Bay Area to race him back to the Hawaiian islands if he succeeded in making it into port before the scheduled start a month later.

Twenty-eight days out of Honolulu, a weary Clarence Macfarlane spotted San Francisco harbour. Through the binoculars he could see the docks, but no sign of welcoming pilot boats. He found this odd, but comforted himself with the thought that he was 'one up' on the San Franciscan yachtsmen and had sneaked in long before they expected. His jubilant crew furled the sails, then went below decks for breakfast, to await their reception. The reception never took place.

A sombre San Francisco port doctor arrived, as per the customs regulations, to examine Macfarlane and his crew shortly after they had anchored. Macfarlane told the doctor that he was disappointed at not having being welcomed, as was custom, by the local sailing enthusiasts, and asked if his crew could at least be escorted to the Occidental Hotel. The doctor responded, 'Coming in, did you notice anything strange?'

'Yes,' Macfarlane confirmed, he had. The harbour had seemed deserted on their arrival, but he had not given it a second thought. The doctor led Macfarlane to the deck and pointed to shore. No buildings could be seen in the distance. Smoke rose from smouldering fires scattered throughout the city. Long lines of people waited near a tent encampment. The yacht had arrived in San Francisco several hours after the

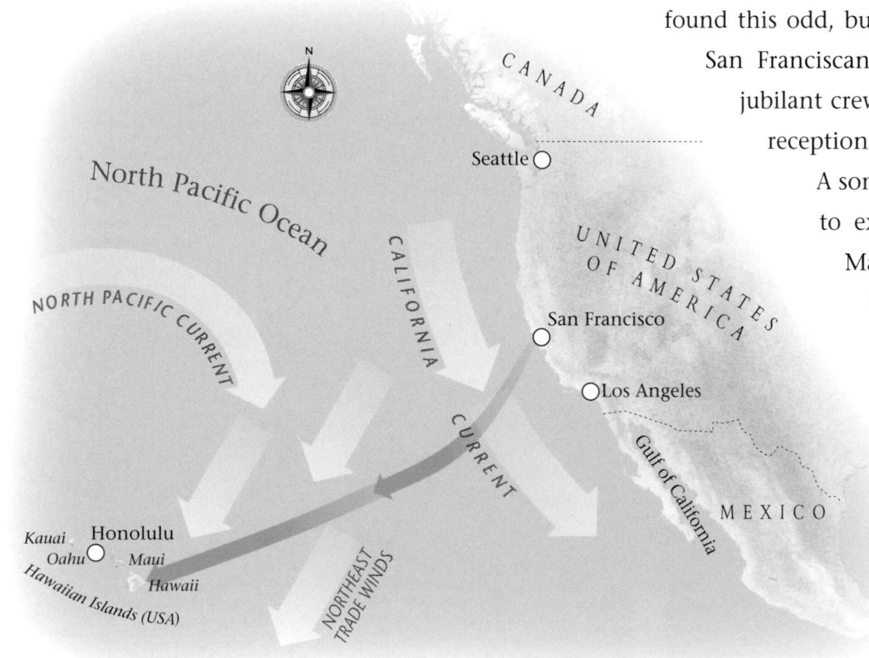

Top BOWMAN PASCAL BLOUIN DOING REPAIRS ON THE SPINNAKER POLE OF *COMMODORE EXPLORER*, CO-SKIPPERED BY JULES VERNE TROPHY WINNERS FRENCHMAN BRUNO PEYRON AND AMERICAN CAM LEWIS IN THE 1997 TRANSPAC RACE. THEIR NAVIGATOR WAS SKIP NOVAK, WHO HAD SKIPPERED IN THE WHITBREAD. *COMMODORE EXPLORER* WAS THE RACE-WINNER IN THE MULTIHULL DIVISION.

Opposite *PYEWACKET* COMPETING IN THE 1995 RACE; IT WAS TO SET TWO TRANSPAC RECORDS IN THE ENSUING YEARS – IN 1997 AND 1999.

devastating 1906 earthquakes; the terrifying tremors and fires that accompanied the natural disaster had all but levelled the city.

'To find your hotel amidst this,' the doctor told Macfarlane, 'would be some trip'.

Realizing the commodore had had no way of knowing about the disaster, he politely added, 'What kind of a trip did you have?'

'One helluva trip,' came the cursive reply. At this point not quite fully aware of the extent of the devastation, Macfarlane followed up with, 'What kind of a fire did you have?'

'One helluva fire,' was the answer.

While San Francisco was being rebuilt, the first official Transpacific Yacht Race was rescheduled to take place on 11 June 1906, with its start in San Pedro, south of Los Angeles.

Above BRACK DUKER'S SANTA CRUZ 70, *EVOLUTION*, COMPETING IN THE TRANSPAC RACE OF 1995. SAILING DOWNWIND WITH HER MASTHEAD SPINNAKER, SHE CAN ACHIEVE TREMENDOUS SPEEDS.

Although the early years saw only three or four boats entering, numbers steadily increased, building up to 71 entries in 1967 and 80 in 1979. Today, an average of 40 boats participate in the race. With the exception of the war years, this biennial event has increasingly attracted sailors from all over the world. The spirit of adventure, and the unsurpassable Hawaiian welcome – aloha – that embraces them after nearly two weeks at sea, has ensured that the Transpac is still one of the most popular long distance

yacht races. It is a pursuit race, meaning that the smaller boats are given sufficient head start to close in on the finish line, with some small boats starting nearly a week before the superior, turbo-charged racers. While predominantly a down-wind race – a 2225-mile (4121km) high-speed surf down the long Pacific swells – for the first few days the boats are either close-hauled (sailing as close to the wind as possible) or close-reaching (sailing 60–90° off the wind) until they reach the Pacific trade winds.

A NEW BOAT CLASS FOR THE TRANSPAC

The Transpacific Yacht Club Perpetual Trophy, better known as the Barn Door, is the most prestigious US West Coast ocean racing prize. It is awarded to the monohull that gets from Los Angeles to Honolulu in the shortest elapsed time. A result of this challenge has been the development of a superfast downwind boat design, known as a Sled (first created by Santa Cruz [California] yacht designer Bill Lee). Similar to the snow sled, these Sled Class yachts are designed for high-speed rides of over 20 knots down mountains of blue water. Lee created several yachts of various sizes – but all long, light and narrow, and ideally suited to the downhill slide conditions so characteristic of the race. The best known Sled Class yacht is probably Lee's own 20m (67ft) *Merlin*, which in 1977 set a record in the Transpac of 8 days 11 hours 1 minute 45 seconds (since broken).

Over time, boats from this class continued to compete against each other: taller masts, longer poles, bigger spinnakers, and more sail area were added to try to get an edge in the duel for line honours. Transpac officials grew understandably nervous, with a growing concern as to where this 'first to finish' obsession might ultimately lead. In an effort to end this duel, in 1983 the Transpacific Yacht Club (TPYC) established a maximum rating limit of 70.0 for the Transpac Race to be held that year, as determined by the International Offshore Rule (IOR). This decision gave birth to a new class of Sleds specifically designed to the rating limit – the ULDB 70s (70ft/21m Ultra Light Displacement Boat).

During the next decade, more than 30 ULDB 70s were built, optimized to the maximum rating limits imposed, and all the designs placed special emphasis on the downwind performance that is so important on the Transpac course. The success of this new Sled Class was attributable to how much fun the boats were to sail. They accelerated incredibly fast; with a breeze of 20–30 knots, the boats slid off the waves attaining 20-plus knots with complete control.

By 1994, however, the 70.0 rating limit of the International Offshore Rule was virtually obsolete, and new Maxi boats were being built to the parameters of the International Measurement

IMS MAXI vs TURBOSLED

When one compares a TurboSled to a true IMS (International Measurement System) Maxi like *Morning Glory*, it is obvious that the IMS design is bigger, heavier and more powerful. An IMS Maxi is about 24m (79ft) long – 3m (11ft) longer than either variety of Sled. Also, it displaces about 24,490kg (54,000 lb) – twice the weight of the Sleds. The IMS Maxi boats have about 50 per cent more sail area than TurboSleds, and their 4m-plus (13^{+}ft) keels draw 1m (3ft) more water.

Although TurboSleds and IMS Maxis rate very much the same, the Maxis are much quicker in buoy racing around marks.

THE 1997 TRANSPAC CREATED A NEW DIVISION FOR ULTRA LIGHT DISPLACEMENT TURBOSLEDS (TOP), WHICH ARE BUILT FOR FAST DOWNWIND SAILING. MAXI YACHTS SUCH AS *STEINLAGER* (ABOVE) MAKE UP FOR EXTRA WEIGHT WITH A LARGER SAIL AREA AND LONGER WATERLINE.

System (IMS). In an effort to attract these new boats to the Transpacific Yacht Race, the TPYC Board of Directors increased race rating limits for the 1995 event. With this revision, it became apparent that a ULDB 70 would not be the first boat to the islands of Hawaii.

Most of the ULDB 70 owners were upset by the ruling, but two American sailors saw it as an opportunity to improve their odds at winning the Barn Door.

The first, Dr Hal Ward, had been in the process of building a new ULDB 70; before it was even taken from the mould, Ward asked his designer Alan Andrews to modify the plans – ignoring the restrictions of the ULDB 70 Class – to optimize his new yacht, *Cheval*, and adapt it for the revised Transpac rating limits.

The second US sailor, Roy Disney, was also quick to act. He ordered a huge, new, fractional carbon fibre mast for his Santa Cruz 70, *Pyewacket*, and had a deeper keel designed.

Both Ward and Disney were 'turbo-charging' their Sled hulls and the term TurboSled was invented. The TPYC had been responsible first for the creation of the Sled Class after they had imposed rating limits for the 1983 race; they had now succeeded in influencing a second new class by increasing the rating limits.

These new TurboSled sailors were not interested in handicap systems or corrected time. They simply wanted to be the first boat to cross the finish line – for them, this was ultimately what the race was all about.

TurboSleds are light boats with extensive sail area, designed specifically for the Transpac's downwind sailing conditions. The hulls of all TurboSleds are built in one of two existing moulds – the same ones used to produce ULDB 70s – but this is where the similarity ends. TurboSleds have tall fractional carbon fibre spars compared with the Sleds' shorter masthead rigs, usually made of aluminum. The headsails for both classes have almost identical dimensions, but a TurboSled mainsail is typically 3–3.5m (10–12ft) taller. Also, all TurboSleds carry oversize spinnaker poles and masthead spinnakers, so their spinnakers are about 50 per cent bigger. Their keels are correspondingly heavier and deeper – .5m (1.5ft) deeper – than Sleds to provide additional righting moment for their larger sail plan.

A 20-YEAR RECORD FALLS

During the course of the 1995 Transpacific race, things had been going particularly well for US boat *Cheval 95*, and the following was reported by an elated crew member, John Kolius.

'We're aboard Cheval *surfing the trade winds along the Hawaiian island of Molokai and nearing the finish of the Transpac Race. Dawn has just broken on what will be our final day at sea, and all twelve crew members are juiced because we're in a position to claim offshore sailing's hat trick: first to finish, first in class, and first in fleet. Life is good!'*

The finish was only 35 miles (65km) away when a block in the backstay system exploded during a gybe in a wind that hit 25 knots, and the mast crashed over the side. The crew drew on their experience and reacted with efficiency. They were fast approaching a reef off the point of Molokai; the life rafts were immediately moved on deck, and then the rigging was cut away. A jury rig was hastily erected using the 8m (26ft) spinnaker pole lashed to the mast stump and the sails were hoisted up sideways. No longer doing 17 knots, the boat still managed a creditable 8-knot average, surfing off one wave at 11.6 knots. *Cheval 95* managed to win the race by a narrow 20 minutes, but 13.5 hours behind *Merlin*'s (Bill Lee) record run of 1977.

Only in 1997 did suitable conditions exist for record-breaking runs, and the first to go was *Merlin*'s 20-year-old record. Bob Lane's 17m (56ft) *Medicine Man* from Long Beach, California, took hours off the record with a corrected time (that is, on handicap) of 8 days 6 hours 31 minutes. He averaged 11.2 knots across the course. In the Sled Class, Roy Disney's 21m (70ft) TurboSled, *Pyewacket II*, became the first monohull to finish the race in less than eight days with a time of 7 days 15 hours 24 minutes 40 seconds. The multihull record was smashed by more than 30 hours by Bruno Peyron of La Baule, France, on his 26m (86ft) catamaran *Explorer*. He catapulted to first place in 5 days 9 hours 18 minutes 26 seconds.

In 1999, only one multihull (*Double Bullet II* owned and skippered by Bob Hanel) was on the start line. Twelve hours later, while flying a hull in 30-knot winds, she flipped. The crew set off the EPIRB and within hours were located, huddled inside the upturned catamaran. They were airlifted to safety, while the boat was recovered and towed to port several days later.

Disney returned in 1999 with *Pyewacket III* to take almost 4 hours off his record of 1997, thereby setting up a new challenge for the record breakers of the future.

Above IN THE 1995 TRANSPAC, LARRY ELLISON'S NEWLY LAUNCHED FARR 70, *SAYONARA*, HAD A MASTHEAD RIG DESIGNED TO ALLOW THE SPINNAKER TO BE HOISTED TO THE TOPMOST POINT OF THE MAST.

Opposite DESPITE BEING DISMASTED, THE FIRST TO FINISH IN 1995 WAS DR HAL WARD'S TURBOSLED *CHEVAL 95*, WHICH OUTPERFORMED *SAYONARA* AND *WINDQUEST* TO WIN THE BARN DOOR TROPHY.

6269
CHEVAL
LONG BEACH, CA

POR
500
Portugal Telecom

CAPE TO RIO

The Cape to Rio is the longest international yacht race in the Southern Hemisphere. It is held every three to four years. The race was created by the South African Ocean Racing Trust after the chairman of the Board of Trustees, Admiral H H Bierman, suggested at a welcoming dinner for South African yachtsman Bruce Dalling that a race from Cape Town to Rio de Janeiro be established. Dalling had just excelled in the 1968 Ostar (*Observer* Single-handed Transatlantic Race).

The direct route from Cape Town, at the southwesternmost tip of South Africa, northwest to Rio de Janeiro, in Brazil on South America's east coast, crosses the Atlantic Ocean. The Atlantic is the second largest of the three major oceans, but because it is easier to cross in comparison to the Indian and the Pacific (the world's largest and deepest), it is commonly know among yachtsmen as 'the pond'. There is also a scarcity of islands within this deep gully which divides the American and African continents, resulting in regular, gently rolling ocean swells. Yachts sailing this route are hindered by the Atlantic High – a high pressure body of air, or anticyclone – whose windless patches within are avoided by yachts which arch their course northwards to skirt the High. Thus the precise route of each race, as well as the actual distance covered, is dictated by the position of the Atlantic High at the time of the race.

In addition to the competition between boats and crew, the winner is therefore also determined by the skipper who most successfully interprets the weather data at his or her disposal. The Cape to Rio Race of 1996 had a plethora of imported multinational talent functioning as 'routers': Australian Andrew Cape on *Warrior*, Hollander Marcel van Triest (whose tactical navigation decisions won the 1993 race for *Broomstick*) on *Corum*, New Zealander Mike Quilter on *Morning Glory*, and South Africa's own Dr Lynneth Beckly on *Wizard*. The gamble lies in how daring the routers think they can afford to be in cutting corners around the Atlantic High, so lessening the actual ground distance. The risk, however, is in being becalmed whilst the competition sails northwards and away!

Although the Cape to Rio Race is more than a dash across the South Atlantic Ocean, the entry list features more than a minority share of small, family-sized cruisers taking the opportunity to be escorted on the first leg of a long-planned extended cruise. Another large portion of the fleet enters simply to have fun, to make the journey in one piece and achieve personal challenges.

The spectator excitement lies, as always, in the racing fleet, the big boats sponsored by big money, all aiming for line honours and setting a new speed record.

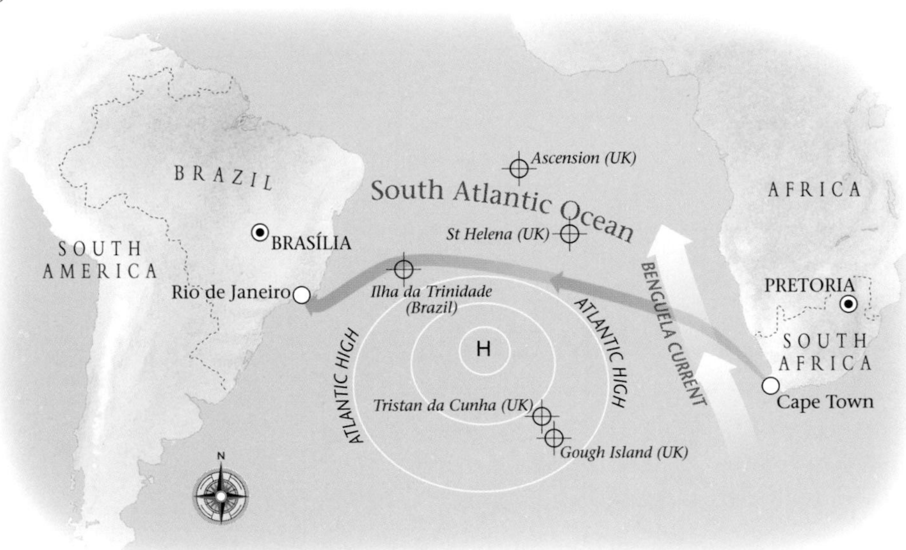

Opposite PRE-RACE FAVOURITE IN THE 2000 CAPE TO RIO RACE, *PORTUGAL-BRASIL* GETS OFF TO A LONELY SECOND START AFTER SHE BROKE HER BOOM LESS THAN FIVE HOURS AFTER THE OFFICIAL START. SHE WAS FORCED TO RETURN TO CAPE TOWN TO EFFECT REPAIRS TO HER CARBON FIBRE RIGGING (WORTH OVER R1 MILLION IN SOUTH AFRICA) BEFORE SHE FINALLY GOT UNDERWAY AGAIN, WITH A 26-HOUR DISADVANTAGE.

Top *AEGIS INSURANCE* (23M; 76FT), SKIPPERED BY SPRINGBOK YACHTSMAN ROB MEEK, WAS THE LARGEST YACHT IN THE 1993 CAPE TO RIO FLEET.

BECALMED IN 1971

The first Cape to Rio Race, held in 1971, was a great surprise in terms of the number of entries and the extraordinary public enthusiasm. The anticipated 10 to 15 entries multiplied to 58, and by the time the race started at 14:30 on 16 January 1971, no single sporting event (not even a crucial rugby, football or cricket test match, which is usually the supreme focus of interest in South African life!) had generated as much enthusiasm as the start of the race.

A famous 50- to 60-knot 'southeaster' blew the competitors on their way, but caused serious damage to the mast of *Albatross II* (skippered by South African John Goodwin). Her gutsy crew sought shelter in the small harbour of Robben Island, just off Table Bay, effected repairs to a badly bent mast, and bravely set off again. But even with lost time and a mast in dubious shape, she went on to win the first race on handicap. Not so lucky was the crew on board the 10m (33ft) sloop, *Pioneer*, which hit a whale at midnight 11 days out of Cape Town. Their yacht sunk very quickly and they spent 16 hours in a tiny life raft before a quirk of fate provided a rescuer in the form of a ship – way out of the

Above AMERICAN HUEY LONG'S MAXI RACER *ONDINE* CHASES FRENCH SAILING LEGEND ERIC TABARLY ON *PEN DUICK* OUT OF TABLE BAY IN THE 1976 CAPE TO RIO; LONG WAS THE RACE WINNER.

Left *ALBATROSS II*, SKIPPERED BY SOUTH AFRICAN JOHN GOODWIN, WAS THE WINNER OF THE INAUGURAL CAPE TO RIO RACE IN 1971, DESPITE HAVING TO DELAY IN TABLE BAY TO REPAIR A DAMAGED MAST.

usual shipping lanes – which fortunately spotted their smoke signal and hauled them aboard.

The worst situation for any boat in the Rio race is to sail into a windless patch, which is what *Cariad* did. (The long passage across the South Atlantic under infuriatingly light winds was so monotonous in 1971 that few skippers were prepared to commit themselves to the second race.) Said Joan Ayles of *Cariad*: 'In thirty-three days our fifteen-member crew read a total of more than 400 books – at least a book a day each – and drank 3000 cups of tea, cocoa and coffee.' Even the few porpoises that tried to surf their bow wave gave up in disgust.

The 39-strong fleet that left Cape Town for the 1973 Cape to Rio was predominantly a fleet designed to take on the race's light downwind conditions. Because of the race of 1971 – described as a 'drifter' by those heavy displacement yachts whose luck ran out, leaving them to wallow their way to Rio – very few of the same ilk were prepared to take it on again. Stories from the crew of one boat, which claimed that the wind was so light they had been in sight of Ilha da Trinidade for eight days, were a dead turnoff.

And so the streamlined fleet set off, with some serious contenders for the laurels. Race favourite was American Huey Long's 54-ton, 22m-long (73ft) *Ondine*, reputed to be one of the world's top three line-honours boats. But the crew's calculated risk in taking the direct route and thus the shorter course after misinterpreting the pattern of the ever-shifting Atlantic High was a gamble that didn't pay off. However, who better to lose to than 73-year-old Hollander Kees Bruynzeel, who had suffered three heart attacks in the year leading up to the race. He took along a nurse specially trained in heart emergencies and two experienced watchmasters, and cleaned up with line honours as well as a handicap win on his 16m (52ft) yacht, *Stormy*. At the time, no boat had won both titles in the Cape to Rio race.

A TIME FOR NEW RECORDS

Due to South Africa's political isolation, 16 years separated the 1993 event from the last one in 1976. The race favourites for the 1993 Cape to Rio Race were predominantly South African yachting greats, well known for their prowess around the buoys, and this race offered them an opportunity to put completely different skills to the test. The line-up of heavily financed boats with high-tech advantages added an edge to some intense competition. The 92 boats on the start line were confident that this race would see the demise of Huey Long's 17-day, 5-hour record set in 1976. With nearly two decades of technological development and design refinement on their side, it was simply a matter of which of the big boats would win the battle. Spinnakers popped and ripped all around as the fleet set off in a fresh southeaster. Race favourite *Broomstick*, skippered by Capetonian Hanno Teuteberg, covered an astonishing 329 nautical miles (609km) in the first 24 hours, with arch rival *Parker Pen* closing in on 312 miles (578km).

The race press was dominated by the contest between *Broomstick*, *Parker Pen* and *Namsea Challenger* with, on average, less than 20 miles (37km) between them. But it was *Broomstick* that

Above A BLUSTERY CAPE TOWN SOUTHEASTER SENT THE 1993 FLEET OF 83 YACHTS OFF ON ITS 5630KM (3500-MILE) RACE TO RIO. *PARKER PEN* WAS THE FIRST YACHT TO GYBE AROUND THE FIRST MARK.

clinched a double win: line honours and a race record of 15 days, 3 hours. On board was Dutch navigator Marcel van Triest, who successfully took *Broomstick* through the centre of the huge Atlantic High. Their chances of a handicap win were snatched first by South African Padda Kuttel's *Namsea Challenger* by 56 minutes, which was in turn taken up by Hasso Plattner's *Morning Glory*, with *Namsea Challenger* second.

Three years later, in 1996, South Africa's handicap hopes lay in the brand-new yacht *Warrior*,

skippered by Capetonian Rick Nankin, and in the 18m (60ft) category, *Wizard*, skippered by Jan Reuvers (also of South Africa). But the glamour of the Maxis – in Germany's *Fancourt Morning Glory* and Sweden's *Nicorette* – and the tussle for line honours was a press drawcard.

A split start offered the smaller eight out of 57 entries a chance to lessen the gap between the line honours victor and the last boat in, and thus ensure a fun finish for all. While the race focus was on the major contenders fighting for

Top FIRST SOUTH AFRICAN YACHT ACROSS THE LINE IN RIO IN 1996 WAS *WARRIOR*. SHE WAS PLACED THIRD, BEHIND GERMAN ENTRY *FANCOURT MORNING GLORY* AND SWEDISH ENTRY *NICORETTE*.

Above *PARKER PEN* AND *BROOMSTICK*, WAY AHEAD OF THE PACK IN 1993. THE FORMER HEADED OFF ON A NORTHWEST COURSE, WHILE *BROOMSTICK*, TO HER ADVANTAGE, TOOK A MORE WESTERLY PATH.

Opposite top *WARRIOR* (FOREGROUND), SKIPPERED BY RICK NANKIN, CAME IN SECOND ON HANDICAP IN 1996 WHEN *RENFREIGHT* TOOK THE LAURELS WITH A DAY TO SPARE ON CORRECTED TIME.

line honours and handicap laurels, it was the tiny (10ft) 33ft Charger, *Renfreight*, skippered by Norge Kennedy, that sneaked in on handicap after 22 days 10 hours. *Fancourt Morning Glory* skippered by Hasso Plattner took line honours and yet another speed record was set: 14 days 14 hours 52 minutes.

Morning Glory's breakthrough was short-lived: in the 2000 race, the Maxi *Zephyrus IV* smashed her record with a line honours and handicap finish of 12 days 16 hours 49 mins 41 secs.

Right AT THE 2000 RACE START, CO-AUTHOR ANTHONY STEWARD, WITH SOUTH AFRICA'S FIRST DEVELOPMENT TEAM TO CROSS AN OCEAN, WAS FIRST ACROSS THE LINE ON *THE BETTER CONNECTION*.

AUCKLAND–FIJI

formerly Auckland–Suva

THE ROYAL AKARANA YACHT CLUB, organizing body of the original Auckland–Fiji yacht race in 1956, was first established in November 1895 at Devonport Wharf, Auckland, New Zealand. Situated on the north mouth of Waitemata Harbour, it was initially named the North Shore Yacht Club. In 1922 it was renamed Akarana Yacht Club, and it relocated its club rooms to Waitemata's southern shores. During 1937 Akarana was granted a royal warrant by King George VI, after which the club proudly became the Royal Akarana Yacht Club. The club enjoyed some magnificent years of sailing before vacating its very modest accommodations at Mechanics Bay and moving to its present premises at Okahu Bay in 1953.

The first Trans-Tasman Cup had been organized by Akarana in 1931 and, over the ensuing years, in conjunction with its Australian sister clubs, a further 12 Trans-Tasman races were organized. In-between these events the club also ran the popular early Auckland–Suva (in Fiji) races with, on several occasions, fleets of over 70 boats crossing the start line. As a result of this racing activity, the Royal Akarana Yacht Club became known in New Zealand as the Home of Blue Water Racing, and still plays host to what has today become an Ocean Classic: the Auckland–Fiji race.

BIRTH OF THE AUCKLAND–FIJI OCEAN CLASSIC

The first official Auckland–Fiji yacht race (the early races were, in fact, named Auckland–Suva) took place on 12 May 1956. Thirteen yachts entered for a fee of five guineas. The largest boat was 11m (36ft) in length and the simple aim, as per the official sailing instructions, was to sail from Orakei Wharf in New Zealand's Okahu Bay to Suva, the capital and chief port of Fiji, on the southeast coast of Viti Levu in the southwest Pacific, with no time limit.

A northwesterly gale, however, forced the withdrawal of several race favourites. The 9m (29ft) *Kehua*, from Whangarei, skippered by Toby Clements, was one of the yachts to pull out; on her return journey to New Zealand she relied on 'dead reckoning' (estimating one's position without celestial navigation, using logs, course, distance, and so on) as her principle navigation tool. Some miscalculating resulted in the ketch missing her plotted landfall. *Kehua* was wrecked much further south, near Whakatane, in the Bay of Plenty. Another yacht, the *Aoma* from Christchurch (skippered by Ron Smith), was dismasted after rolling, but returned safely under jury rig (makeshift rigging).

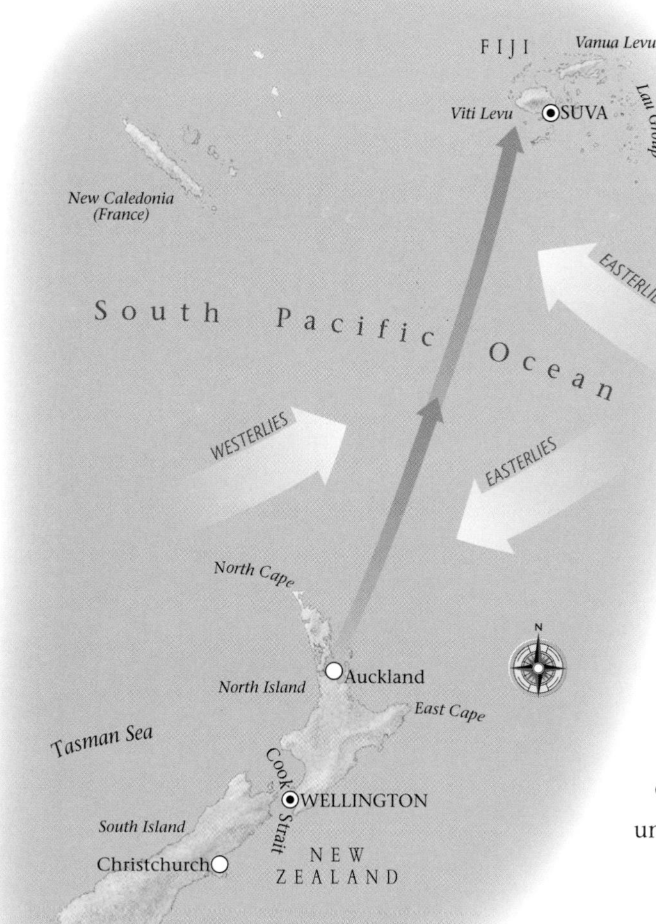

Top 1995 RACE WINNER *ANTAEUS* ONCE AGAIN SETS THE PACE DURING THE 1997 AUCKLAND–DENARAU RACE (THE FIRST YEAR TO SEE THE FINISH IN DENARAU) AND LEADS THE FLEET OUT OF WAITEMATA HARBOUR, AUCKLAND. *ANTAEUS*, DESIGNED BY LAURIE DAVIDSON, AND OWNED AND SKIPPERED BY CHARLES ST CLAIR BROWN, SET A NEW ELAPSED TIME RECORD IN 1998 OF 4 DAYS 8 HOURS 53 MINUTES 14 SECONDS.

Opposite ROBERT CROFT'S *COPPELIA* TOOK THE HANDICAP LAURELS IN 1999 AND WAS FIRST OVER THE LINE IN HER DIVISION.

The Wanderer, with Auckland-based skipper Tom Buchanan at the helm, was previously believed to be the slowest boat in the fleet, but the crew reduced sail to a small jib only, and sailed on through 50-knot winds and 7.5m (25ft) seas. After the storm, she picked up strong westerly winds, arriving at Suva in Fiji on 24 May as the confirmed line honours winner with an elapsed time of 11 days 12 hours 33 minutes.

It was another 10 years before the next race to Fiji was held. In 1966, 31 boats lined up at the start. Already in the early stages of the race, the fleet sailed into bad conditions when 130kph (80mph) winds were being recorded. Only 24 yachts finished; several pulled out of the race with damage at both ends of the spectrum, from broken masts to sinking (*Tatariki* sank while being towed in). *Roulette*, skippered by Fred Andrews, took two days off the 1956 race time with a time of 9 days 12 hours 50 minutes.

Three years later, in 1969, there were 27 starters for the Auckland–Fiji race, in which skipper Lawrence Nathan and his crew, on *Kahurangi*, took a further two days off the record with a time of 7 days 14 hours 51 minutes.

The peak years attracting a substantial fleet to the race were 1973 (when 70 boats entered and good weather prevailed for most of the way), 1977 (107 boats started out and 1973 line honours winner, *Ta'Aroa*, skippered by Doug Bremner, took two days off the previous elapsed-time record), and 1979.

The large number of entries in 1979 forced the race destination to be split between Suva and Lautoka (also on Viti Levu, Fiji). *Anticipation*, which had taken line honours in 1977, was again first over the line in Suva in 1979, but head winds prevented the breaking of any records. *Kishmul*, a yacht from Whangarei with Richard Tapper and Lester Smith at the helm, won on both IOR and PHRF handicapping systems (see page 12), whilst winner of the alternate route to Lautoka was *Quasar*, also from Whangarei and skippered by C Rapley.

Left RACE VETERAN *TA'AROA* FIRST TOOK PART IN THE AUCKLAND–FIJI RACE OF 1969. SHE WAS THE LINE HONOURS WINNER IN 1973, WITH A TIME OF 5 DAYS 12 HOURS 52 MINUTES.

Many of the entrants returned to New Zealand shortly after the race in such appalling weather conditions that three vessels sustained damage, *Ponsonby Express* (skippered by Noel Angus) and its crew disappeared without trace, and *Snow White* sank after hitting a whale, although the crew were all picked up by another yacht.

In 1983, a reduced number of boat entries for the race (one contributing factor was prohibitive insurance costs for many boat owners) resulted in Suva reverting to its role as the single, final, race destination. *Urban Cowboy* was first to finish in 7 days 18 hours 21 minutes.

As had already occurred before in the Auckland–Suva race, the return passage in 1983 proved onerous for the race entrants. Two yachts encountered disaster when they hit stormy weather. *Southern Raider*, with John Stephenson as skipper, was abandoned and a crewman died during the rescue. *Lionheart* hit rocks while attempting to enter Whangaroa Harbour and seven crew members lost their lives through exposure to the cold and drownings. The remainder of the yachts realized that going out to sea during the storm was a wiser move, and they eventually sailed into port further south on New Zealand's coast.

Race records were broken in 1985, and again in 1989 (*Urban Cowboy* achieved a passage of 5 days 8 hours 53 minutes in 1985, while in 1989 *Future Shock* was first on handicap and also took line honours in a brilliant time of 4 days 14 hours 42 minutes). A decision had been taken to combine the latter race with the Auckland to Fukuoka race (Fukuoka is a port in Kyushu, southwest Japan). Of the 46 entrants, the majority headed for Suva only, while the remainder continued on to Japan.

The 1993 race event, once again combined with the additional leg to Fukuoka, Japan, and attracting 40 entrants, was marked by excessively calm conditions as a result of a high pressure system lying between New Zealand and Fiji. Extremely slow sailing even forced a number of boats to ration their food and water stores during the last days of the race. The inclusion of New Zealander Chris Dickson's two brand-new W60s (see page 108), which were undergoing sea trials, served to heighten interest in the race.

1995 – A WINNING YEAR

Although a relatively small fleet of 13 boats competed in the race in 1995 – this time from Auckland to Suva only – the event (*Antaeus* took line honours with a time of 4 days 19 hours 31 minutes) was punctuated with excitement. Team New Zealand, led by Russell Coutts, was challenging the America's Cup in San Diego, USA. Crews arriving in Suva after their own race from Auckland had little time to recuperate before the celebrations recommenced after they watched Team New Zealand's success against regular cup-holder, American Dennis Conner, on Fiji television.

Above THE NZ$10,000 PRIZE OFFERED BY RAYC TO THE FIRST YACHT TO CROSS THE DENARAU FINISH LINE WITHIN FOUR DAYS WAS MATCHED IN 1999 BY ST CLAIR BROWN (OF *ANTAEUS*, ABOVE), TO BE AWARDED TO THE BOAT THAT BEATS HIS RECORD.

AUCKLAND–DENARAU OCEAN CLASSIC

Concerned by the declining entries in the Suva race, the 1997 organizing committee for the Auckland–Suva Ocean Classic decided that the Denarau Island Resort on the western coast of Fiji could provide a popular alternative destination. The resort owners, Tabua Investments, had made a substantial commitment to developing the Denarau Island region, and the inclusion of a new marina and yacht club enhanced its attraction as an exciting yachting destination.

On 20 June 1997, 17 yachts left Auckland for a thrilling ride to Denarau, with the front runners exceeding speeds of 20 knots in the early stages. However, this was followed by two days of light airs in the middle of the race, eliminating the chance of a new race record to Fiji. *Hydroflow* set the inaugural race time to Denarau of 5 days 12 hours 5 minutes 22 seconds.

It was a small fleet that followed the successful 1997 race with a second event in 1998. *Antaeus*, skippered by Charles St Clair Brown, recorded a top speed of 23 knots (achieved while skimming down a wave). Three spinnakers were shredded during the race and the spinnaker track tore off the mast in winds that were hitting 45 knots. Contending with such resistance, the yacht's best run was 350 miles (648km) in 24 hours! Yet she still managed to set a new Auckland–Denarau race record of 4 days 8 hours 53 minutes 14 seconds, winning the Auckland Harbour Board Cup (awarded to the line honours winner) as well as the Mercury Cup (handed to the PHRF winner).

In 1999, *Lew Anne*, the smallest boat in the fleet and with only a two-handed crew, came in first on handicap; according to the race rules, however, she did not qualifty for the win as she had used her self-steering gear – certainly permissible in the Two-handed Division, but once used, the boat is rendered ineligible to compete in any other division. As the only entry in the Two-handed Division, she was awarded a special prize for her effort. Grant Wharington took line honours on *Wild Thing*.

Right GRANT WHARINGTON'S IMS MAXI *WILD THING* (21M; 69FT) WAS SPECIFICALLY DESIGNED FOR THE SYDNEY–HOBART RACE.

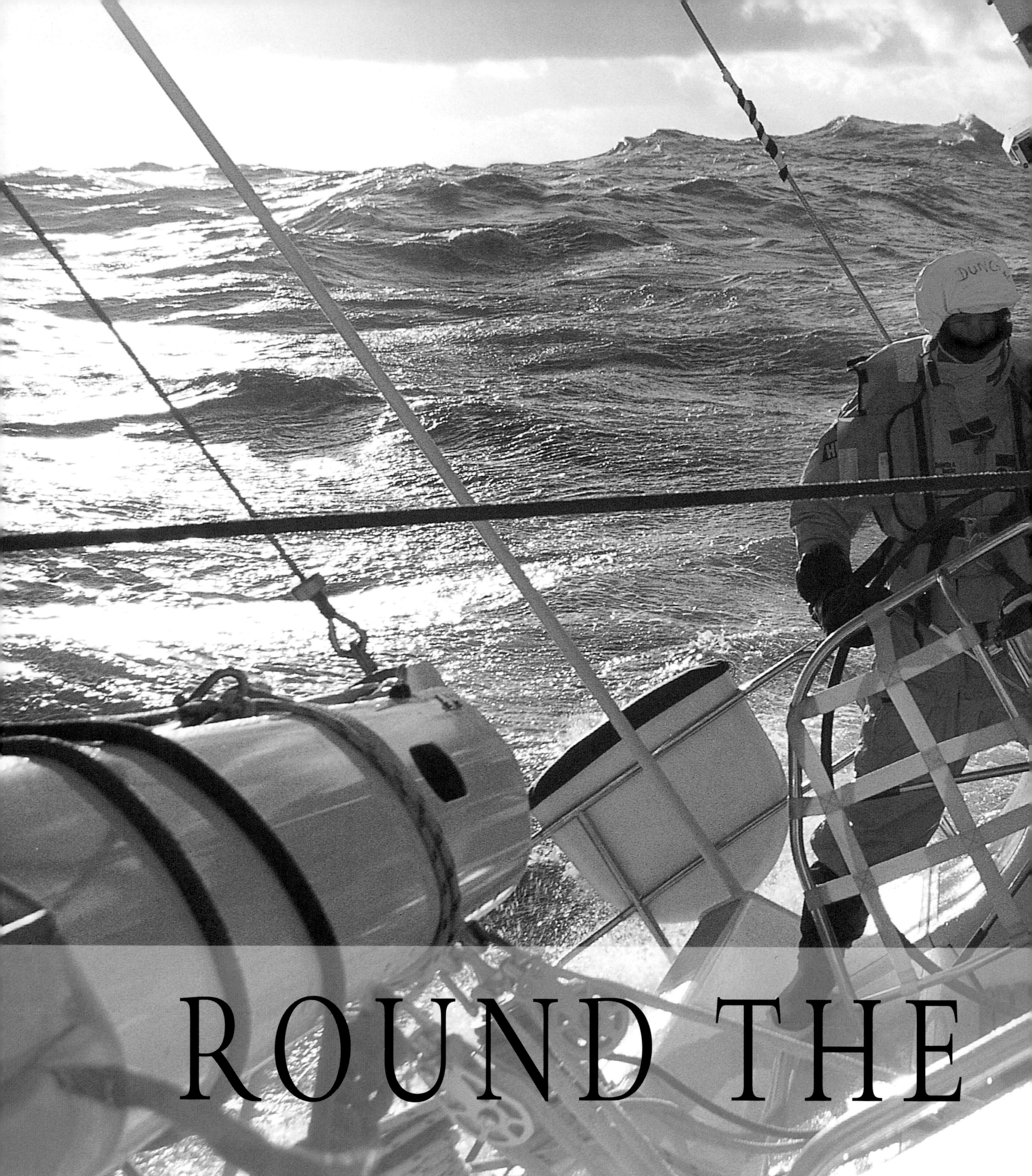

ROUND THE

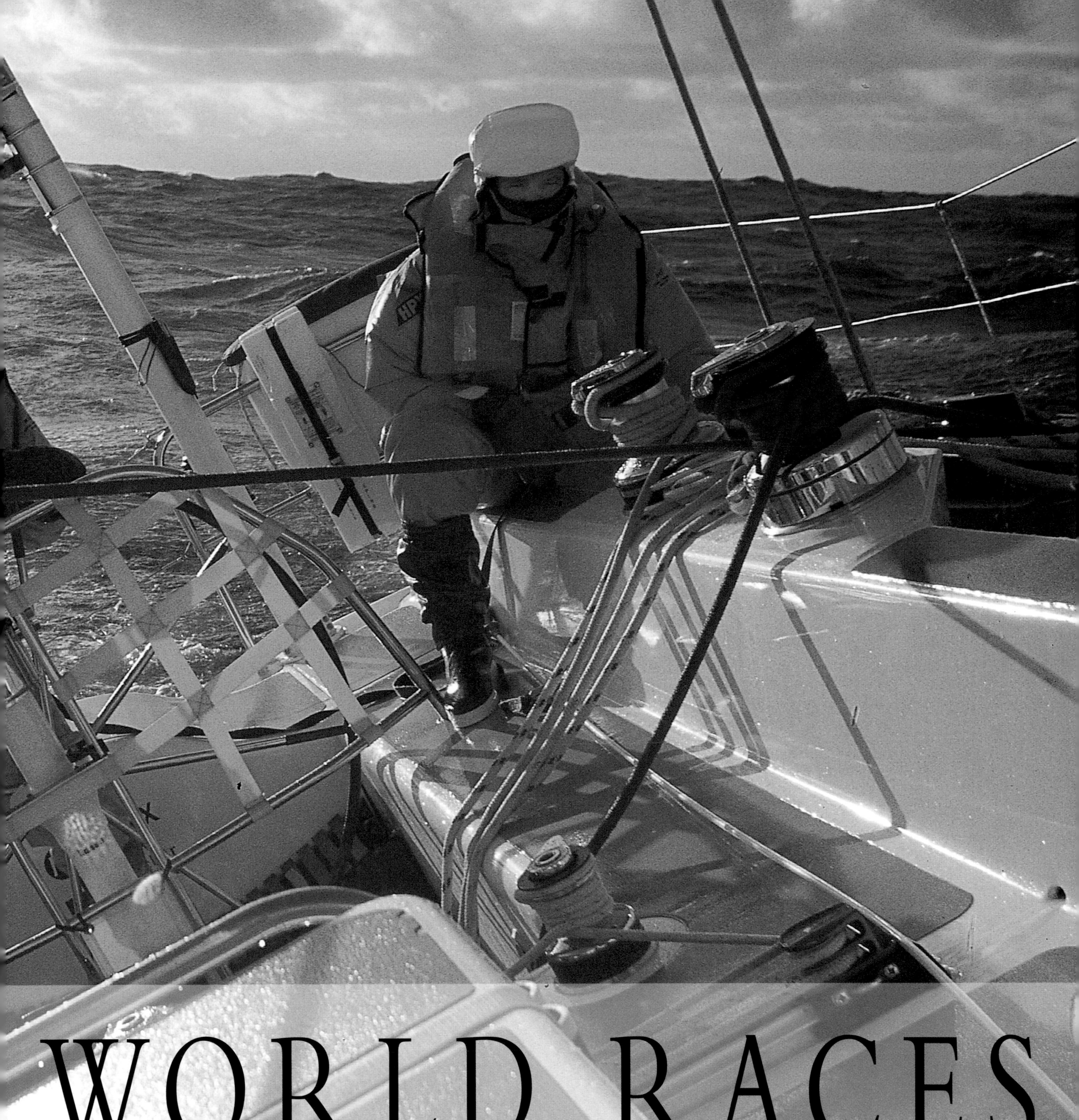

WORLD RACES

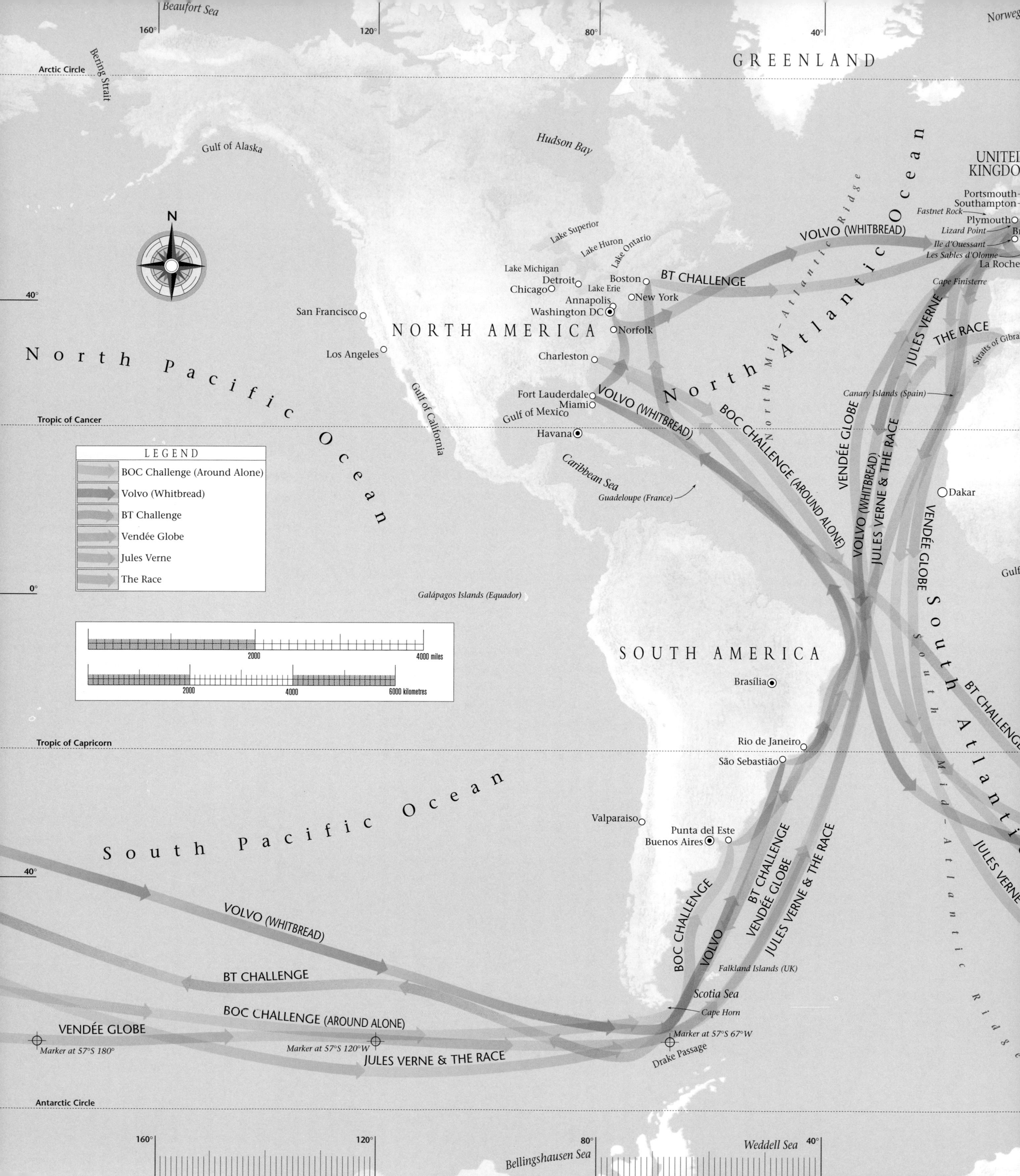

LEGEND
BOC Challenge (Around Alone)
Volvo (Whitbread)
BT Challenge
Vendée Globe
Jules Verne
The Race
2000
4000 miles
2000
4000
6000 kilometres
N
GREENLAND
NORTH AMERICA
SOUTH AMERICA
North Pacific Ocean
South Pacific Ocean
North Atlantic Ocean
South Atlantic
North Mid-Atlantic Ridge
South Mid-Atlantic Ridge
Beaufort Sea
Arctic Circle
Bering Strait
Gulf of Alaska
Hudson Bay
Tropic of Cancer
Tropic of Capricorn
Antarctic Circle
Lake Superior
Lake Huron
Lake Ontario
Lake Michigan
Lake Erie
Detroit
Chicago
Boston
New York
Annapolis
Washington DC
Norfolk
Charleston
San Francisco
Los Angeles
Gulf of California
Fort Lauderdale
Miami
Gulf of Mexico
Havana
Caribbean Sea
Guadeloupe (France)
Galápagos Islands (Equador)
Brasília
Rio de Janeiro
São Sebastião
Valparaiso
Punta del Este
Buenos Aires
Falkland Islands (UK)
Scotia Sea
Cape Horn
Marker at 57°S 67°W
Drake Passage
Marker at 57°S 180°
Marker at 57°S 120°W
Bellingshausen Sea
Weddell Sea
Dakar
Canary Islands (Spain)
Cape Finisterre
Portsmouth
Southampton
Fastnet Rock
Plymouth
Lizard Point
Ile d'Ouessant
Les Sables d'Olonne
La Rochel
Straits of Gibral
Norweg
UNITED KINGDO
VOLVO (WHITBREAD)
BT CHALLENGE
BOC CHALLENGE (AROUND ALONE)
VENDÉE GLOBE
JULES VERNE & THE RACE
JULES VERNE
THE RACE
BOC CHALLENGE
VOLVO
160°
120°
80°
40°
0°

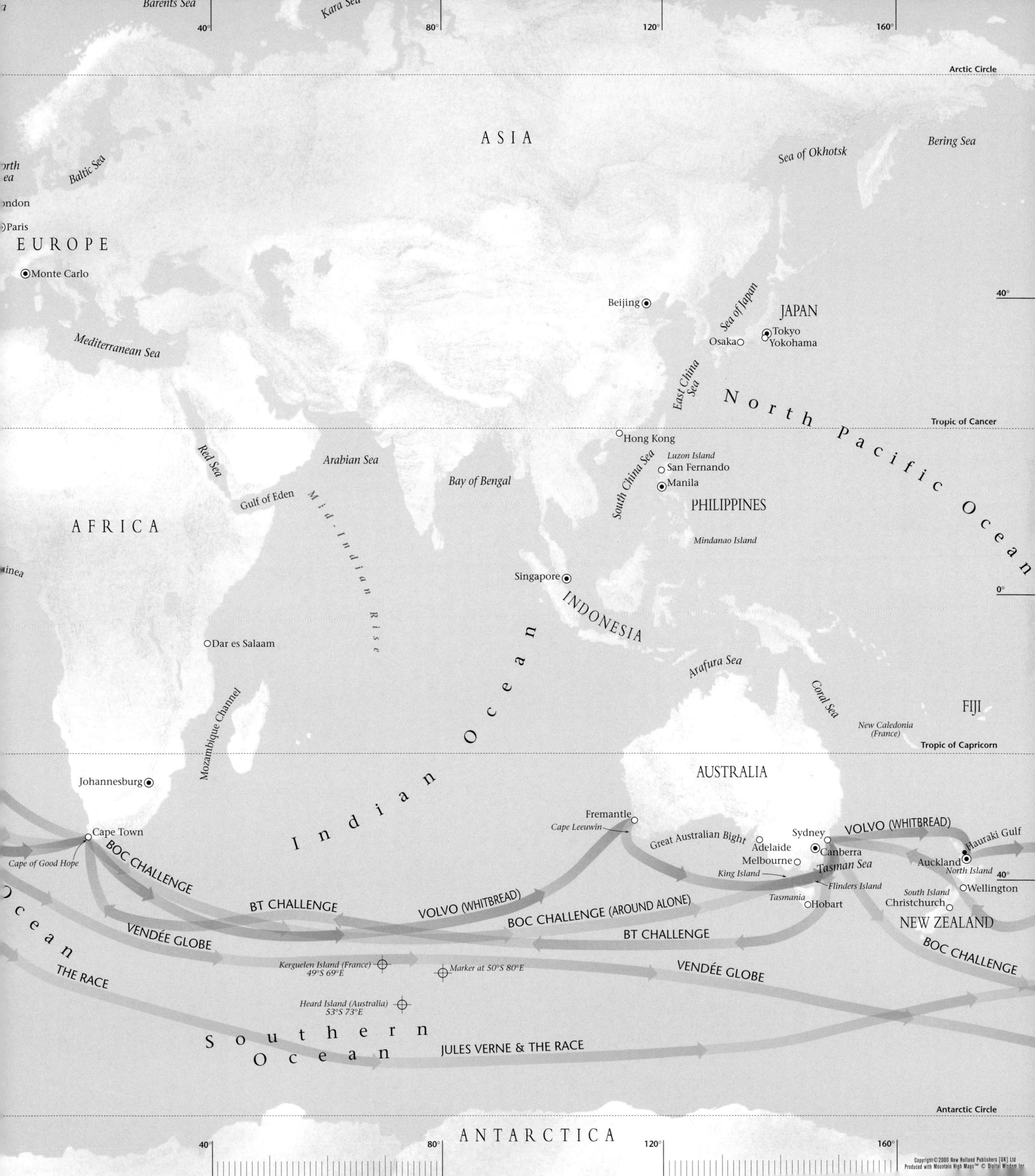

Barents Sea
Kara Sea
40°
80°
120°
160°
Arctic Circle
ASIA
Bering Sea
Sea of Okhotsk
Baltic Sea
Paris
EUROPE
Monte Carlo
Beijing
Sea of Japan
JAPAN
Tokyo
Osaka
Yokohama
Mediterranean Sea
East China Sea
North Pacific Ocean
Tropic of Cancer
Hong Kong
Red Sea
Arabian Sea
Luzon Island
San Fernando
Bay of Bengal
South China Sea
Manila
Gulf of Eden
Mid-Indian Rise
PHILIPPINES
AFRICA
Mindanao Island
Singapore
0°
INDONESIA
Dar es Salaam
Indian Ocean
Arafura Sea
Coral Sea
Mozambique Channel
FIJI
New Caledonia (France)
Tropic of Capricorn
AUSTRALIA
Johannesburg
Fremantle
Cape Leeuwin
Cape Town
Great Australian Bight
Sydney
VOLVO (WHITBREAD)
Hauraki Gulf
BOC CHALLENGE
Adelaide
Canberra
Cape of Good Hope
Melbourne
Tasman Sea
Auckland
North Island
King Island
Flinders Island
Wellington
Tasmania
Hobart
South Island
Christchurch
BT CHALLENGE
VOLVO (WHITBREAD)
BOC CHALLENGE (AROUND ALONE)
NEW ZEALAND
VENDÉE GLOBE
BT CHALLENGE
BOC CHALLENGE
Kerguelen Island (France) 49°S 69°E
Marker at 50°S 80°E
VENDÉE GLOBE
THE RACE
Heard Island (Australia) 53°S 73°E
Southern Ocean
JULES VERNE & THE RACE
Antarctic Circle
ANTARCTICA

MERIT CUP · MERIT CUP
MONACO

VOLVO CHALLENGE

formerly Whitbread

'For any yachtsman or woman, the Southern Ocean is the ultimate sailing experience. Enormous waves unimpeded by any land mass roll around the bottom of the world, providing crews with a sailing experience that cannot be found anywhere else.' — GLEN SOWRY, THREE-TIME WHITBREAD VETERAN

WHEN THE BRITISH ROYAL NAVY TOOK DELIVERY of several 17m (55ft) yachts in April 1972, the hunt was on soon thereafter to secure a major sponsor for a crewed round the world race. The Royal Navy announced it would support the race whether or not there was a sponsor, and this vote of confidence led to a deal with corporate giant, Whitbread PLC, a purveyor of food, drink and leisure products employing over 70,000 people. The first Whitbread Race was held in 1973/74, and has since taken place every four years.

The first race saw 17 yachts cross the start line off Portsmouth, on England's south coast, opposite the Isle of Wight. Unlike the only other round the world race established at the time (the single-handed Golden Globe Race of 1967, sponsored by the *Sunday Times*), some of the boats were manned by crews of up to 14. Furthermore, some of the boats were 22m (73ft) in length, offering some degree of comfort and stability, and emphasizing that this first event was a yacht race rather than a test of endurance. The course of the first race was divided into four stages:

- Portsmouth, UK, to Cape Town, South Africa (7350 nm/13,600km)
- Cape Town to Sydney, Australia (6550 nm/12,120km)
- Sydney to Rio de Janeiro, Brazil (8370 nm/15,490km)
- Rio de Janeiro to Portsmouth (5560 nm/10,290km)

The array of boats on the race start line was an apt representation of the type of sailor involved. Most were production-line cruiser boats manned by amateur sailors, eager to follow in the footsteps of the great pioneers like Britons Sir Francis Chichester, Sir Robin Knox-Johnston, and Sir Chay Blyth, but there were also professional sailors, like Blyth himself, and French sailing hero Eric Tabarly.

For his crew, Chay Blyth had selected a dozen paratroopers for their toughness and stamina rather than any sailing experience, while Ramón Carlín, a wealthy Mexican washing-machine manufacturer, had chosen experienced and competent crew members to compensate for his 'family' yacht, a Swan 65 named *Sayula II*, and his own limited experience. The race was costly. Three men were lost overboard: Dominic Guillet, the French skipper of *33-Export*, Paul Waterhouse, a British crew member on board

Opposite *MERIT CUP*, WITH SKIPPER GRANT DALTON AT THE HELM, BEATS TO WINDWARD WITH THE CREW ON THE WEATHER RAIL (OR HIGH SIDE) AS THE BOAT STARTS OUT FROM FREMANTLE, WESTERN AUSTRALIA, DURING THE 1997/98 WHITBREAD ROUND THE WORLD RACE.

Top to bottom ACTION STATIONS ON BOARD *MERIT CUP* AS THE CREW BUSY THEMSELVES ON LEG FOUR OF THE WHITBREAD; THE CREW CANNOT AFFORD ANY IDLE TIME DURING THIS RACE, AND ARE CONSTANTLY AT WORK IN ALL TYPES OF WEATHER CONDITIONS. THE PROTECTIVE CLOTHING WORN BY ONE OF THE CREW MEMBERS (BOTTOM) HELPS WITHSTAND THE ICY CONDITIONS IN THE NOTORIOUSLY TURBULENT SOUTHERN OCEAN.

Pages 98–99 *NUCLEAR ELECTRIC* IN THE 1996/97 BT CHALLENGE; THE CREW ON DECK IS KEPT TO A MINIMUM BECAUSE OF THE EXTREME COLD.

Italian yacht *Tauranga*, and UK paratrooper Bernie Hosking from Blyth's *Great Britain II*. The rolling seas and the violent storms were typical of the Southern Ocean, while the crew on board Ramón Carlín's winning boat passed through such a dense snow storm that the men on deck built a snowman!

In the fifth Whitbread race, held in 1989/90, crew member Gordon Maguire comments of his race aboard *NCB Ireland*:

'The Whitbread Race is a race of extremes. Nothing can compare with the thrill and exhilaration of an almost out of control rollercoaster ride in the twenty-foot waves and forty-knot winds of the Southern Ocean. There was also the excitement of dodging growlers, sometimes the size of a small house, floating just below the surface of the water.

'In a boat on the face of one of those mountainous waves, flying full-size spinnaker and full mainsail, in screaming Gale Force winds that make communication virtually impossible, in pitch darkness so black that nothing outside the boat is visible, in temperatures low enough to produce freezing flakes of snow – you have a ride straight from hell.'

The similar, evenly matched, state-of-the-art racing boats – permanently driven to the limit and beyond by large professional crews (a signature of the Whitbread) – have contributed to it becoming recognized as the most competitive round the world sailing event. It has been described as the race during which the crew surf 'on the edge of sanity at thirty knots, enduring pain and courting disaster'.

Above ICEBERGS ARE A COMMON SIGHT IN THE SOUTHERN OCEAN. THE SMALLER ICEBERGS – KNOWN AS GROWLERS – FLOATING JUST BELOW THE SURFACE, POSE AN EXTREME DANGER TO THE BOATS.

Centre SKIP NOVAK OF THE USA AND HIS RUSSIAN CREW BECALMED ABOARD *FAZISI*. WAITING FOR WIND IN THE DOLDRUMS IS WORSE PUNISHMENT TO A CREW THAN THE RIGOURS OF THE SOUTHERN OCEAN.

Top A YACHT TACKLES CHOPPY SEAS OFF CAPE HORN, IN THE 1993/94 WHITBREAD. ICY AND RELENTLESS STORM CONDITIONS OFF THE TIP OF SOUTH AMERICA MAKE THIS LEG THE MOST GRUELLING.

Above SNAPSHOTS OF MOMENTS AT SEA CAPTURED OVER THE YEARS DURING VARIOUS WHITBREAD ROUND THE WORLD RACES. OCCASIONS OF NOTE INCLUDE THE CREW OF *EF LANGUAGE* CELEBRATING THEIR WINNING FINISH IN 1997/98 (TOP ROW, CENTRE); A CHAMPAGNE CELEBRATION AFTER ROUNDING CAPE HORN (CENTRE ROW, LEFT); KING NEPTUNE AND HIS 'MERMAID' PARTICIPATING IN A CEREMONY TO COMMEMORATE THE CROSSING OF THE EQUATOR (CENTRE ROW, CENTRE); THE CREW OF DUTCH ENTRY *FLYER* (BOTTOM ROW, RIGHT) REPAIRING THEIR BROKEN BOOM WHILE UNDER SAIL IN 1981/82 (THEY WENT ON TO WIN THE RACE).

Above MAXI CLASS WINNER, *NEW ZEALAND ENDEAVOUR*, WITH GRANT DALTON AS SKIPPER, HAS HER SAILS PERFECTLY SET TO CATCH AN EARLY MORNING BREEZE DURING THE 1993/94 WHITBREAD RACE.

A RACE THAT ALLOWS NO SLEEP

After the 1993/94 Whitbread Race, Grant Dalton, skipper of the *New Zealand Endeavour*, was quoted as saying:

'Within twenty-four hours of the start it was evident that the race was a bloodbath. In the last race we had downtime, it was something you accepted. On leg one this time, we didn't even lose a second. We couldn't afford to. The level is right up there. If you have downtime, you'll be left for dead.'

It is not uncommon for crews to skip their off-watch period to help sail the boat at top speed through a favourable weather system. For example, in the 1997/98 Whitbread race, most of the fleet went without their sleep to push on a 'full-race watch system' during leg seven (in this particular year, the race was extended) – the 870-nautical-mile (1611km) stretch to Baltimore, in Chesapeake Bay on the USA's east coast. During the same race, the crew of *Tokio* were hard hit by what's become known as the 'Dicko Method of Whitbreading'. Their skipper Chris Dickson's simple philosophy was based on the statement he once made after a race: 'You were so tired you slept when you hit the bunk. If you weren't tired you hadn't been working hard enough.' Keeping the boat as light as possible for maximum speed, he was very strict about what the crew were allowed to bring on board. 'Yes, we had a number of books on board; we're all very familiar now with the code signals and the water-maker book. The medical handbook's a favourite,' quipped Dickson. Whitbread Race crews, challenging the powers of the Southern Ocean and not infrequently coming within an inch of a 'death roll', or even a broach, are adrenaline junkies, putting up with weeks of cramped, ice-cold conditions, perpetual damp, discomfort and constant fear.

Skipper Gunnar Krantz of Sweden, a two-time race veteran of *Swedish Match*, describes some of the emotions experienced:

'Screaming down the waves, we couldn't tell if the blips on the radar were white caps or growlers. At that moment, being responsible for twelve lives as well as their families gets to you. It's a feeling of having to survive just another minute, just another minute. . .'

Of the downwind surfs, he describes the boat as 'leaping off waves and landing on its transom like a powerboat'.

Despite the exhortations each time the yachts complete their crossing of the Southern Ocean, such as: 'That was the last time I'll ever be down here', or 'I'm never going into that hole again', it seems that the same people go back every time to tackle the Whitbread Race once more.

With the race becoming progressively competitive, it has also become necessary to elect skippers and crews that have the courage to be more daring. In order to win, it is essential to keep pushing the boat to its maximum speed limits round the clock, throughout each leg. 'Taking it easy' at any time or place is not listed in the racing sailor's vocabulary. It is this 'white knuckle' sailing that keeps Whitbread competitors revisiting the punishment of the Southern Ocean time and again.

As a result of the competitiveness engendered by the race leading to ever faster craft, as well as the successful appearance in the 1993/94 Whitbread Race of a few of the then newly

Right PRE-RACE FAVOURITE IN 1993/94, *TOKIO* WITH CHRIS DICKSON AT THE HELM. THE BOAT LOST ITS RIG OFF SOUTH AMERICA, THUS DASHING ANY CHANCES OF WINNING THE RACE.

A PORTFOLIO OF WHITBREAD WINNERS

Above THE BRITISH ENTRY *HEATH'S CONDOR* WAS DISMASTED IN THE FIRST LEG OF THE 1977/78 RACE. ON BOARD WAS NEW ZEALAND'S SIR PETER BLAKE, WHO WENT ON TO WIN THE 1989/90 WHITBREAD.

Top centre IN THE 1973/74 WHITBREAD RACE, *GREAT BRITAIN II* WAS SKIPPERED BY WELL-KNOWN SCOTTISH SAILOR SIR CHAY BLYTH. THE 24M (80FT) BOAT CAME IN SIXTH OVERALL ON HANDICAP.

Above THE 20M (65FT) ALUMINIUM KETCH *FLYER* WAS SKIPPERED IN 1977/78 BY OWNER CORNELIS VAN RIETSCHOTEN. HE PUSHED HIS BOAT TO A WIN IN THAT YEAR'S EVENT.

Left VAN RIETSCHOTEN RETURNED IN 1981/82 WITH A BRAND-NEW 23.5M (77FT) SLOOP RIG (ALSO *FLYER*) AND ONCE AGAIN CAME IN FIRST. HE IS THE ONLY SKIPPER TO HAVE WON THE WHITBREAD TWICE.

designed 19m (62ft) Whitbread 60s – which proved to be closely matched – this design was adopted for the 1997/98 event. Thus different to the previous races in that only one class – the Whitbread 60 – was permitted, this ensured seriously close racing. The top five boats finished leg three in Sydney, Australia, within five minutes of each other, after travelling 2250 nautical miles (4167km) from Fremantle on the continent's west coast, while the rest of the fleet finished within two hours! The performance difference between the boats is absolutely minimal – and of the nine entries, eight were designed by one boat architect, New Zealander Bruce Farr.

TWO HOTLY CONTESTED DESIGNS

Two class divisions were permitted only in the Whitbread race of 1993–94: the 21m (68–70ft) Maxis and the Whitbread 60s (W60). The first in each division to cross the finish line was considered a winner, thus avoiding the confusion of corrected time, used to calculate past winners.

According to skipper Ross Field of the Japanese/New Zealand entry *Yamaha* (winner of the 1993/94 Whitbread Race), the difference between a Maxi and a Whitbread 60 in the Southern Ocean can be described in the following way: the Maxi is a big stable platform, whilst the Whitbread 60 is like a saucer, sliding everywhere. The faster a W60 goes, the trickier it gets, so the crew work is far more vital than on a Maxi. Like conservative versions of the radical Open Class 18m (60ft) craft that race in the Vendée Globe and BOC challenges, the W60s are slightly longer with more displacement and water ballast, and having less beam and a higher freeboard. The water ballast allows them to pump the equivalent weight of 35 men up to the weather side of the boat, which enables them to perform at their peak in heavy weather. Additionally, their light weight and hull shape allow them to plane really easily. Today, however, only Whitbread 60s are the permissible class.

Due to political, tactical and practical reasons, various changes have been made over the years to the actual course of the Whitbread Race. For

Left *TOKIO* ARRIVING IN FREMANTLE IN THE 1993/94 RACE, WHICH WAS THE LAST ONE WHERE EACH LEG HAD AN EQUAL RATING. THEREAFTER, RACE LEGS WERE RATED ACCORDING TO THEIR DIFFICULTY.

Top FROM THE START, *EF LANGUAGE* LED THE BOATS THROUGH THE SOLENT IN THE 1997/98 RACE, A PSYCHOLOGICAL VICTORY WHICH HELPED HER WIN LEG ONE AS WELL AS THE ENTIRE EVENT.

Right *INNOVATION KVAERNER* AND *TOSHIBA* AT THE SOUTHAMPTON START IN 1997. *TOSHIBA* CAME IN SIXTH IN THE FIRST LEG – SKIPPER CHRIS DICKSON RESIGNED AND PAUL STANBRIDGE TOOK OVER.

the 1997/98 race, when only the W60 Class made up the entrants, extra stopovers were introduced, bringing the total to nine legs.

- ▲ Southampton to Cape Town, South Africa (7350nm/13,600km)
- ▲ Cape Town to Fremantle, west coast, Australia (4600nm/8520km)
- ▲ Fremantle to Sydney, east coast, Australia (2250nm/4160km)
- ▲ Sydney to Auckland, New Zealand (1270nm/2350km)
- ▲ Auckland to São Sebastião, Brazil (6670nm/12,340km)
- ▲ São Sebastião to Fort Lauderdale, Florida, USA (4750nm/8790km)
- ▲ Fort Lauderdale to Baltimore, east coast, USA (870nm/1610km)
- ▲ Baltimore to La Rochelle, France (3390nm/6270km)
- ▲ La Rochelle to Southampton, UK (450nm/830km)

A NEW AGE OF SPONSORSHIP

The nature of the race has also shifted. Whereas the US$500,000 fee per boat in the Whitbread Race's earlier years used to pay the way through a four-leg survival test, the sponsors now recognize and reward teams that can endure intense bursts of 'all-out' sailing over nine legs.

The race of 1997/98 was the swansong of the Whitbread sponsorship, and enjoyed unprecedented media attraction: more than 2.6 billion homes in 193 countries followed the event on television (it was the most widely televised sailing event ever). However, after 25 years, Whitbread PLC took the decision to sell the sponsorship rights to the race because the event and the exposure had outgrown the company's primary UK market. Enter Swedish car manufacturer Volvo. This concern has a wide global reach, selling in 130 countries with 62 international production sites. Volvo's decision to buy the naming rights of this sailing event was based on the values embodied in the race, which matched their own company ethics: strength, endurance, teamwork, leading edge technology, safety, excitement, and achievement.

Top *SILK CUT*, SKIPPERED IN 1997/98 BY LAWRIE SMITH, SAILS IN A STIFF BREEZE OFF FREEMANTLE. THE YACHT AND ITS CREW CAME IN FOURTH DURING THIS LEG (TWO) OF THE RACE.

Left TESTIMONY TO THE INCREDIBLE SPECTATOR SUPPORT EXPERIENCED GENERALLY BY WHITBREAD ROUND THE WORLD RACES IS THIS AERIAL VIEW OF THE SOUTHAMPTON START IN 1997.

Right A BIRD'S EYE VIEW FROM THE MASTHEAD OF *TOSHIBA* IN THE RACE OF 1997/98. FOR THE FOURTH LEG, IT WAS DENNIS CONNER'S TURN TO TAKE OVER FROM PAUL STANBRIDGE AS SKIPPER.

AROUND ALONE

formerly BOC Challenge

'For the rest of your life don't waste any time. Make the best of what you may before you turn into clay.'
— *HARRY MITCHELL (UK), LOST AT SEA IN 1994/95 ON BOARD HIS YACHT* HENRY HORNBLOWER

THE FIRST CHALLENGE, SPONSORED BY THE BOC GROUP (formerly British Oxygen Company, which dealt in industrial gases and healthcare), was launched in 1982. British Oxygen Company saw the opportunity to promote business in key markets around the world, and with UK round the world sailor Robin Knox-Johnston as race director for the first BOC event, 17 race entrants set off on this single-handed challenge on 28 August 1982 from Newport, Rhode Island, in the USA.

The BOC sponsorship fell away in 1998/99, and the race is now referred to as the Around Alone. Boat entries are restricted to either of two class categories, Class 1 (15.5–18m; 50+–60ft) or Class 2 (under 15.5m; 50ft). The legs of the race have varied. The 1998/99 course had four: beginning in Charleston, southeast South Carolina (USA), boats headed for Cape Town (South Africa), on to Sydney (Australia) for leg two, to Punta del Este (South America) for leg three, and then returned to Charleston (leg four). The race is an endurance marathon, requiring the more obvious skills of navigation, weather forecasting, race tactics, and an ability to carry out major repair work en route combined with the less obvious ability to juggle a minimum amount of sleep with keeping the boat at peak performance. The history of the BOC has witnessed shipwrecks, sinkings, dramatic rescues – and two deaths. In 1986/87, Frenchman Jean-Jacques de Roux's yacht was found, drifting off South Australia with no-one aboard, and in 1994/95, no trace of Harry Mitchell nor his boat *Henry Hornblower* was ever found after the boat went missing at sea.

THE BOC'S HARDY PERSONALITIES

France's Isabelle Autissier was the first woman ever to win a leg of the BOC Around Alone Challenge. She stepped into the limelight after winning the first leg – from Newport (Rhode Island) to Cape Town (South Africa) – of the 1994/95 BOC race when she beat the standing record set by compatriot Alain Gautier by more than two days. She also beat her closest competitor by over five days!

Autissier does not place great emphasis on being the first woman to win this leg. 'It's nice to feel it might be important for women', she concedes, but firmly qualifies this with 'I'm the winner and that's enough'. She is patently aware of her disadvantages in terms of sheer muscle strength. The 18m (60ft) yacht is a powerful craft and she admits to not being as strong as some of the men in the race. On the other hand, her boat *Ecureuil* was specially tailored for her, and she therefore found it easy to handle. She is also disciplined in keeping a constant vigil on boat maintenance and the very few technical

Left PREPARING FOR A SPINNAKER HOIST ON *COYOTE* IN 1994 (TOP); FRANCO-AMERICAN J P MOULIGNÉ, A RESIN SALESMAN, WON CLASS II COMFORTABLY ON *CRAY VALLEY* (CENTRE) IN 1998/99; JOSH HALL ON ILL-FATED *GARTMORE* IN 1994 – HE HAD TO ABANDON HIS BOAT AFTER HITTING A CONCEALED OBJECT IN THE WATER AND WAS RESCUED FROM HIS LIFE RAFT BY FELLOW RACE COMPETITOR ALAN NEBAUER.

Opposite FRENCHMAN PHILIPPE JEANTOT ON HIS BOAT *CRÉDIT AGRICOLE*. HE WON THE INAUGURAL EVENT IN 1982/83 AND AGAIN IN 1986/87.

PICOLE
85

problems she has encountered at sea during the course of her sailing career are a tribute to her meticulous preparation.

Having successfully completed the first leg, and with a five-and-a-half day lead in the Class I, Autissier's voyage from Cape Town to Sydney, on Australia's east coast, was fraught with mishaps. She was dismasted but managed to make her way under jury rig to the Kerguelen Islands, a territory of France in the south Indian Ocean, where another mast was installed. But 2750 nautical miles (5088km) southwest of Adelaide, South Australia, disaster struck once more. In Autissier's own words:

'The wind and sea were very rough. . .fifty to sixty knots. I had no sails up and was doing eight knots. I was inside the boat, and the boat did a huge roll. It went right over, through 360 degrees. I could feel it rolling. I fell on the bulkhead, then on the ceiling, then on the other bulkhead. When I opened my eyes, the boat was full of water. If I had been on deck, I would have been washed away.'

Ecureuil was ravaged: both masts were gone and the cabin house had been wrenched apart, leaving a gaping hole. Her emergency beacons alerted the race headquarters and approximately 16 hours later she was spotted by a Royal Australian Air Force (RAAF) Hercules C-130 plane. A full-scale rescue ensued. For two and a

Left ALAIN GAUTIER ON *GENERALI CONCORDE* AT THE START OF THE THIRD LEG, FROM SYDNEY TO PUNTA DEL ESTE, IN 1990/91. HE WON THE LEG (IN 31 DAYS) AND WAS PLACED SECOND OVERALL.

Above ISABELLE AUTISSIER, ON *ÉCUREUIL POITOU CHARENTES,* LOST HER MAST ON THE CAPE TOWN TO SYDNEY LEG IN 1990. SHE WAS EVENTUALLY PLACED SEVENTH OVERALL IN THE RACE.

half days the planes stood by until the Royal Australian Navy frigate HMAS *Darwin* reached her and sent its helicopter to airlift Autissier to safety. She is recorded as saying, 'This is the first time I have had to leave my boat. It was very difficult. I have spent all these three years thinking [about] and preparing this boat.'

Fellow Frenchman Christophe Auguin took up the lead in the Southern Ocean after Autissier dropped out of the race. Auguin started sailing at the age of five with his schoolteacher father on a 6.5m (21ft) Muscadet. When the family moved close to Saint Malo in Brittany in the northwest of France, he became a regular at the yacht club and was soon immersed in sailing every regatta, including the infamous Fastnet Race of 1979 (see page 18). It was the Figaro race that propelled his credibility towards the sponsorship stakes: his first attempt placed him ninth, in 1985 he was placed fifth, and one year later – first. With this win under his belt, he was able to give up his job teaching electrics and mechanics to become a full-time professional yachtsman.

His first BOC Challenge attempt in 1990/91 was aboard a 5.8m-wide (19ft) Sled, the most extreme 18m (60ft) monohull ever seen at this stage. It displaced only 10 tonnes of water and had the capacity to carry up to 3.5 tonnes of water (ballast) on each side for stability. Victory for Auguin in his first BOC was no mean feat, as Alain Gautier was leading for the first three legs. Auguin took the lead only in the final leg, off the coast of Brazil. However, he set a new course record of just over 120 days.

In the same race, during the fourth week of leg three, while concern was mounting about the whereabouts of UK yachtsman Harry Mitchell, race headquarters received a message from Briton Robin Davie aboard *Cornwall*: '*Cornwall* dismasted at 55°58"38'W. No assistance required. Down but not out.'

Forty-five minutes later: 'Cleared the decks and cut away all the rig. Only two spinnaker poles remain. Just having a cup of tea. Then think I'll turn in until daylight. No damage to hull and decks that I've seen. Repeat, no assistance required.'

While Robin Davie limped towards the Falkland Islands, east of the southernmost tip of Argentina in the South Atlantic, another entrant, Australian Arnet Taylor, on *Thursday's Child*, developed a serious split at the base of his mast so he, too, aimed for the Falklands in order to effect repairs.

Josh Hall of the UK put out a distress call after his 18m/60ft craft *Gartmore* crash-landed on an unseen object, splitting the hull and taking on more water than the pumps could bail out. Fellow racer Alan Nebauer helming *Newcastle Australia*, which was 90 nautical miles (167km) from Hall's position off the Brazilian coast, made his way over and picked up the Briton from his life raft just in time to watch *Gartmore*'s final sinking.

HARRY MITCHELL'S DISAPPEARANCE

There was no greater character in the history of the BOC than Harry Mitchell from Portsmouth, in South England. A retired car-hire manager, he was fondly known as the 'Brit with true grit', as well as The Old Man of the Sea and the Ancient Mariner. He said once, 'The BOC is the only race where [I] can take part and prove that youth isn't the final answer to motivation'.

He was everybody's favourite personality, the life and soul of every party. He attempted his first BOC Challenge at the age of 62 on the famous Admiral's Cup boat, *Yeoman XX*, which was affectionately nicknamed Kiss Kiss; it was

Top left *SCETA CALBERSON*, SKIPPERED BY FRENCHMAN CHRISTOPHE AUGUIN, AT THE FINISH IN CHARLESTON, USA, AFTER SAILING TO VICTORY IN THE 1994/95 BOC CHALLENGE.

Top right AN AERIAL VIEW OF *FILA*, AN OPEN 60 WHICH, AT THE HANDS OF CHARISMATIC AND MUCH-LIKED ITALIAN SAILOR GIOVANNI SOLDINI, WON THE 1998/99 AROUND ALONE RACE.

ISABELLE AUTISSIER

Autissier was born on 18 October 1956, the fourth of five daughters. She grew up in Paris and began sailing at the age of eight, when her father, an architect, bought a cruising boat. At age 18, she moved to Rennes to study as an agricultural engineer, specializing in the economics driving the fishing industry. During this time, she built herself a yacht, *Parole*, and went cruising in the West Indies and off Brazil with friends. After undertaking the return journey single-handed, the solo sailing bug hit hard.

At the late age of 31, she took up yacht racing and entered the single-handed Mini–Transat in 1987. She won the first leg and was placed third overall, an astonishing feat against the fleet of seasoned, dedicated single-handers. In 1988 and 1989 she competed in the leading French single-handed triangle race, Figaro, which drew her closer to her dream of sailing the BOC Challenge. After competing in her first Vendée Globe Challenge, she persuaded her sponsors to buy Jean-Luc van den Heede's 18m (60ft) yacht *36.15 Met,* with which she sailed herself into seventh overall position in the 1990/91 BOC race. It was only then that she started sailing professionally, analyzing her strengths and weaknesses and taking a close look at what makes people win or lose. Like Philippe Poupon, another great French sailor, Autissier is a technician, and her training in problem solving has been of great benefit to her.

Having dedicated her life full-time to sailing, she commissioned French architect Jean Berret to design a lightweight, easy-to-handle yacht which would perform well in light conditions. She worked closely with weather and routing experts (including Pierre Lasnier, acknowledged as the top French weather router), thus improving her own skills. Eighteen months before the start of the 1994/95 BOC race, her new yacht *Écureuil* was launched, ready to be put to the test for the 1993 season. She won two out of three legs in the Round Europe Race, and subsequently put on an astounding performance by breaking the tough New York to San Francisco clipper ship record by an incredible 14 days.

Autissier has been portrayed in the media as a kind, highly intelligent and articulate woman. It is a credit to her that, after her highly rated achievement in the 1994/95 BOC Challenge, she was somewhat surprised at the considerable fuss made of her first leg victory.

Above and top ISABELLE AUTISSIER CELEBRATES HER VICTORY IN LEG ONE OF THE 1994 BOC CHALLENGE (ABOVE); SHE SETS OFF FROM CAPE TOWN, SOUTH AFRICA, ON THE SECOND LEG (TOP).

Above AUTISSIER PARTICIPATING IN THE VENDÉE GLOBE RACE IN 1996/97. THINGS DID NOT GO TOO WELL FOR HER, AS SHE LATER HIT AN OBJECT UNDER THE WATER AND LOST HER RUDDER.

Above THE SOUTHAMPTON TO CAPE TOWN LEG OF THE 1994/95 BOC MADE PEOPLE SIT UP AND NOTICE AUTISSIER – SHE WAS FIVE DAYS AHEAD (1000 MILES/1820KM) OF AMERICAN STEVE PETTENGILL.

renamed *Double Cross* by Mitchell for his BOC attempt in 1986/87. He was, however, forced to retire more than halfway around the world when he ran aground in New Zealand. His second attempt, in 1991/92, was on a new boat called *We Are Lovers* (in the hope that she would respond to Harry's touch), but she was struck by a cargo ship on the way to the Newport start! Undeterred, he joked that she'd given him a 'bloody nose' instead, and sent off his entry fee for the next BOC Challenge.

And so, at the age of 70, Harry found himself at the start of the 1994/95 BOC race, aboard his repaired yacht, this time renamed *Henry Hornblower*. On 2 March 1995, 1450 nautical miles (2685km) west of South America's Cape Horn, during a violent Southern Ocean storm he triggered his EPIRB (Emergency Position Indicating Radio Beacon). The rescue coordination centre in Valparaiso, Chile, diverted a bulk carrier which had arrived in the vicinity of Mitchell's boat two and a half days after the first signal had been sent. She swept the area twice, making a grid search, sounding fog signals and firing flares in the hopes of eliciting a response, but her attempts were unsuccessful. A week later another ship was also diverted from her path to Cape Horn, but after a 36-hour search it was released by the rescue centre. Her search area had been extended to cover a 60-sq-nm-area (200km^2) but with winds once again increasing to Storm Force and seas rising to 12m (39ft), she was experiencing structural stress and was overloading her propulsion and steering systems.

A few days later, yet another ship was diverted to look for Harry Mitchell. At this stage, race director Mark Shrader said there was still hope that the yacht had been incapacitated with no communications and was somehow proceeding to Cape Horn, indicating that Mitchell had been somehow separated from his EPIRB, whose four days of signals had all emanated from a 4-mile (7km) radius.

Five days after the EPIRB activation, it happened to be Harry Mitchell's 43rd wedding anniversary. 'He'll show up because he always does,' said his wife Dianne. 'I cannot just stop believing that he is all right. I don't know where Harry is, or whether he will be found. He is in the hands of God now.'

Top FRENCHMAN MARC THIERCELIN ON HIS BOAT *SOMEWHERE*, WHICH WON LEG FOUR OF THE 1998/99 AROUND ALONE. HE ALSO RECORDED THE BEST 24-HOUR RUN IN CLASS I.

Left HARRY MITCHELL ON HIS BOAT *DOUBLE CROSS* DURING THE 1986 BOC CHALLENGE. ON LEG TWO, HE FELL AND KNOCKED HIMSELF OUT FOR SIX HOURS, SUFFERING CRACKED RIBS AND A SPLIT SCALP.

HOOD
Y3
TACK
HEATH GROUP

BT CHALLENGE

formerly British Steel Challenge

'I have talked to the boys who do the Whitbread, and they don't exaggerate – it is that bad. But they have the advantage of going with the wind, whereas we face a 6000-mile slog to windward.'
— *John Roberson (UK) on board* Courtaulds International

For those whose dream has always been to race on an enormous racing yacht and take on the Seven Seas. . . or to conquer the Southern Ocean. . . the BT Challenge was definitely created for them. Sold as the 'adventure of a lifetime', the BT Challenge is the brainchild of Scottish sailing fanatic Sir Chay Blyth, and the intent was to run it every four years. This famous sailor's contribution to yachting has been phenomenal; his most outstanding feat was in 1971, when he became the first person to sail alone and nonstop around the world against the prevailing winds and currents. He had already rowed across the Atlantic Ocean and has competed in the Whitbread (now Volvo) Round the World Race. The first race, held in 1992/93, was known as the British Steel Challenge. However, British Telecom, a UK-based telecommunications company, sponsored the next race in 1996/97, when it became the BT Challenge. It was always Blyth's view that yachting was an elitist sport, his aim, therefore, was to enable the ordinary human being to achieve what was previously impossible – race around the world the 'wrong' way. For those able to snatch at the opportunity to achieve that elusive dream, the cost is £18,750, paid per berth – the equivalent of two years' salary for some of the competitors.

Sailing into the wind – 'bashing your brains out', as seasoned sailors often describe it – does seem mindless and sadomasochistic. When a boat sails into the wind, the correct nautical term, 'beating', expresses it all. It is a lot slower than sailing with the wind, and extremely uncomfortable, as the boat literally beats into every wave and heels right over. But there is method behind this apparent madness of sending novices off on a round-the-world beat. If a crew member falls overboard, the rest of the crew have a far better chance of being able to pick him or her up because the boat is going more slowly; they can do this a lot sooner too. Also, the fleet tends to stick together, so boats are within an attainable distance from each other should there be, in a worst-case scenario, the need for rescue.

Racing into the wind means, too, that a less experienced sailor can take the helm without any threat of damaging the boat as he or she goes through the paces of trial and error. There is probably nothing more dangerous than doing the opposite – racing with the wind. The Whitbread/Volvo boats operate on a knife edge, thundering down the face of each wave at incredible speeds. With no room for error, the crew has to be constantly alert to any change. It is only the skill of the helmsman and the finely honed backup from his/her vastly experienced crew that sees a Volvo boat safely around the world.

Opposite AFTER CREWING ON *HEATH INSURED* IN THE FIRST BT CHALLENGE (1992), BRITON SAMANTHA BREWSTER WENT ON TO BECOME THE FIRST WOMAN – AS WELL AS THE YOUNGEST PERSON – TO CIRCUMNAVIGATE THE 'WRONG' WAY ROUND THE WORLD, ALONE.

Top to bottom CREWS OF VARIOUS YACHTS WORK TO GET THE BEST PERFORMANCE OUT OF THEIR CRAFT IN BT CHALLENGE EVENTS. ROUTINE MAINTENANCE PROCEDURES AND CAREFUL MONITORING OF WEAR AND TEAR ARE ESPECIALLY IMPORTANT ON LONG STRETCHES AT SEA.

The boat class selected for the BT Challenge is a 20m (67ft) steel cutter, designed by British designer, David Thomas, to be an 'upwind workhorse'. All the BT yachts were built at a boat yard in Plymouth and much went into ensuring that none had any design or technical advantages over any other in the fleet. These boats are heavier, therefore less likely to break up, and in an effort to maximize their speed on the beat they are reefed down (the sail area is reduced by gathering it in, in folds at the foot of the sail). Less pressure is thus placed on the rigging system – mast and sails – reducing the risk of dangerous breakages.

Because the race is about sailing skills – not design or big money – the boats, instead of being lightweight racing machines, are heavier and safer than they could be. Although they are slower by design, it is a setback they all suffer, and they therefore start off on an equal footing.

Within three weeks of the BT Challenge first being marketed for a 1992 start, over 5000 people had applied to take part in the race. From these, only 140 crew members were chosen, plus 200 alternates – and only 30 per cent of the entire selection had ever been on a yacht before. The first race was a phenomenal success, capturing the public's imagination.

The crews for the next BT Challenge, scheduled for 1996 – comprising six legs, and starting and ending in Southampton – were recruited early in 1994. By April of that year, there was a waiting list of more than 2000 people willing to pay almost £19,000 to take part. Together with the paid berths and the corporate sponsorships, there was as much as £20 million being pledged for the race. Chay Blyth's original idea of selling sponsorship packages – 'putting the dream within the grasp of the ordinary man' – as well as berths on the racing fleet had already been imitated successfully. The Clipper Race (leaving from and returning to English shores) has the same approach, but Blyth's offer hinges on his brainchild being the world's toughest race (though still within reach) for the novice.

Before the 1996 race had even been completed, the waiting list for the year 2000 BT Challenge was already starting to climb. A fleet of new 22m (72ft) yachts was being built for the millennium race, with the intention that 14 boats would be at the start line with a fully international crew.

'We're not taking the Whitbread on. The more [professional races] there are, and the more

Top IT WAS VETERAN YACHT *BRITISH STEEL II* THAT CARRIED CHAY BLYTH NONSTOP AROUND THE WORLD. HERE, SHE LEADS THE FLEET AT THE START OF THE FIRST BT CHALLENGE IN 1992.

Above THE 1996 BT CHALLENGE FLEET MOORED IN ST KATHERINE DOCK, LONDON. THE EVENT IS EXTREMELY WELL MARKETED AND CLOSELY FOLLOWED BY THE PUBLIC WORLDWIDE.

Opposite *BRITISH STEEL II* IN THE SOLENT DURING THE CHALLENGE OF 1992/93. SKIPPER JOHN CHITTENDEN ON *NUCLEAR ELECTRIC* ACHIEVED THE BEST ELAPSED TIME IN THE EVENT.

l. Challenge

'grand prix' they are, the more they put these races out of the reach of the ordinary person,' Chay Blyth is once quoted as saying.

A RACE THAT CHANGES PEOPLE'S LIVES

For the crews taking part in this race, there are extraordinary degrees of motivation, expectations and dedication rarely found in any workplace. The four years of anticipation – years that crew members and their families spend preparing for the race, making all kinds of personal sacrifices – end up becoming one of the largest commitments they've ever made in their lives.

The pressure on the skippers is enormous. They carry the hopes and expectations of the entire crew; their technical skills in sailing, navigation, the trimming of sails, and so on are not the most critical elements of success. The dangers lie in crushing the expectations of the crew. 'I'll never forgive him for taking the gloss off my race,' one crew member has once said of her skipper. She and her fellow crew had felt underused, mismanaged and let down. One of the sailing crew on *Ocean Rover* in the 1997 race, Humphrey Walters, is chief executive of a large management training company. He describes the uniqueness of the race: 'It has all the elements: duration, confinement, leadership, teamwork, risk and danger. The only other thing like it is warfare, and I didn't want to go to war!'

Being taken deep into the Southern Ocean becomes without fail the pinnacle of any sailing experience for people who generally lead quite ordinary lives. Of his first experience of the Southern Ocean's ferocity, sailor John Roberson, sailing on *Courtaulds International*, writes:

'It was mid-morning in this watery wilderness as I stood behind the wheel, my eyes on the sixty-odd feet of deck and a huge expanse of greyness. My vision shifted further upwards and further up, until at last I could see the sky. Then the bow started to lift and we began to climb until the boat herself felt as if she was standing vertically on her transom [the stern]. As we neared the top of this mountain, I realized to my horror that the top was breaking and, in the next instant, the foredeck was under a mass of foaming grey whiteness which was soon swirling around the mast and heading rapidly towards me.

'I felt my grip on the wheel tighten, and just as the wall of water hit me, the bow of the boat went into free fall; there was no back to the wave for her to slide down.'

That the race is a life-changing experience there is no doubt. While some returning sailors embrace the everyday familiarities they once took for granted, others find their return to normal life intolerable, feeling perpetually restless, discontented and wanting more from their lives.

'When I came back I found it very difficult to do anything. Everything seemed very mundane.

Above left *TIME & TIDE*, CREWED BY A PHYSICALLY DISABLED TEAM, HEELS RIGHT OVER AS SHE HEADS INTO STRONG WINDS AT THE START OF THE 1996 BT CHALLENGE OFF SOUTHAMPTON.

Left 1992 WINNER *NUCLEAR ELECTRIC* AT THE START OF THE 1996 CHALLENGE; HER MAINSAIL IS REEFED DOWN TO PREVENT HER FROM BEING OVERPOWERED IN STRONG WIND.

Returning to nine-to-five did my head in. I'd find myself wandering off, trying to get that buzz back,' admits London-based builder Nigel Bray after competing aboard *British Steel II* in the first race of 1992. 'I've been treading water ever since. I'm still trying to find something to recreate the fun and excitement of what we did. When you have adrenaline pumping through you, it's hard to readjust.'

Samantha Brewster, a Suffolk (UK) farmer's daughter and an outdoor pursuits instructor, was also a recruit in the first BT Challenge. Her traumatic circumnavigation on *Heath Insured*, which included the suicide at sea of a fellow crew member, did not dampen her sailing appetite. After returning to normal life, Samantha went on to become the first woman – and the youngest person – to circumnavigate the world, single-handedly, the 'wrong' way around (against the prevailing winds and tides) in 247 days.

While James Hatfield, having completed a single-handed circumnavigation, was receiving his MBE from Queen Elizabeth II, she asked him what he wanted to do next. His reply was, 'To skipper a disabled crew around the world'.

And so he did. In 1996, the entire crew of Hatfield's entry, *Time & Tide*, overcame life-threatening illnesses and disabilities to take part in the challenge, and became the first crew with disabilities to sail – never mind race – around the world. An incident two days into the race reflects the humour they have learnt to apply to their daily lives. Hatfield reported that crew member Nigel Smith had broken his right leg just above the knee joint, exposing the joint. The radio communication went as follows:

'. . .the medic cleaned the wound and gave it a squirt of WD40. Paul Burns and David Tate, the sail repair team, were asked for their opinions. It was decided to Sikaflex the inner scar tissue to give a firm base for the sail repair thread to bind into, then duct tape the whole thing till we get to Rio.'

(Amputee Nigel Smith commented afterwards that the prosthetic legs he was using were inclined to break frequently!)

The crew finished an amazing 10th, beating four able-bodied crews and astonishing the entire fleet. Hatfield maintains that his team had already faced their toughest test in life by facing up to their disabilities; the race was simply an adventure.

34-year-old Paul Burns, a member of the British parachute regiment, lost his left leg in the 1979 IRA bomb blast in Warren Point, England. He spent two years in hospital, after which he stayed on with his regiment and went on to complete 700 sky dives. Among the donors of his £18,750 entry fee for the 1996 race, the most celebrated are former UK prime minister Margaret Thatcher and British multimillionaire Richard Branson (owner of the Virgin group of companies). Burns parachuted into Branson's back garden to collect his donation!

It is an inspiration to all that Chay Blyth's 'normal' people did indeed become incredible people when faced with the challenge that he set. Perhaps an event like the BT Challenge gives credibility to the theory that all people have indomitable character traits and unknown reservoirs of strength, but the challenge lies in finding the trigger.

Above TIME TO DRY OUT THE OILSKINS ON A RARE SUNNY DAY IN THE SOUTHERN OCEAN ON BOARD *BRITISH STEEL II*, HERE PARTICIPATING IN THE FIRST BRITISH STEEL CHALLENGE, IN 1992.

Above IN THE 1996/97 CHALLENGE, CREW MEMBERS ABOARD *NUCLEAR ELECTRIC* ADJUST ONE OF THE SHROUDS THAT FORM PART OF THE STAINLESS STEEL RIGGING SUPPORTING THE MAST.

Top *COMMERCIAL UNION* ROMPS ACROSS THE SEA UNDER SPINNAKER; SAILING DOWNWIND REQUIRES CONCENTRATION AND FULL TEAMWORK. IT IS ESPECIALLY DIFFICULT FOR A NOVICE CREW.

VENDÉE GLOBE CHALLENGE

A definition of the Vendée Globe challenge is very simple: to sail nonstop around the world, solo, and without assistance. Both the start and finish are at Les Sables d'Olonne on the west coast of France. Simple in concept, ruthless in nature, the solo round the world race is an exceptional human adventure. From the calm seas of the Equator to the storms and extreme weather conditions of the Southern Ocean, each racing sailor meets his or her limits, experiencing feelings of exhaustion and discouragement. Requirements are that the boat be a monohull of a maximum of 18m (60ft) in length, that sailors head to the east, and that they not be permitted to stop or receive outside assistance – either physical or routing.

The race is an enormous challenge – more men have circled the world as astronauts than sailed around it nonstop and single-handed, as sailors. In fact, the Vendée Globe is acknowledged as the world's toughest single-handed event in any sport. It was created to meet the needs of sailors who wished to push themselves to the limit, and unites yachtsmen from all over the world. The winner is the first sailor to cross the finish line at Les Sables d'Olonne.

The predecessor to the Vendée Globe Challenge competition was the feat accomplished by Canadian-born sailor, Joshua Slocum, who was the first person ever to sail single-handedly around the world, on his boat *Spray*. Starting in 1895, he needed three years to complete his voyage whereas today, little more than three months is sufficient to follow a trail of 22,700 nautical miles (42,000km) around the planet. The compulsory passage points are:

- Les Sables d'Olonne, France
- The Canary Islands (off Africa's northwest coast)
- Antarctica to starboard
- Heard Island (Southern Ocean) to starboard
- Marker located at 50°S90°E to starboard
- Marker located at 57°S180° to starboard
- Marker located at 57°S120°W to starboard
- Marker located at 57°S67°W to starboard
- Cape Horn, South America, to port
- Les Sables d'Olonne, France

The race is organized by Sail Com, with the technical assistance of UNCL (Union Nationale pour la Course au Large) and the SNS (Sport Nautique Sablais).

In the first Vendée Globe Challenge, on 26 November 1989, there were 13 sailors at the start line at Les Sables d'Olonne. This first race would take 120 days (and nights), with no interruption. Of the 13 entrants, seven finished officially, three completed the course but had had to stop during the race, and three abandoned the race due to severe damage caused to their boats.

Top to bottom AMONG THE MASSES OF SPECTATORS (TOP AND CENTRE) ARE FAMILY AND FRIENDS WITH WHOM THE YACHTSMEN WILL HAVE THEIR LAST PERSONAL CONTACT UNTIL THE FINISH IN LES SABLES D'OLONNE, IN WEST FRANCE; PETE GOSS ON *AQUA QUORUM* (BOTTOM).

Opposite 1996/97 RACE WINNER CHRISTOPHE AUGUIN ON GÉODIS – A BOAT OF THIS SIZE NORMALLY HAS A MASSIVE STEERING WHEEL, BUT AUGUIN (TOGETHER WITH ISABELLE AUTISSIER) HAS A TWIN RUDDER SYSTEM AND TENDS TO PREFER THE DIRECT RESPONSE THAT CHARACTERIZES A TILLER.

Frenchman Titouan Lamazou was the first to cross the finish line of the 1989/90 round the world race on his 18m (60ft) monohull, *Écureuil d'Aquitaine II*. His time established a new world record of 109 days 8 hours 48 minutes 50 seconds, this after 24,120 miles (44,620km).

Despite Frenchman Loïc Peyron having to rescue compatriot Philippe Poupon off the Cape of Good Hope, Cape Town, South Africa, when his boat *Fleury Michon* capsized, Peyron still took second place on the podium. It was his first trip in southern oceans. French/Belgian Jean Luc van den Heede finished third, and Philippe Jeantot – who played the role of both competitor and organizer – fourth.

LIVES LOST IN 1991/92

In the second race, held in 1991/92, this time it was 14 sailors who set out to experience the legendary Vendée Globe Challenge. Two tragedies, however, served to remind everybody of the difficulties of such an extreme challenge. On Sunday 22 November 1991, a tanker, having left the harbour of Les Sables d'Olonne, spotted the capsized hull of American Mike Plant's *Coyote* 800 nautical miles (1482km), or an hour, west of the start; it had been making its way to participate in the race. He had not been heard from for over a month after having left New York, alone, on 16 October. On 25 November, a French Navy tug reached *Coyote* and the divers who boarded her found only a partially inflated life raft; there was no sign of Mike Plant.

Meanwhile, off Cape Finisterre, on the northwest coast of Spain, Vendée challenger Nigel Burgess of the UK activated his Argos distress beacon, but was later found dead, floating in his survival suit with the beacon around his neck, the victim of a severe head injury. His boat was later recovered intact.

The prevailing vicious low-pressure weather system dismasted one other competitor and sent five others back to Les Sables for repairs. Back at the race headquarters, the questions, which were all the same, bore testimony to the extreme nature of the Vendée Globe: 'What kind of event takes the lives of two sailors and beats back six others in less than three days?'

The race was dominated from start to finish by Alain Gautier of France. Only Philippe Poupon threatened Gautier, on the way back, in the southern Atlantic. But Poupon was dismasted 1500 nautical miles (2775km) from the finish, forcing him to complete the course with a makeshift rigging, thus placing him third after Belgian Jean Luc van den Heede.

More than 200,000 people were waiting to greet the competitors on their return to Les Sables d'Olonne.

DRAMA IN 1996/97

The third Vendée Globe represented Frenchman Christophe Auguin's third round the world solo victory; he was also a two-time BOC winner. He completed the 26,000-nautical-mile, singlehanded, nonstop marathon in a record-breaking 105 days 20 hours 31 minutes 23 seconds on his yacht *Géodis*. Fifteen entrants started the ocean trial, and only six returned to the starting point in France some 106 days later.

'It's like Formula One. When you push too much, you break your motor,' Auguin said of the enormous pressure he was under from fellow competitors Yves Parlier and Isabelle Autissier, both of France. Parlier, with his pow-

Top FRENCHMAN YVES PARLIER ON *AQUITAINE* IN THE 1996/97 RACE. HIS BOAT IS LITERALLY 'FLYING' OVER THE SURFACE, APPARENT FROM THE BOW WHICH IS LIFTING CLEARLY ABOVE THE WATER.

Left ALAIN GAUTIER, ON *GENERALI CONCORDE* IN THE 1989 VENDÉE GLOBE, HAS PUSHED HIS BOOM RIGHT OUT TO ALLOW THE MAINSAIL TO CATCH AS MUCH WIND AS POSSIBLE FROM THE PORT STERN.

erful wing-masted rig, set a lightning pace in the opening stages of the race, while Autissier raced Auguin neck and neck for two weeks in the south Atlantic before hitting an underwater object and losing a rudder.

Auguin's *Géodis* has been likened to an ocean-going surfboard, with her plumb bow and stern, massive beam, low freeboard and acres of deck space. She was not the newest boat in the race, and there were three others that were potentially faster, but Auguin's advantage was sheer determination and a touch of good luck.

Alain Gautier, his major rival on the single-handed sailing circuit and defending champion of the Vendée Globe, says of him:

'I think to win three round-the-world races is incredible. No-one has done that. Christophe has big determination to win this race. You need that. When he wants something, he goes for it one hundred per cent. He has a good feeling with tactics and meteorological problems.'

Weather forecasting was undoubtably the most important part of Auguin's day, with at least three hours every day being dedicated to poring over weather faxes, looking at options on his Maxsea Routing software, analyzing what was ahead of him and reviewing all his options. It was time well spent – and it paid off.

A severe storm in 1996/97 (see panel on Tony Bullimore, right) also affected race competitor, Frenchman Thierry Dubois, who had capsized three times even before the real drama began. The first time, he pitch-poled (stern over bow),

Top FRENCH SAILOR CHRISTOPHE AUGUIN ON HIS YACHT *GÉODIS*, MAKING RADIO CONTACT AT HIS NAVIGATION STATION DURING THE VENDÉE GLOBE CHALLENGE OF 1996/97.

TONY BULLIMORE'S DRAMATIC RESCUE

The dramatic rescue during the 1996/97 race of 57-year-old Briton Tony Bullimore from within the hull of his 'turtled' boat was miraculous. His boat *Exide Challenger* was discovered after he had set off the distress call on 5 January 1996 from his Emergency Position Indicating Radio Beacon (EPIRB). It was upside down and it was evident that the keel had snapped off, but there was no sign of Bullimore. It was race organizer and two-time BOC Challenge winner, Frenchman Philippe Jeantot, who suggested that the safest place for Bullimore to be would be inside the boat. On 8 January, an Orion PC-3 dropped sonar devices around the hull, and it was believed that light tapping sounds could be heard, but there was no certainty as to whether these were being made by Bullimore. The boat, HMS *Adelaide*, was dispatched to investigate further and a crew on an inflatable rapped on the hull. They were rewarded with an answering rap, soon followed by Bullimore himself, who did not wait to be rescued but dived out from under his boat unassisted! He described his six days of being trapped within his boat as 'being sloshed around like a ping pong [ball] in a washing machine'. His only dry spot was a shelf in the forward storage compartment (a surface of about .5x1m/1.5x4ft, with .5m/1.5ft clearance). 'I have got an attitude which is inbuilt. I've been in lots of scrapes in the past, and I don't panic.'

It is clearly evident that it was Bullimore's attitude and sense of humour that helped him see his ordeal through. (Bullimore had severed the tip of his little finger in an attempt to free his lifeboat, and when the pain bothered him he simply put it in the water for 10 minutes until it became numb from the cold!)

He had been sailing under bare poles (no sails up) in a 60-knot gale when he lost his keel (which he termed 'the almighty'). He described the actual capsize in the following words:

'. . .All of a sudden there was a crack; literally, like, CRACK. It happened, bang, quickly and instantly – amazingly quickly – within two or three seconds, the boat had gone Pow! and was upside down. It wasn't a slow capsize. It turned over at a million miles an hour, and that's what happened. I wasn't hurt even a little bit.'

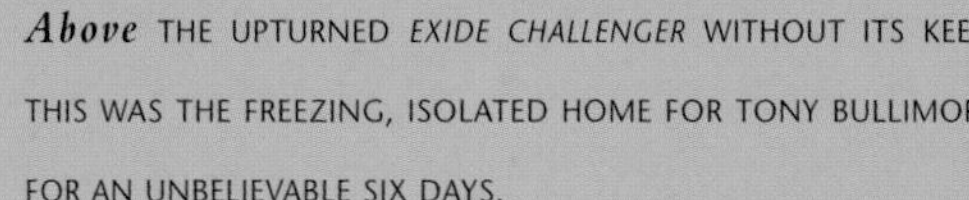

Above THE UPTURNED *EXIDE CHALLENGER* WITHOUT ITS KEEL. THIS WAS THE FREEZING, ISOLATED HOME FOR TONY BULLIMORE FOR AN UNBELIEVABLE SIX DAYS.

Above THE AMAZING RESCUE OF TONY BULLIMORE (LEFT) AND THIERRY DUBOIS, HERE ARRIVING IN WESTERN AUSTRALIA, INVOLVED THE AUSTRALIAN NAVY, AIR FORCE AND RESCUE SERVICES.

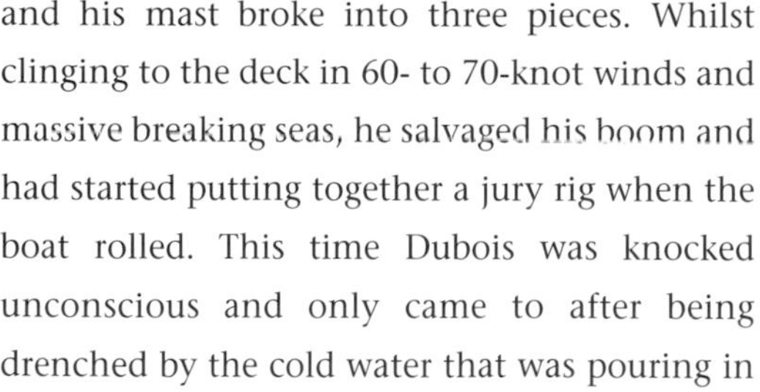

and his mast broke into three pieces. Whilst clinging to the deck in 60- to 70-knot winds and massive breaking seas, he salvaged his boom and had started putting together a jury rig when the boat rolled. This time Dubois was knocked unconscious and only came to after being drenched by the cold water that was pouring in through his damaged – previously watertight – hatch (the latch had been ripped off). By now it was, in his own words, 'very rough'.

Realizing his position was perilous, he wedged himself in by jamming a mattress against the chart table, hoping to sit out the storm in safety before taking further action. Some 24 hours later Dubois heard the approach of an enormous wave. The boat was rolled over as if in slow motion, enabling him to walk around the hull until he was standing on the inside of the roof. It became clear that the boat was going to remain upside down, so Dubois put on his survival suit and moved into the aft watertight compartment with his emergency beacons. In order to ensure the signal had a good chance of being transmitted he moved outside, through the transom hatch, with the beacons. He hung on between the rudders; it was a huge task just to stay aboard as the boat gyrated wildly but with no sign of righting. Dubois managed to half-inflate his life raft before it was blown away by the strong winds.

Ironically, because of the ongoing search for Tony Bullimore, a rescue plane flew over Dubois within two hours, although, at the time, it was unaware of Dubois' plight. The Australian Air Force plane dropped a life raft to Dubois, which unfortunately missed him and, on landing, immediately capsized and blew away. On the second attempt the aircraft dropped a pair of

Above left YACHTSMAN BERTRAND DE BROC GETTING SOME REST DURING THE 1996/97 RACE. HIS RADAR SYSTEM WILL ALERT HIM TO ANY ONCOMING HAZARDS.

Top THE BUBBLE DOME OF YVES PARLIER'S CABIN AFFORDS HIM A 360-DEGREE VIEW OF HIS BOAT ABOVE-DECK WITHOUT HIM HAVING TO LEAVE THE WARMTH AND SAFETY OF HIS COCOON-LIKE CONFINES.

rafts, tied together, but the rope tangled during the drop and one raft inflated before hitting the water. Dubois swam from his boat to try to get into the other raft – which also broke up, having been damaged during the drop! This was the worst point of the yachtsman's plight – he was in the water, without a life raft, and a long way from his boat.

He now thought it likely that he was going to die. He kept a cool head, however, swimming slowly but hopelessly after his drifting boat in the freezing water. Thankfully, 30 minutes later the plane returned and dropped a final pair of rafts. This time the drop was successful; the rafts fell upwind of Dubois and when he got to them, they were still intact. He climbed in and prepared for the long, freezing-cold, two- to three-day wait for help to arrive in the form of the HMS *Adelaide* with its helicopters.

During the same race, on 25 December 1996, Briton Pete Goss turned his 15m (50ft) yacht, *Aqua Quorum*, back into a Hurricane Force headwind to rescue French sailor Raphael Dinelli. He risked his life and any chance of winning. Instead, he was awarded France's highest honour – the Légion d'Honneur – and an MBE (Member of the Order of the British Empire) in the 1998 New Year's Honour List.

Above ONE OF THE TRANQUIL MOMENTS DURING THE 1996/97 RACE – A GENTLE BREEZE FROM BEHIND CATCHES THE SAILS OF CHRISTOPHE AUGUIN'S BOAT *GÉODIS* AT THE CLOSE OF DAY.

Right PATRICK DE RADIGUES PARTICIPATING IN THE SAME RACE ON *AFIBEL*. THE BOAT'S NARROW STERN DIFFERS DRAMATICALLY FROM THE SAUCER-LIKE HULL SHAPE OF *GÉODIS*.

Commodore
Commodore Explorer
Commodore Explorer
Commodore Explorer

JULES VERNE TROPHY

The Jules Verne Trophy, or Trophée Jules Verne, was originally conceived by Frenchman Yves Le Cornac (a sailor himself) as a challenge to circumnavigate the world by boat in 80 days. It has established itself as the first yacht race of its kind: rather than boat against boat, it is boat against time. The Jules Verne is not an event as such; it has no fixed start time – or even a start line. It is an open invitation to any yachtsman to take on the challenge, with the only criterium being that the boat starts and ends between Ile d'Ouessant, an island off the province of Brittany in northwest France, and the Lizard, a peninsula projecting into the English Channel (forming the southernmost point of Great Britain).

The first winner, in 1993, of the Jules Verne Trophy (79 days 6 hours 15 minutes 56 seconds on his boat *Commodore Explorer*) – and thus the first person to break the round-the-world speed record – was Frenchman Bruno Peyron, who boasts an impressive sailing résumé. He was ranked the number one Oceanic Multihull Skipper in four consecutive years, from 1987 to 1990. He broke the Transatlantic Single-handed record in 1987 and again in 1992. Always seeking to break more records, it was Peyron who invented a new planetary race event for the year 2000: The Race (see page 132) is an invitation to the fastest sailing racers in the world to take part in a no-limits round the world race, with the firing of the start gun on 31 December 2000.

In his Jules Verne challenge, Peyron was partnered by American sailor Cam Lewis, one of the most well known and respected personalities in competitive sailing, particularly in multihulls – earning him the 1993 Rolex Yachtsman of the Year Award. A resident of Lincolnville, USA, Lewis includes among his numerous accolades the winning of the America's Cup in 1988 on board fellow countryman Dennis Conner's *Stars & Stripes*, and being ranked the top American ocean racer in March 1997 by the Fédération Internationale de la Course Océanique (FICO).

TWO WORLD-CLASS SAILING VETERANS

A year after Bruno Peyron's successful claim to the Jules Verne Trophy, ocean racing veterans Robin Knox-Johnston of the UK and Peter Blake of New Zealand teamed up for the second attempt. Their 26m (85ft) catamaran, *Enza New Zealand*, smashed the record with a time of 74 days 22 hours 17 minutes.

Just like Jules Verne's fictitious character Philæas Fogg, Knox-Johnston and Blake are legends in their own right: Sir Robin Knox-Johnston was the first to race nonstop, single-handed, around the world (for which the UK *Sunday Times* awarded him a Golden Globe Trophy), completing his epic voyage in 1969 on his ketch *Suhaili*. Sir Peter Blake's numerous achievements include two Sportsman of the Year awards and four Yachtsman of the Year awards, which he earned in his native country New Zealand. He was named a Member of the Order of the British Empire (MBE) in 1983 for his service to yachting, and in

Opposite *COMMODORE EXPLORER* COMPETING IN 1993. THE 26M (85FT) CATAMARAN WAS DESIGNED AND BUILT BY FRENCHMAN GILLES OLLIER.

Top to bottom *COMMODORE EXPLORER* (TOP), SKIPPERED BY BRUNO PEYRON AND CAM LEWIS, WAS THE FIRST WINNER OF THE JULES VERNE TROPHY, BEATING THE 80-DAY CUTOFF IN 79 DAYS 6 HOURS 15 MINUTES 56 SECONDS. PETER BLAKE AND ROBIN KNOX-JOHNSTON (CENTRE) ON *ENZA NEW ZEALAND* IN THEIR FIRST ATTEMPT AT THE JULES VERNE CHALLENGE IN 1993. THEY RETIRED AFTER A COLLISION ON 26 FEBRUARY IN THE INDIAN OCEAN. *ENZA NEW ZEALAND* AT THE 1994 FINISH (BOTTOM). IN THIS ATTEMPT, BLAKE AND KNOX-JOHNSTON BEAT THE TIME SET BY PEYRON AND LEWIS.

JULES VERNE (1828-1905)

Jules Verne was born on 8 February 1828 in Nantes, a city just inland of the Loire River mouth in north-east France. Together with his brother, a younger Jules used to sail on the Loire, often following it down to the sea. In the boy's active imagination, their leaky boat was transformed into a palatial yacht, and every stretch of scenic landscape was an important geographic discovery he'd made. His father, a lawyer, wanted Jules to follow in the same profession. but when Jules was sent to school in Paris, he studied literature instead of law. He also had an endless fascination with science, and read the latest books and journals on the subject, while pumping the scientists he encountered for the most recent and up-to-date information. Whenever he hit upon an interesting discovery, he speculated on what could come of it. From these speculations grew his famous novels. In 1869 Verne wrote *20,000 Leagues Under the Sea* – 30 years before the submarine had been invented. The force that powered Verne's submarine was electricity which, at the time, was a mere curiosity in the scientific laboratory. He researched in libraries and aquariums, and even undertook a transatlantic steamship journey. He wrote most of the book on his sailing boat, to make sure he accurately caught the feel of the sea.

The startling inventions described in Jules Verne's novels seemed quite fantastic to the readers of his time; today he is regarded as a prophet. His dreams of undersea and air travel have materialized, and Verne's story *Around the World in Eighty Days* now feels like a record of a leisurely trip. In the tale, the main character, Philæas Fogg, accepts a wager to defy the premise that he cannot travel around the world in 80 days – an incredible feat at that time.

However, in more recent times, it was French yachtsman Bruno Peyron who himself took up the challenge on his Maxi catamaran *Commodore Explorer.* His epic modern-day nautical adventure took him around the world in a record-smashing time of 79 days 6 hours 15 minutes 56 seconds.

Above *ENZA NEW ZEALAND* FINISHING IN BREST, FRANCE, DURING THE 1994 JULES VERNE CHALLENGE. THE CATAMARAN BECAME THE SECOND TITLE HOLDER OF THE JULES VERNE TROPHY.

Below, left and right OLIVIER DE KERSUASSON IS THE CURRENT HOLDER OF THE JULES VERNE TROPHY. IN 1997 HE DID A CIRCUMNAVIGATION ON *SPORT-ELEC* WITHIN THE 80-DAY TARGET. IN AN EARLIER ATTEMPT IN 1994, ON *LYONAISSE DES EAUX*, HE CLOCKED UP 77 DAYS, BUT *ENZA NEW ZEALAND* BETTERED THIS WITH ITS 74-DAY RECORD.

1991 received a knighthood from Queen Elizabeth II, when he was also honoured with the title of Officer of the Order of the British Empire (OBE), again for services to yachting. Blake sailed the first five Whitbread Round the World Races (see page 103) and in the 1989/90 Whitbread, skippered *Steinlager* to an unprecedented clean sweep. His racing crew walked off with line, handicap and overall honours on each of the race's six legs.

At the head of the 1995 Team New Zealand syndicate competing for the America's Cup, Blake's leadership in the art of meticulous planning helped his team win the race, only the second time in the event's 144-year history that a non-American team had won the silver trophy. With Blake on board as a crew member, the Team New Zealand boat crossed the line first in all but one race, defeating Team Dennis Conner of the San Diego Yacht Club 5–0.

SETTING A NEW RECORD

In 1997, on his seventh attempt, Frenchman Olivier de Kersuasson succeeded at taking the Jules Verne Trophy for sailing the fastest around the world. His 27m (90ft) trimaran *Sport-Elec* crossed the finish to set a record of 71 days 14 hours 18 minutes, beating *Enza*'s (Knox-Johnston/Blake) time by over three days.

Despite beating the record by such a large margin, *Sport-Elec* actually recorded a lower average speed. Her average of 14.6 knots was surpassed by *Enza*'s round the world average of 14.7. *Sport-Elec*'s success in shaving off three days was due to the favourable weather conditions, which allowed her to navigate a course that was 1500 miles (2778km) shorter than *Enza*'s 26,413-mile (48,917km) course.

The weatherman on board *Sport-Elec* was Bob Rice, who had also been a major influence in Blake's America's Cup Challenge as well as his Jules Verne record. Sir Peter Blake was, in fact, on the quayside at Brest, France, to welcome the yacht and her crew in.

Right A BIRD'S EYE VIEW OF *ENZA*. SKIPPERS KNOX-JOHNSTON AND BLAKE HAVE BEEN KNIGHTED FOR THEIR SERVICES TO YACHTING. THEIR 74-DAY RECORD OF 1994 WAS BEATEN BY DE KERSUASSON (71 DAYS).

THE RACE

'The Race would be the most extravagant demonstration of extreme sports at sea. . . That race is going to be the ultimate encounter between ocean racers. Nothing will compare with this fastest circumnavigation on the biggest racing yachts ever built.' — *New Zealander Ross Field, winner of the Whitbread 1993/94*

The challenge thrown out by Bruno Peyron, France's top catamaran sailor, to skippers manning the fastest boats in the world is what laid the foundations for The Race. As audacious as its name, the challenge is a nonstop sprint around the world with no rules governing boat construction materials, number of hulls, weight, and length of the competing boats. Unlike the Jules Verne challenge (see page 129), The Race has a fixed start date. This forsakes the opportunity to wait for suitable race conditions, meaning that precious days could be lost upfront in the race should inclement weather conditions so dictate.

The only prequalifier for The Race is that the entrants must be able to sail an ocean passage at an average speed of more than 20 knots. There are three qualifying courses: New York on the USA's east coast to Lizard Point, the southmost point on the southwestern tip of England; Los Angeles on the US west coast to Honolulu in Hawaii; and Yokohama in Japan to San Francisco on the west coast of the USA.

The Jules Verne Trophy winner of May 2000 automatically qualified for The Race. The start of the first event is scheduled for 31 December 2000, in order not to conflict with the America's Cup (as did its original starting date of 1 January 2000). The race begins and finishes in the Straits of Gibraltar, the passage between Spain and Morocco (North Africa), and as boats leave the Cape of Good Hope (South Africa), Cape Leeuwin (at the southwest extreme of Western Australia) and Cape Horn (the southernmost point of South America) respectively, they do so keeping the land to port (that is, ensuring the continent is to the left-hand side of the boat when heading out).

There are also no design limits – launching designers into an effort to research the fastest conceivable sailboat while making it durable enough to handle the rigours of a global race. Regardless of class or technical specifications, these 'clippers of the year 2000' will be 35–40m (115–131ft) long, capable of doing 40 knots and covering a distance of more than 600 nautical miles (1110km) in record-breaking time. This need for such high-level performance is the essential criterion for assuring the quality and impact of the event.

Designwise, the 'no limit' concept means that for the first time in the history of round-the-world sailing races, boats of different design will be able to compete. The heated debate which has characterized the event since its conception has focused on the type of boat that is most likely to win the prestigious race. Combining the pioneering spirit of the 20th century with the technology of the 21st, The Race promises to feature the largest, swiftest and sleekest yachts yet designed.

Top to bottom CHALLENGER TRACY EDWARDS' JULES VERNE ATTEMPT ON *ROYAL & SUNALLIANCE* ENDED IN MARCH 1998 WITH A DISMASTING; HI-TECH NAVIGATIONAL EQUIPMENT IS THE ONLY LUXURY IN *PLAYSTATION'S* INTERIOR; RACE CONTENDER BRUNO PEYRON ON *COMMODORE EXPLORER* FOR HER JULES VERNE CIRCUMNAVIGATION ALMOST CAPSIZED IN THE SOUTHERN OCEAN AND SURVIVED A 70-KNOT STORM OFF CHILE.

Opposite STEVE FOSSETT'S ULTRAMODERN CATAMARAN *PLAYSTATION* IS THE 2000 RECORD HOLDER FOR THE NEWPORT–BERMUDA RACE.

USA 2
PlayStation
PlayStation

Most competitors will be entering catamarans, which can generally average 20 knots and are capable of reaching 40 knots plus, enabling them to encircle the globe in less than 70 days. The required stability and sailpower on a 30m-plus (100ft) multihull necessitates two masts, one on each hull. Cam Lewis, Jules Verne Trophy winner in 1993, says, 'Most designers think that 125 feet [38m] is the optimum length, that any longer is wasted waterline'. Besides the question of design, Bruno Peyron is encouraging an open attitude to the unfettered imagination and the greatness of challenge, as well as a more universal approach to ocean racing. His dream is that the event, far from being a short-lived display of skills or simply another sports performance, will define the spirit of humankind in the new millennium. To Peyron, The Race represents universalism, open-mindedness and tolerance, breaking away from past tendencies towards domination, partitioning and protectionism: a no-rules event for spectators and media followers all over the world.

These criteria are also not quite enough. Competitors will be asked to make a commitment that goes far beyond the strict observation of race rules. They are required to make The Race's values their own and promote them: these include education on and future preservation of the environment and increasing public awareness of the world's maritime heritage.

EuroDisney outside Paris, Europe's answer to the USA's Disneyland, is backing the event, for which the budget is £15 million. So far, 23 syndicates from 11 countries have registered their interest in giving financial support. The prize is US$1 million. In the words of Jean-Jacques Aillagon, president of La Mission pour la Célébration de l'an 2000: 'The Race would be the bearer and ambassador to the world of the spirit that France wanted to give year 2000 celebrations: opening to the world, solidarity between the peoples of the Blue Planet, spirit of innovation, a taste for enterprise.'

BT (British Telecom), a major telecommunications company in the UK, has committed itself to sharing their satellite technology by transmitting all the action to television viewers worldwide, and race crews will supply daily updates to websites via the Internet, give live television interviews, and question and answer

Top WHERE MOST CONTENDERS ARE BUILDING NEW CRAFT FOR THE RACE, ROMAN PASZKE'S ENTRY IS ONE-TIME JULES VERNE RECORD HOLDER *EXPLORER* (EX-BRUNO PEYRON).

Bottom US BILLIONAIRE STEVE FOSSETT EXCELS IN SETTING RECORDS; HOT-AIR BALLOONING, DOG-SLED RACING AND MOUNTAIN CLIMBING ARE JUST SOME OF THE SPORTS HE HAS EXCELLED IN.

sessions will be conducted for the public. The anticipation that precedes The Race is inherent in a statement made by UK sailor Tracy Edwards, skipper of the first all-female crew in the Whitbread Race and contender in the Jules Verne Trophy on the Maxi catamaran *Royal & SunAlliance*: 'To be on the starting line with the best boats and the best crew, this is what we are working on. Personally, I can't wait to take up the challenge.'

THE RACE PLAYERS

- Nigel Irens of the UK is the boat architect of Tracy Edwards' catamaran *Royal & SunAlliance* (New Zealander Peter Blake's ex-*Enza*) and Loïc Peyron's trimaran *Fujicolor II*.
- US billionaire and well-known hot-air balloonist Steve Fossett has entered his 36.5m (120ft) VLC (Very Large Cat), *Playstation*.
- Five-time Whitbread veteran, New Zealander Grant Dalton, will be skippering a 33.5m (110ft) catamaran *ClubMed* (yacht specifications are a closely guarded secret, but Frenchman Gilles Ollier's design team is involved). Project manager Jean Maurèl has competed in four Route de Rhum events and 24 Transat races.
- Roman Paszke of Poland has purchased *Commodore Explorer* from Bruno Peyron for his entry in The Race.
- UK boat designer Adrian Thompson has designed a 38m (125ft) 'wave piercer' Maxi catamaran for Pete Goss.
- Cam Lewis of Maine, USA, has also chosen Gilles Ollier for his 33.5m (110ft) catamaran, which is to have a 46m (150ft) mast. He aims to maintain speeds of 40 knots per hour.
- Dutch sailor Henk de Velde is the only sailor to have completed three circumnavigations on a catamaran. His boat is a 40m (131ft) catamaran designed by Australian team Crowther; each hull will sport a self-bearing AeroRip sprit mast.
- Bruno Peyron's brother, Loïc – one of his generation's most talented oceanic multihull skippers – was one of the first five yachtsmen to confirm his race entry. His architect, fellow Frenchman Marc Lombard, has put together a 32m (105ft) foiler trimaran.

BRUNO PEYRON

This yachtsman from La Baule, a town lying north of the Loire River mouth on France's west coast, built his first catamaran *Jaz* with a bipod rig (twin side-by-side masts) at the age of 22. A serious single-handed sailor, he has raced four Figaro Solos and three Route de Rhum races (in which he twice finished second). He has made more than 34 Atlantic Ocean crossings, 12 of which were achieved single-handed – and two of which were new transatlantic records (1987 and 1992). From 1987 to 1990 Peyron held the unbroken title of number one Oceanic Multihull Skipper in the world. The highlight of his astonishing career was becoming the first person (at the age of 38) to win the Jules Verne Trophy (see page 129), which he did in 1993, setting a time of 79 days 6 hours 15 minutes 56 seconds on his Maxi cat *Commodore Explorer*. Peyron has accumulated more than 240,000 nautical miles (over 444,000km) of ocean sailing.

Below BRUNO PEYRON'S (ABOVE) *COMMODORE EXPLORER* APPROACHES SAN FRANCISCO. SHE HAD RECENTLY ACCOMPLISHED A NEW TRANSATLANTIC RECORD IN HER CAMPAIGN FOR THE RACE – CONCEPTUALIZED BY PEYRON.

INSHORE

CLASSICS

25
25 MUMM
CHAMPAGNE

ADMIRAL'S CUP

The Admiral's Cup was created in 1957 by Sir Miles Wyatt, who at the time was Admiral of the UK-based Royal Ocean Racing Club (RORC) – the oldest club in the world, formed purely to promote offshore yacht racing. It was in that year that Wyatt had decided, together with four friends, that international yachts needed to be encouraged to come to UK waters to race against local yachts in Cowes Week, where the trophy would be presented.

Cowes, situated in the north of the Isle of Wight, at the entrance to the Medina River, faces Southampton across the Solent. London is approximately 129km (80 miles) away. In the 19th century, Cowes became the traditional centre of yacht racing; the Regatta was a glittering and festive event in the social season, patronized by European royalty. Queen Victoria lived at Osborne House near Cowes, and her large family, together with the monarchs of Germany, Russia and Spain, raced against each other in the Solent. Cowes' history is closely linked with that of the Royal Yacht Squadron, whose castle has guarded the approach to the town for more than a century.

Cowes Week is organized by Cowes Combined Clubs, and is held during the first week of August, while the Admiral's Cup is organized every two years by the Royal Ocean Racing Club. Until 1999, the Admiral's Cup was run over a two-week period, the second week coinciding with Cowes Week. The long offshore race, which formed part of the sailing events, was the Fastnet Race, starting on the last Saturday of Cowes Week.

After 1997, the decision was made to move the Admiral's Cup out of Cowes Week, hence its timing since then being two weeks earlier. This allowed the Cup's inshore racing to take place in the Solent and gave it the exclusivity competing nations deserved when taking part in this prestigious battle. The decision was also made not to change the Fastnet Race, which would still take place at the end of Cowes Week, and a new event, the Wolf Rock Race, became the long offshore race for the Admiral's Cup.

The Cup is a series of races held in the UK between different nations, competing on offshore racing yachts. The races occur over a period of two weeks in mid-July, in odd-numbered years. Each nation is permitted to send one team, consisting of three yachts – one each in three specified size categories. The categories are a Mumm 36 (One Design), a Sydney 40 (One Design) and the 'Big Boat' Open Class (13–15m, or 44–50ft, handicap racers).

The Mumm 36 (sponsored by the Mumm champagne house) – fast, demanding to sail and exciting to watch – has become a well-established offshore One Design Class in its own right. Evolved from trophy racing at the top level, the yacht was developed by Farr International as a result of a design competition held by the RORC to find a new IMS (International Measurement System) racing yacht for the Admiral's Cup. Over 100 of these racing yachts were built within two years, winning top regattas on handicap and racing as a class in sailing circuits in Europe, the USA and the Pacific Ocean. The boat is 11m (36ft) in length, light, fast, seaworthy, and has a crew weight limit of 655kg (1444 lb).

Previous pages HELMSMAN BOUWE BEKKING ON *MEAN MACHINE*, PART OF THE DUTCH TEAM THAT WON THE ADMIRAL'S CUP OF 1999.
Opposite *INNOVISION 7*, OWNED BY HANS ECKOFF, ANOTHER DUTCH ENTRY THAT WAS PART OF THE 1999 TEAM, SAILING CLOSE UPWIND.
Top to bottom IRELAND (FOREGROUND) WAS REPRESENTED BY A THREE-BOAT TEAM, *JAMESON I, II* AND *III*, IN THE 1995 EVENT; *CHERNIKEEFF* (COMMONWEALTH TEAM) DURING THE 1999 RACE; THE JUBILANT SKIPPER FROM THE US TEAM, WINNERS OF THE ADMIRAL'S CUP IN 1997.

The premise of the term 'One Design' is that each yacht is designed with exactly the same parameters and the racing is undertaken in 'real time', that is, results are measured on a strict 'first across the line' basis. The racing is also very close, with much of the fleet arriving at the turning mark at the same time. The difference is skill – which is why this design class attracts the top professional yacht racers.

Surprisingly, owning and racing a Mumm 36 is less expensive than the former IOR (International Offshore Rules) boats. The advantage of the One Design format is that competitors can race anywhere in the world by chartering a Mumm 36 locally and then flying over their own sails and crew members.

Above THE GENOA AND MAINSAIL ARE QUICKLY ADJUSTED TO ENABLE SCANDINAVIAN ENTRY IN 1997, *INVESTOR*, TO DIP BELOW THE YACHT AHEAD, WHICH ON A STARBOARD TACK HAS RIGHT OF WAY.

When participating in Mumm 36 regattas, competitors favour two and three short offshore races a day, over a period of three to four days, thus achieving the maximum amount of racing in the shortest possible time.

The Sydney 40 is the mid-size boat of each competing team in the Admiral's Cup. Like the Mumm 36, it is a strict offshore One Design, designed and developed in Australia.

Third and biggest boat of each team is the IMS 'Big Boat' Class – the latest generation of IMS 45s and 50s on the sailing circuit. The Admiral's Cup has always been raced according to the handicapping system of the day. By retaining a handicap class – the Big Boat Open Class – the organizers have succeeded in keeping the event open to any nation's designers and builders. This class represents the glamour of yacht racing.

Below THE AMERICAN TEAM ON *BLUE YANKEE PRIDE*, A SYDNEY 40, IN THE 1999 ADMIRAL'S CUP. THIS CLASS FORMS A PART OF EACH THREE-BOAT TEAM COMPETING IN THE CUP.

Above IMAGES FROM THE ADMIRAL'S CUP. TOP ROW, LEFT TO RIGHT: *APOLLO IV* RUNNING AGAINST THE CURRENT IN 1979; THE AUSTRALIAN TEAM ON *SWAN PREMIUM* (RIGHT) LEAD THE FLEET IN 1987; *NADA* IN 1975. CENTRE ROW, LEFT TO RIGHT: FINISH OF THE FIRST RACE IN 1985 WITH THE ROYAL YACHT SQUADRON IN THE BACKGROUND; ONBOARD ACTION IN THE 1987 EVENT; *PINTA,* IN 1985, PREPARING TO GYBE THE SPINNAKER. BOTTOM ROW, LEFT TO RIGHT: THE FLEET SURFING UNDER SPINNAKER IN 1985; *SPEAKEASY* PLOUGHS HER WAY UPWIND IN 1997; AN EXCITING DOWNWIND SPINNAKER RUN ON *TRILOGY II* IN COWES WEEK 1990.

The major yachting nations of the world send their best sailors to participate in the Admiral's Cup: a typical fleet will have half a dozen Olympic medal winners, as well as America's Cup skippers and sailors, among the crews. The yachts are usually owned by wealthy individuals. Others are sponsored by companies who name the yacht and display a limited amount of advertising. The key crew members on each yacht are either professional racing sailors paid by the owner or sponsor, or professionals in the yachting industry (such as sail makers) loaned to the yacht by their companies.

A NEW FORMAT FOR THE CUP

All the inshore races are held in the Solent, keeping the racing close to the base at Cowes. The offshore races consist of a middle-distance race over the middle weekend of the event and the new replacement for the Fastnet, the Wolf Rock Race, which is the final and sternest test, the objective being to feature a race of between 48 and 72 hours. The Wolf Rock itself is situated off the Isles of Scilly off Land's End, the south-westernmost tip of Great Britain, and the full course takes the boats along the English south coast and back to Cowes by way of a series of

Left THE IRISH YACHT *JAMESON II* IN THE SOLENT FOR THE ADMIRAL'S CUP IN 1995. THE EVENT WAS WON BY THE ITALIAN TEAM OUT OF A TOTAL OF EIGHT NATIONALITY ENTRIES.

Above DURING THE 1999 EVENT, *JEANTEX* AND ITS GERMAN CREW, IN THE MUMM 36 CLASS, IN A TIGHT MARK-ROUNDING WITH THE VICTORIOUS DUTCH TEAM ON *MEAN MACHINE* ACROSS THEIR BOWS.

turning marks in mid-Channel. Like the Fastnet, however, the Wolf is a stern and classic test of offshore sailing and includes many of the great obstacles of the former race.

The Wolf Rock Race starts and finishes at the Royal Yacht Squadron line in Cowes, again keeping the event at one venue and saving teams, supporters and press from being forced to decamp and re-establish themselves in Plymouth, as used to be necessary in the old Fastnet Race.

In the evolving story of this great series, many variations on the theme of start and finish points have been tried. In the early days of the competition, Cowes was the natural starting and stopping point for the Channel offshore race. In intervening years, finishing points outside the Solent became fashionable. A welcome move to revert to a Cowes finish does, however, find purists fretting that finishing a long offshore race back in the Solent, with its fickle breeze and rushing tidal streams, can unfairly distort the pattern of the race. Boats tend to anchor up at the entrance, waiting for a change in the current (although yachts do return to the Solent through its wider eastern entrance, where the currents run less fiercely than in the western arm; in the latter, Hurst Narrows, particularly, can produce conditions similar to a sluice gate).

Today's Cowes finish for the Admiral's Cup English Channel offshore race, as well as the long offshore race (Wolf Rock), succeeds in bringing the racing course full circle.

Above BRITISH ENTRY *ARBITRATOR* LEADS THE FLEET IN THE S40 CLASS IN THE EARLY PART OF THE 1999 SERIES. THE BOAT HAD A BAD FINAL RACE AFTER AN EXCELLENT START TO THE ADMIRAL'S CUP.

Left SINCE THE ROYAL SHIP *BRITTANNIA* WAS DECOMMISSIONED, IT NO LONGER PROVIDES A DOMINATING PRESENCE AT COWES WEEK CELEBRATIONS AS IT ONCE DID FOR MANY YEARS.

AMERICA'S CUP

THE AMERICA'S CUP WAS ORIGINALLY DESIGNED by London jeweller Robert Garrard in 1848 as a stock item. The cup was purchased by the first Marquess of Anglesey, who presented it as a racing trophy to the Royal Yacht Squadron based in Cowes, on the north shore of the Isle of Wight, lying off the south of England. Here it first became known as the 100 Guinea Cup, before it took on the name of the America's Cup.

In 1851, the new trophy was put up for a contest between the US schooner *America* and a fleet of Royal Yacht Squadron boats, which were to race around the Isle of Wight. The purpose of this sailing exhibition was to celebrate Britain's supremacy at the height of the Victorian era. British naval power – the notion of Britannia ruling the waves – lay at the heart of British self-confidence, and it was this challenge to a country's national pride that provoked America into taking them on.

The *America* had been commissioned by a syndicate of wealthy New Yorkers, led by John C Stevens, commodore and founder of the New York Yacht Club (NYYC). They were determined to demonstrate that American yachts and skippers were a match for the British.

The Earl of Wilton, commodore of the Royal Yacht Squadron, on hearing of the project formally invited Stevens to bring the New York syndicate's vessel to Cowes. In his letter of acceptance, Stevens, adopting a ploy of psychological warfare, promised he would 'take with good grace the sound thrashing we are likely to get by venturing our longshore craft on your rough waters'. Stevens' aim was to flatter the British and so build a sense of false security; he had no intention of losing.

Although *America*'s good looks and flat sails drew admiration, before having even left the USA she had not, in fact, fulfilled the design brief – to be the 'fastest yacht afloat'. Pitted against Stevens' personally owned yacht, *Maria*, a 33m (110ft) centreboard sloop, the *America* was outsailed.

After arriving in France, the *America* set off across the English Channel to the UK. As she closed the English coast, she was met by the cutter *Laverock*, one of the newest and fastest boats in UK waters. Under the watchful gaze of the British yachting elite – and to their great consternation – *America* sailed past *Laverock* with ease.

The result was that nobody would take on any of the challenges Stevens posted on the Royal Yacht Squadron's noticeboard, until *The Times*, outraged at the cowardice of British yachting circles, wrote a stinging editorial. Thoroughly provoked, the British accepted the challenge to race *America* around the Isle of Wight for the inaugural 100 Guinea Cup.

Sixteen yachts competed and, although they ranged in type and size (from 47 to 392 tons), no handicaps applied. In those days, yacht races began with all the competitors anchored and the sails down. *America* was slow to get away but eventually set off in pursuit of her UK rivals.

Because the race instructions were not absolutely clear, *America* sailed a shorter course than the British boats, having cut inside the Nab lighthouse, while the others sailed the longer, outside, route. Several

Top to bottom *STARS & STRIPES* VS TEAM NEW ZEALAND IN THE 1988 AMERICA'S CUP; A PAINTING OF THE SCHOONER *AMERICA*, WHICH TOOK ON THE ROYAL YACHT SQUADRON IN 1851; 'SEWERMAN' ON *WHITE CRUSADER* IN THE 1987 EVENT; TEAM NEW ZEALAND, VICTORIOUS IN 1995.

Opposite THE ADVANTAGE OF SIGNIFICANT SPEED AND EXCELLENT BOAT HANDLING BY TEAM NEW ZEALAND IN THE 2000 RACE RESULTED IN A ONE-SIDED FINAL WITH A 5–0 VICTORY OVER THE ITALIAN TEAM ON *PRADA*.

NZL-60
NZL-60
Telecom
NEW ZEALAND
Steinlager
TOYOTA
ONE
LOTTO
ITA 45
ITA 45
PRADA
PRADA

of the best UK entries put themselves out of the race – one by running aground, another by making itself available for the rescue operation. A further two contenders collided with each other.

As history records, *America* was the first home. Legend has it that Queen Victoria, who had watched proceedings from the royal yacht, was dismayed at the result and, hoping for some consolation, enquired who was second. To which came the famous reply, 'Your Majesty, there *is* no second'. Interestingly enough, *Aurora*, the smallest boat in the fleet, was second across the line, eight minutes behind *America*. Had handicaps applied, *Aurora* would have thoroughly beaten the schooner.

The trophy took up residence at the NYYC, taking on the name of the winning schooner and ultimately occupying place of honour in a specially designed circular room just off the main lobby of the club's impressive headquarters in downtown Manhattan. It was to remain there for 132 years, as the club successfully withstood 25 challenges from all around the world.

Most persistent of the challengers was Irish tea baron, Sir Thomas Lipton who, between 1899 and 1930, mounted five successive challenges, and was busy planning his sixth when he died in 1931. Lipton had become enormously popular in the USA during this time and cannily used his America's Cup campaigns to advertise his tea, sales of which soared in that country. His last challenge, at the age of 80, was beaten in 1931 by Harold Vanderbilt (46 at the time), a member of the wealthy US family.

For being among the most tenacious challengers, Frenchman Baron Marcel Bich would have to be the rightful successor to Lipton. Creator of the disposable ballpoint pen and razor, he eventually invested more than US$10 million (which in the 1970s was quite a sum) to finance the building of four boats for his four separate challenges. Always playing very carefully by the rules, he only ever used 'national' equipment onboard; he helmed the boats himself, sometimes assisted by the likes of Eric Tabarly and other talented French sailors of that time. It was his foresight that brought a wider international interest to the America's Cup, and created the necessity for a challenger elimination series, which was the forerunner of the Louis Vuitton Cup.

THE CRUSHING DEFEAT OF 1983

Ultimately, of course, it was inevitable that the NYYC would be defeated. In 1983, seven yacht clubs from five different countries presented simultaneous challenges for the America's Cup. (At this point, regulations determining boat class for the race had been revised: from J Class to the 12 Metre Class.) Because of the number of challengers, it was necessary to organize, for the first time, a selection series to decide which one of the seven would go forward. French design house, Louis Vuitton, decided to link its name officially with this challenge, becoming in the process co-organizer of the elimination series. The honour of racing the America's Cup-holder thus fell to the winner of the Louis Vuitton Cup. The format for the latter contest includes three round robin elimination series, a semi-final elimination series and a final match.

It was Australian magnate Alan Bond's radical new white boat *Australia II* and the royal-blue and gold *Victory '83*, from the UK, that eventually went forward to the Louis Vuitton Cup final. Throughout the action of the exciting race, there were plenty of off-the-water allegations and much questioning of the legitimacy of 'something' apparently being hidden every night behind a tarpaulin on the Australian boat. The mysterious 'something' was a breakthrough 'winged' keel design, and the Louis Vuitton elimination series had allowed the Australians to fine-tune and optimize their boat against some real competition. It also succeeded in distracting the Americans from their own preparation for the defence of the America's Cup.

Above left *LIBERTY* LEADS *COURAGEOUS* IN 1983, DURING THE ROUND ROBIN ELIMINATION EVENTS OF THE LOUIS VUITTON CUP, IN WHICH A CHALLENGER FOR THE AMERICA'S CUP IS ESTABLISHED.

Above right *AUSTRALIA II* WITH ITS SECRET 'WEAPON' – AN INNOVATIVE WINGED KEEL – AND WORLD-CLASS SKIPPER JOHN BERTRAND WINS THE CHALLENGER TITLE FOR THE AMERICA'S CUP IN 1983.

Opposite IT WAS AN UNPRECEDENTED VICTORY WHEN *AUSTRALIA II* WRESTED THE AMERICA'S CUP FROM THE US TEAM, DISLODGING IT FROM ITS 132-YEAR-OLD HOME AT THE NEW YORK YACHT CLUB.

Australia II beat *Victory '83* to win the Louis Vuitton Cup and went on to line up against the USA's *Liberty*. Alan Bond had arrived in Newport, Rhode Island, for his fourth attempt at the cup, and was wielding a golden spanner which he swore he would use to unbolt the America's Cup from its perch of honour in the NYYC.

During the customary America's Cup battle to log up wins in the best of seven races, *Australia II*, skippered by John Bertrand, flashed its revolutionary winged keel, while off-the-water public relations turned complicated and nasty as Bond outmanoeuvred every attempt by the NYYC to outlaw his keel – winning the battle hands down. On the water, it was more of a struggle. Up against the consummate modern America's Cup skipper, Dennis Conner, the Australians looked unlikely victors when the score for races won reached 3–1 in the NYYC's favour. *Australia II* was demonstrating superior speed, but didn't look strong enough to stay intact and finish the course. With gear failure causing the yacht to slip to its 3–1 down position, it now needed to win every race to stay in the running; one more win to Conner and the cup would be safe from Bond's golden spanner. Unbelievably – from a seemingly impossible situation – *Australia II* fought its way out of the corner, winning the next three races to beat the Americans, thus ending their 132-year winning streak – the longest one in sporting history.

In accordance with protocol, the America's Cup itself and the organization of the event were handed to the Royal Perth Yacht Club, for the first time turning the defenders into challengers. It made world news.

The Louis Vuitton Cup and the Australian victory had the double effect of globalizing the America's Cup race and mobilizing challengers from an even larger number of countries for the next event – which had become an international race against technology.

AMERICA WINS BACK THE CUP

In the next event, held three years later in 1986, an unprecedented 13 challengers arrived in Fremantle, Perth, in Western Australia, determined to take the cup away from its new residence in the Royal Perth Yacht Club. Alan Bond, notching up his fifth America's Cup campaign to match Sir Thomas Lipton's record, lost in the defender elimination contest. Dennis Conner, the loser of the last cup, represented San Diego Yacht Club and won the Louis Vuitton Cup against New Zealand's *Kiwi Magic*, setting the stage for a great comeback.

The series that took place in Fremantle was probably the most spectacular of all to watch as the 12 Metre Class yachts crashed and burned through the heavy winds and great Indian Ocean seas that pile up on Australia's western coastline. Endless sun, powerful winds, rough seas and white water lent a new visual appeal to what had been, up till now, a rather sedate event. It was televised, taking on a whole new dimension as a spectator sport.

Dennis Conner's *Stars & Stripes*, perfectly honed after four months of seemingly endless duels against the other challengers, was more than a match for the Australian defender, *Kookaburra III*. The USA succeeded in wresting the America's Cup back from Australia with an emphatic 4–0 score. After only four years, the cup had been reclaimed.

San Diego Yacht Club held the trophy for eight years, successfully defending it twice. It faced its first challenge only a year after the Fremantle victory, when New Zealand's Sir Michael Fay lodged his *Big Boat* challenge in 1988. This surprise invitation from the large

Left *STARS & STRIPES* LEADS *KIWI MAGIC* IN THE 1987 LOUIS VUITTON CUP. WINNING US SKIPPER, DENNIS CONNER, WENT ON TO REDEEM HIMSELF BY TAKING BACK THE AMERICA'S CUP FROM AUSTRALIA.

Above CONNER'S CREW ON *STARS & STRIPES* – THE US SKIPPER HAS SAILED IN SEVEN AMERICA'S CUP CHALLENGES AND WON FOUR OF THEM (IN 1974, 1980, 1987 AND 1988).

monohull was met controversially by Dennis Conner's catamaran *Stars & Stripes* – an obvious mismatch which fuelled a case that was dragged through an endless succession of court battles. Finally, the courts concluded the arguments with a ruling that San Diego should retain the cup.

Out of that inglorious episode, a new class of yachts was introduced to replace the 12 Metres, used since World War II. The International America's Cup Class (IACC) yacht, still in use today, first contested the cup in 1992, when billionaire Bill Koch's *America*^{3}, sailing for the San Diego Yacht Club, defeated *Il Moro di Venezia*, financed by Italian billionaire Raul Gardini and his US$150 million syndicate.

Above COMPETING AGAINST NEW ZEALAND IN 1988, DENNIS CONNER'S CATAMARAN ENTRY *STARS & STRIPES* – AN OBVIOUS MISMATCH FOR THE CONTENDING MONOHULL *BIG BOAT* – CAUSED A FURORE.

The race in 1995, in San Diego, witnessed a return of most of the players from 1992, but there was one syndicate that stood out early on: Team New Zealand and their black boat (which matched the colour of the first boat to challenge the cup back in 1851 – the US schooner *America*) looked undeniably impressive. New Zealander Russell Coutts steered his team through the four round robins, semi-finals and final, dropping just one race to an opponent, and taking the Louis Vuitton Cup in style. The world – and the entire population of New Zealand – braced themselves for the next move. Team New Zealand went on to dish out one of the most humiliating defeats the America's Cup has ever encountered.

Massive street parades and a national outpouring of joy greeted team leader Sir Peter Blake, Russell Coutts and their crewmates as they brought the cup home to New Zealand. The smallest nation ever to engage in the America's Cup saga had brought home the laurels. The Royal New Zealand Yacht Squadron thus became the fourth custodian of the cup.

Left USA AND NEW ZEALAND FIGHT IT OUT IN THE 1995 AMERICA'S CUP. NEW ZEALAND'S RELENTLESS ATTACK IN THE PRECEDING LOUIS VUITTON SERIES GAVE THEM THE CONFIDENCE TO WIN THE CUP 5–O.

In March 1997, another dramatic episode left its dent – literally – on the cup. Benjamin Piri Nathan entered the Squadron premises and attacked the trophy with a sledge-hammer, severely damaging it. Nathan, who had a record of criminal offences, claimed his act was politically motivated, but he was subsequently convicted and imprisoned. Instantly, news of the attack travelled around the world. Amongst the many calls expressing outrage and sympathy to the Royal New Zealand Yacht Squadron was an offer from the UK jeweller, Garrard, who had created the silver trophy back in 1848, to restore the cup free of charge. For the next three months, silversmiths from Garrard devoted all their skills to the delicate task of restoring the prized trophy (had it been a car, the cup would have been declared a write-off).

When it was ready and being returned to New Zealand by air, perched on its own seat in First Class, the managing director of Garrard, Richard Jarvis, explained simply why his firm had undertaken such a massive task at no charge:

'The reason is really quite straightforward. It's the America's Cup.'

In 1999, 18 challengers from 10 nations battled for the honour of taking on New Zealand for the America's Cup in Auckland. Australia, the UK, France (three boats), Hong Kong, Italy, Russia, Japan, Spain, and Switzerland (two boats) joined the six challengers from the USA to compete for the Louis Vuitton Cup.

It was the seventh Cup – an all-time high – for Dennis Conner, representing San Diego's Cortez Racing Association (at the time he was, however, the only American to have lost the cup: once in 1983 and again in 1995).

Sir Peter Blake, Team New Zealand's steadfast leader, has a long and proven track record. His dominating win in the 1989/90 Whitbread Round the World Race and demolition of the Jules Verne Trophy record (around the world, nonstop) in 1994 were an accomplishment that many Kiwi sailors aspired towards. And his team

Top, left to right A CLOSE RUN BETWEEN THE USA'S *AMERICA ONE* AND JAPAN'S *ASURA* IN THE 1999 LOUIS VUITTON CUP. THE FORMER'S VICTORY SAW HER UP AGAINST *PRADA* IN THE FINAL.

Left AN ELATED TEAM NEW ZEALAND PREPARE TO RECEIVE THE AMERICA'S CUP IN 2000. FOR THE FIRST TIME IN HISTORY, THEY HAVE HELD ON TO THE CUP FOR TWO CONSECUTIVE YEARS.

included Russell Coutts, the world's most talented helmsman. It was the first time in the history of the event, however, that America did not make it to the final. It was Italy's *Prada* that claimed the 2000 Louis Vuitton Cup and the honour of taking on New Zealand – and a highly professional 5–0 win by *Team New Zealand* allowed the jubilant crew to maintain control of the prestigious America's Cup.

Above *BRAVO* AND *6IEME SENS* COMPETING IN THE 1999 CUP.

Right *STARS & STRIPES* TAKES THE LEAD AGAINST SAN FRANCISCO YACHT CLUB'S *AMERICA TRUE* IN THE 1999 LOUIS VUITTON CUP.

HISTORICAL RACE RESULTS

Here, race results are listed according to the availability of historical race records and, in some cases, only the results most relevant to the text have been extracted. In most races, there are various classes as well as handicaps that apply; by not acknowledging the winners in every category, we are in effect committing an injustice to the spirit of racing. However, space limitations and relevance to the content of the book have both played a role in our following summary of yacht race results.

FASTNET (Handicap)

Year	Boat	Owner
1925	*Jolie Brise*	E G Martin
1926	*Ilex*	Royal Engineer Yacht Club
1927	*Talley Ho!*	Lord Stalbridge
1928	*Nina*	P Hammond
1929	*Jolie Brise*	R Somerset
1930	*Jolie Brise*	R Somerset
1931	*Dorade*	R Stephens Senior
1933	*Dorade*	R Stephens Senior
1935	*Stormy Weather*	P Le Boutillier
1937	*Zeearend*	Kees Bruynzeel
1939	*Bloodhound*	I Bell
1947	*Myth of Malham*	John H Illingworth
1949	*Myth of Malham*	John H Illingworth
1951	*Yeoman III*	O A Aisher
1953	*Favona*	Sir M Newton
1955	*Carina II*	R Nye
1957	*Carina II*	R Nye
1959	*Anitra*	S Hansen
1961	*Zwerver*	W N H van der Vorm
1963	*Clarion of Wight*	D Boyer and D Miller
1965	*Rabbit*	R E Carter
1967	*Pen Duick III*	Eric Tabarly
1969	*Red Rooster*	R E Carter
1971	*Ragamuffin*	S Fischer
1973	*Saga*	E Lorentzen
1975	*Golden Delicious*	P Nicholson
1977	*Imp*	D Allen
1979	*Tenacious*	Ted Turner
1981	*Mordicus*	Taylor and Volterys
1983	*Condor*	R A Bell
1985	*Panda*	P T Whipp
▲ 1987	*Juno*	M Peacock
1989	(IMS) *Diane*	R Schwartz
	(IOR) *Great News*	R Short, Jones, Forbes
1991	(IMS) *Iona*	N Brown
	(IOR) *Passage*	G Isett
1993	(IMS) *Encore*	Jim Dolan
	(IOR) *Indulgence*	G Walker
1995	(IMS) *Nicorette*	Ludde Ingvall
	(IOR) *Nicorette*	Ludde Ingvall
1997	(IMS) *Morning Glory*	Hasso Plattner
	(IOR) *Royal Blue*	G Ekdahl
1999	*Whirlpool-Europe 2*	C Chabaud

▲ From 1987 onwards, IMS and IOR handicap winners were introduced

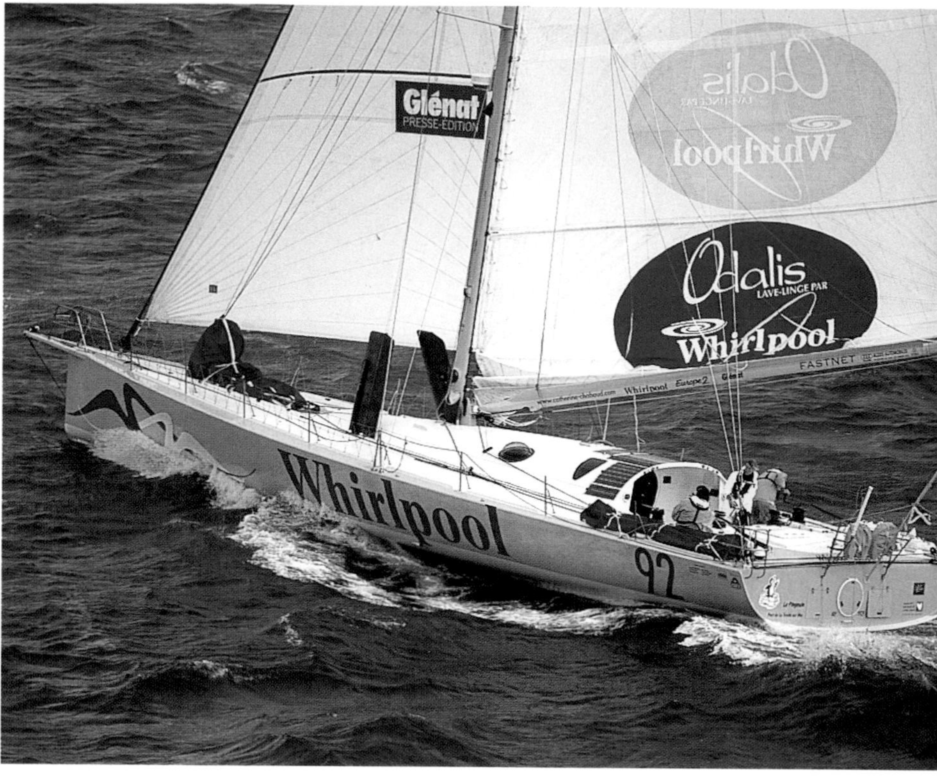

Above WHIRLPOOL, A STATE-OF-THE-ART 18M (60FT) YACHT DESIGNED FOR SINGLE-HANDED SAILING, WAS THE WINNER OF THE 1999 FASTNET RACE.

TOUR DE FRANCE À LA VOILE (Line honours)

Year	Boat	Skipper
1978	*Marseille*	François Pailoux
1979	*Dunkerque*	Joe Setten
1980	*Dunkerque*	Damien Savatier
1981	*Dunkerque*	Damien Savatier
1982	*Marseille*	Jean-Paul Mouren
1983	*Lanveoc-Navale*	Benoït Caignaert
1984	*Europe*	Philippe Hannin (Belgium) & Dominique d'Andrimont
1985	*Côtes du Nord*	Yannick du Petit
1986	*Le Havre*	Benoït Caignaert
1987	*Sète-Languedoc-Roussillon*	Pierre Mas & Bertrand Pace
1988	*Sète-Languedoc-Roussillon*	Pierre Mas & Bertrand Pace
1989	*Ronuc-Saône-et-Loire*	Richard Sautieux
1990	*Wasquehal*	Hans Boulsholte (Netherlands) & Philippe Delhumeau
1991	*La Ciotat*	Laurent Delage
1992	*Sodifac-Roubaix*	Jimmy Pahun
1993	*Saint Quentin-en-Yvelines*	Thierry Peponnet
1994	*Saint Pierre-et-Miquelon*	Alain Fedensieu
1995	*Baume et Mercier-EDC-Mauguio-Carnon*	Bernard Mallaret
1996	*E LeClerc-Région Scaso*	Paul Cayard & Vincent Fertin & Sébastien Destremeau
1997	*CSC-Sun-Microsystems*	Bertrand Pace & Philippe Guigne
1998	*Nantes & St Nazaire-Bouygues Telecom*	Luc Pillot
1999	*Kateie*	Luc De Wulf (Belgium)

Note: All entries French unless otherwise indicated

KEY: IOR = International Offshore Rules | IMS = International Measurement System | * denotes current race record

SYDNEY–HOBART (Line honours & handicap)

Year	Boat	Elapsed time	Handicap
1945	*Rani*, UK	6 days 14hrs 22mins	*Rani*, UK
1946	*Morna*, NSW	5 days 2 hrs 53 mins 33 secs	*Christina*, NSW
1947	*Morna*, NSW	5 days 3 hrs 3 mins 54 secs	*Westward*, TA
1948	*Morna*, NSW	4 days 5 hrs 1 min 21 secs	*Westward*, TA
1949	*Waltzing Matilda*, NSW	10 days 33 hrs 10 mins	*Tradewinds*, NSW
1950	*Margaret Rintoul*, NSW	5 days 28 hrs 35 mins	*Nerida*, SA
1951	*Margaret Rintoul*, NSW	4 days 2 hrs 29 mins 1 sec	*Struen Marie*, NSW
1952	*Nocturne*, NSW	6 days 2 hrs 34 mins 47 secs	*Ingrid*, NSW
1953	*Solveig*, NSW	5 days 7 hrs 12 mins 50 secs	*Ripple*, NSW
1954	*Kurrewa IV*, NSW	5 days 6 hrs 9 mins 47 secs	*Solveig*, NSW
1955	*Even*, NSW	4 days 18 hrs 13 mins 14 secs	*Moonbi*, NSW
1956	*Kurrewa IV*, NSW	4 days 4 hrs 31 mins 44 secs	*Solo*, NSW
1957	*Kurrewa IV*, NSW	3 days 18 hrs 30 mins 39 secs	*Anitra V*, NSW
1958	*Solo*, NSW	5 days 2 hrs 32 mins 52 secs	*Siandra*, NSW
1959	*Solo*, NSW	4 days 13 hrs 33 mins 12 secs	*Cherana*, NSW
1960	*Kurrewa IV*, NSW	4 days 8 hrs 11 mins 15 secs	*Siandra*, NSW
1961	*Astor*, NSW	4 days 4 hrs 42 mins 11 secs	*Rival*, NSW
1962	*Ondine*, USA	3 days 3 hrs 49 mins 16 days	*Solo*, NSW
1963	*Astor*, NSW	4 days 10 hrs 53 mins	*Freya*, NSW
1964	*Astor*, NSW	3 days 20 hrs 5 mins 5 secs	*Freya*, NSW
1965	*Stormvogel*, South Africa	3 days 20 hrs 30 mins 9 secs	*Freya*, NSW
1966	*Fidelis*, New Zealand	4 days 8 hrs 39 mins 43 secs	*Cadence*, NSW
1967	*Pen Duick III*, France	4 days 4 hrs 10 mins 31 secs	*Rainbow II*, New Zealand
1968	*Ondine II*, USA	4 days 30 hrs 20 mins 2 secs	*Koomooloo*, NSW
1969	*Crusade*, UK	3 days 15 hrs 7 mins 4 secs	*Morning Cloud*, UK
1970	*Buccaneer*, New Zealand	3 days 14 hrs 6 mins 12 secs	*Pacha*, NSW
1971	*Kialoa*, USA	3 days 12 hrs 46 mins 21 secs	*Pathfinder*, New Zealand
1972	*American Eagle*, USA	3 days 4 hrs 42 mins 39 secs	*American Eagle*, USA
1973	*Helsal*, NSW	3 days 1 hr 32 mins 9 secs	*Ceil III*, Hong Kong
1974	*Ondine III*, USA	3 days 13 hrs 51 mins 56 secs	*Love & War*, NSW
1975	*Kialoa*, USA	2 days 14 hrs 36 mins 56 secs	*Rampage*, WA
1976	*Ballyhoo*, NSW	3 days 7 hrs 59 mins 26 secs	*Piccolo*, NSW
1977	*Kialoa II*, USA	3 days 10 hrs 14 mins 9 secs	*Kialoa*, USA
1978	*Apollo*, NSW	4 days 2 hrs 23 mins 24 secs	*Love & War*, NSW
1979	*Bumblebee IV*, NSW	3 days 1 hr 45 mins 52 secs	*Screw Loose*, TA
1980	*New Zealand*, New Zealand	2 days 18 hrs 45 mins 41 secs	*New Zealand*, New Zealand
1981	*Vengeance*, NSW	3 days 22 hrs 30 mins	*Zeus II*, NSW
1982	*Condor*, Bermuda	3 days 59 mins 17 secs	*Scallywag*, NSW
1983	*Condor*, Bermuda	3 days 50 mins 29 secs	*Challenge III*, VA
1984	*New Zealand*, New Zealand	3 days 11 hrs 31 mins 21 secs	*Indian Pacific*, NSW
1985	*Apollo*, NSW	3 days 4 hrs 32 mins 28 secs	*Sagacious*, NSW
1986	*Condor*, Bermuda	2 days 23 hrs 26 mins 25 secs	*Extension*, NSW
1987	*Sovereign*, NSW	2 days 21 hrs 58 mins 8 secs	*Illusion*, NSW
1988	*Ragamuffin*, NSW	3 days 15 hrs 29 mins 7 secs	*Sovereign*, VA
1989	*Drumbeat*, WA	3 days 6 hrs 21 mins 34 secs	*Ultimate Challenge*, VA
1990	▲ *Ragamuffin*, NSW	2 days 21 hrs 5 mins 33 secs	*Sagacious V*, NSW
1991	• *Brindabella*, ACT	3 days 1 hr 14 mins 9 secs	(IOR) *Atara*, Ireland (IMS) *She's Apples II*, NSW
1992	• *New Zealand Endeavour*, NZ	2 days 19 hrs 19 mins 18 secs	(IOR) *Ragamuffin*, NSW (IMS) *Assassin*, NSW
1993	• *Ninety Seven*, NSW	4 days 54 mins 11 secs	(IMS) *Micropay Cuckoos Nest*, NSW (IOR) *Solbourne Wild Oats*, NSW
1994	*Tasmania*, TA	2 days 16 hrs 48 mins 4 secs	(IMS) *Raptor*, Germany
1995	*Sayonara*, VA	3 days 53 mins 53 secs	(IMS) *Terra Firma*, VA
1996	*Morning Glory*, Germany	2 days 14 hrs 7 mins 10 secs	(IMS) *Ausmaid*, VA
1997	*Brindabella*, NSW	2 days 23 hrs 37 mins 12 secs	(IMS) *Beau Geste*, Hong Kong
1998	*Sayonara*, USA	2 days 19 hrs 3 mins 32 secs	(IMS) *AFR Midnight Rambler*, Australia
1999	* *Nokia*, Australia/Denmark	1 day 19 hrs 48 mins 2 secs	(IMS) *Yendys*, Hong Kong

▲ *In 1990 the yacht* Rothmans, *from the UK, recorded the fastest elapsed time (since* Kialoa's *record in 1975), but she was penalized for breaching Rule 26 (advertising).*

• *In 1991, 1992 and 1993, two overall handicap winners (IOR/IMS) were declared during the transition from IOR to IMS. Since 1994, only one overall winner has been declared, calculated under the IMS rule.*

Above WELL-KNOWN AUSTRALIAN CONTENDER *WILD THING* WAS THE THIRD BOAT TO HEAD OUT THROUGH SYDNEY HEADS DURING THE DISASTROUS 1998 SYDNEY–HOBART RACE.

Below *BRINDABELLA* FEATURES REGULARLY ON THE AUSTRALIAN YACHT RACING CIRCUIT. HERE, THE CREW MEMBERS ARE BOUNCING THE SPINNAKER HALYARD IN ORDER TO RAISE HER SPINNAKER – SHE CAME IN SECOND OVERALL IN THE SYDNEY–HOBART RACE OF 1998.

CHICAGO–MACKINAC (Mackinac cup handicap winners)

Year	Boat	Owner	Year	Boat	Owner
1898	*Vanenna*	W R Crawford	1953	*Fleetwood*	N J Geib
1899–1903	not contested		1954	*Taltohna*	Edgar B Tolman
1904	*Vencedor*	Fred Price	1955	*Rangoon*	Silberman–Stern
1905	*Mistral*	D Lawrence	1956	*Copperhead*	C L Kotovic
1906	*Vanadis*	G S Steere	1957	*Meteor III*	Henry Burkard
1907	*Vencedor*	G Tramel	1958	*DYNA*	Clayton Ewing
1908	*Valmore*	W H Thompson	1959	*Feather II*	William G Peacock Jr
1909	*Valmore*	W H Thompson	1960	*Freebooter*	Pohn-Pohn
1910	*Valmore*	W H Thompson	1961	*Blue Horizon*	Dick Kaup
1911	*Mavourneen*	E M Mills, Otto C Schoenwerk	1962	*Flame*	James E Doane
1912	*Polaris*	J O Heyworth			
1913	*Olympian*	J O Heyworth	1963	*Meteor III*	Henry Burkard
1914	*Olympian*	Snite & Barcal	1964	*X-Barb*	Dr David Axelrod
1915	*Leda*	G B Currier	1965	*Blitzen*	Schoendorf brothers
1916	*Intrepid*	Snite & Barcal	1966	*Blitzen*	Schoendorf brothers
1917–1920	not contested due to World War I		1967	*Flying Buffalo*	M Declercq & K Ness
1921	*Virginia*	Carlos Alling	1968	*Comanche*	Schoendorf brothers
1922	*Intrepid*	Prather & Farrell	1969	*Flying Buffalo*	M Declercq & K Ness
1923	*Virginia*	J A Hadwiger	1970	*Decision*	D W Howell
1924	*Sari*	B Carpenter	1971	*Endurance*	R H DeRusha
1925	*Virginia*	J A Hadwiger	1972	*Azure*	Lekan & Haagenson
1926	*Intrepid*	Prather & Farrell	1973	*Bay Bea*	Pat Haggerty
1927	*Siren*	Karas	1974	*No Go VII*	Crowley, Siegel
1928	*Comet*	H A Beaumont	1975	*Dora IV*	L A Williams
1929	*Blue Moon*	H T Simmons	1976	*Tortuga*	Creger, Wharton
1930	*Cynthia*	J L Williamson	1977	Mackinac Cup jointly awarded to seven first place winners in seven sections	
1931	*Siren*	Karas brothers	1978	*Scaramouche*	E Kirsch
1932	*Bagheerea*	R P Benedict Jr	1979	*Chocolate Chips*	Lester, Porter
1933	*Siren*	Karas brothers	1980	*Rush*	R K Hicks
1934	*Elizabeth*	L A Williams	1981	*Thunderbird*	Mashke, Erb
1935	*Princess*	Jedzrykowski–Kallgren	1982	*Leading Edge*	Eugene Mondry
1936	*Rubaiyat*	Nathaniel Rubinkam	1983	*Thirsty Tiger*	A G d'Ottavio
1937	*Rubaiyat*	Nathaniel Rubinkam	1984	*Heritage*	Sea Scouts
1938	*Hope*	Herman Karnstedt	1985	*Hilaria*	Robert Stocker
1939	*Gloriant*	A M Herrmann	1986	*Eagle*	Jerome O'Neill
1940	*Bangalore*	Edward Lumbard	1987	*Glider*	J Huff, R Stearns
1941	*Lively Lady*	Otto Dreher	1988	*Jeannine*	Jack Roeser
1942	*White Cloud*	Sorenson	1989	*Insatiable*	Fred Krehbiel
1943	*Gloriant*	Thomas	1990	*Kodiak*	Lloyd Ecclestone Jr
1944	*Bangalore Too*	Lumbard, Kinsey	1991	*Wizo*	Hector J Marchland
1945	*Cara Mia*	L L Karas	1992	*Sensation*	Thomas, Thomas, Chapman
1946	*Blitzen*	Grates, Knapp	1993	*Daybreak*	Robert Chatain Jr
1947	*Cara Mia*	L L Karas	1994	*Windquest*	Richard de Vos
1948	*Taltohna*	E B Tolmon Jr	1995	*Flash Gordon 2*	Helmut Jahn
1949	*Cara Mia*	L L Karas	1996	*Bantu*	Thomas Kuber
1950	*Fleetwood*	Nicholas J Geib	1997	*Wizo*	Willard J Harman
1951	*Gale*	Harry G Nye Jr	1998	*Bacchant*	Jere Sullivan
1952	*Tahuna*	P C McNulty	1999	*Pied Piper*	Richard Jennings

ROUTE DU RHUM (Line honours)

Year	Boat	Skipper	Multihull
1978	*Olympus*	Mike Birch	Trimaran
1982	*Elf Aquitaine*	Marc Pajot	Catamaran
1986	*Fleury Michon*	Philippe Poupon	Trimaran
1990	*Pierre 1er*	Florence Arthaud	Trimaran
1994	*Primagaz*	Laurent Bourgnon	Trimaran
1998	* *Primagaz*	Laurent Bourgnon	Trimaran

Of interest is that an enormous time lapse separates Birch's 1978 record (23 days) and Bourgnon's of 1994 (14 days 6 hrs 28 mins 29 secs)

OSAKA CUP (Line honours)

Year	Entries	Boat	Skipper	Elapsed time
1987	64	*Nakiri Daio*	Warwick Thomson	31 days 19 hrs 6 mins 26 secs
1991	42	*Nakiri Daio*	Ross Fields	28 days 6 hrs 39 mins 10 secs
1995	28	* *Wild Thing*	Grant Wharington	26 days 20 hrs 47 mins 6 secs
1999	20	*Sayernara*	Rob Drury	30 days 3 hrs 39 mins 22 secs

NEWPORT–BERMUDA (Line honours)

Year	Entries	Boat	Elapsed time
1906	3	*Tamberlane*	126 hrs 9 mins
1907	12	*Dervish*	89 hrs
1908	5	*Verona*	100 hrs 19 mins 30 secs
1909	5	*Amorita*	78 hrs 19 mins
1910	2	*Vagrant*	90 hrs 42 mins
1923	22	*Memory*	112 hrs 18 mins 45 secs
1924	14	*Memory*	102 hrs 31 mins 21 secs
1926	16	*Dragoon*	118 hrs 6 mins 45 secs
1928	25	*Rugosa II*	103 hrs 13 mins 48 secs
1930	42	*Yankee Girl II*	98 hrs 29 mins 39 secs
1932	27	*Highland Light*	71 hrs 35 mins 43 secs
1934	29	*Vamarie*	75 hrs 33 mins 32 secs
1936	44	*Vamarie*	114 hrs 50 mins 30 secs
1938	38	*Baruna*	91 hrs 5 mins 42 secs
1946	31	*Baruna*	119 hrs 3 mins 5 secs
1948	36	*Baruna*	87 hrs 9 mins 45 secs
1950	59	*Bolero*	75 hrs 32 mins 9 secs
1952	58	*Royono*	97 hrs 16 mins 28 secs
1954	77	*Bolero*	108 hrs 55 mins 4 secs
1956	89	*Bolero*	70 hrs 11 mins 37 secs
1958	111	*Good News*	102 hrs 23 mins 48 secs
1960	131	*Venturer*	121 hrs 13 mins 12 secs
1962	131	*Northern Light*	80 hrs 46 mins 32 secs
1964	143	*Stormvogel*	92 hrs 10 mins 15 secs
1966	167	*Kialoa II*	105 hrs 2 mins 41 secs
1968	152	*Ondine*	83 hrs 12 mins 35 secs
1970	152	*Windward Passage*	87 hrs 3 mins 47 secs
1972	178	*Robon*	80 hrs 15 mins 15 secs
1974	166	*Ondine*	67 hrs 52 mins 22 secs
1976	150	*Tempest*	88 hrs 16 mins 20 secs
1978	161	*Circus Maximus*	105 hrs 5 mins 46 secs
1980	160	*Bumblebee IV*	70 hrs 7 mins 45 secs
1982	178	*Nirvana*	62 hrs 29 mins 16 secs
1984	115	*Boomerang*	82 hrs 11 mins 50 secs
1986	125	*Condor*	90 hrs 46 mins 47 secs
1988	120	*Congère*	87 hrs 24 mins 8 secs
1990	145	*Boomerang*	87 hrs 20 mins 1 sec
1992	117	*Boomerang*	72 hrs 19 mins 29 secs
1994	149	*Windquest*	72 hrs 15 mins 9 secs
1996	145	* *Boomerang*	57 hrs 31 mins 30 secs
1998	162	*Alexia*	90 hrs 56 mins 16 secs

Above THE CLASS II FLEET START IN 1998 OF THE OFFSHORE CLASSIC, THE NEWPORT–BERMUDA RACE. THIS EVENT TRADITIONALLY ATTRACTS CRUISER RACERS.

COASTAL CLASSIC [AUCKLAND–RUSSELL] (Line honours)

Year	Boat	Skipper	Elapsed time
1982	*Krisis*	Duncan Stuart	18 hrs
1983	*NZ Challenger*	John Mansell	26 hrs 57 mins 35 secs
1984	*Mokihi*	Max Purnell	18 hrs 49 mins 7 secs
1985	*Split Enz*	J Sager, R Dekker, N Strong	17 hrs 6 mins 48 secs
1986	*Bullfrog*	Ian Johnston, Cathy Hawkins	19 hrs 53 mins 6 secs
1987	*Afterburner*	Alastair Russell	12 hrs 39 mins 55 secs
1988	*Afterburner*	Alastair Russell	9 hrs 20 mins 50 secs
1989	*Emotional Rescue*	Graeme Woodroffe	19 hrs 7 mins 26 secs
1990	*Split Enz*	J Sager, R Dekker, J Hughes	18 hrs 20 mins 29 secs
1991	*Future Shock*	Ian Margan	25 hrs 4 mins 58 secs
1992	*Antaeus*	Tony Ruiterman	21 hrs 59 mins 48 secs
1993	*Split Enz*	J Sager, R Dekker, J Hughes	8 hrs 48 mins 31 secs
1994	*Split Enz*	J Sager, R Dekker, J Hughes	19 hrs 17 mins 51 secs
1995	*Afterburner*	Alastair Russell	18 hrs 28 mins 44 secs
1996	* *Split Enz*	J Sager, R Dekker, J Hughes	7 hrs 20 mins 51 secs
1997	*Split Enz*	J Sager, R Dekker, J Hughes	8 hrs 32 mins 33 secs
1998	*Afterburner*	Alastair Russell	7 hrs 56 mins 58 secs
1999	*Afterburner*	Alastair Russell	13 hrs 3 mins 25 secs

SAN FERNANDO (Handicap)

Year	Boat	Owner
1975	*Drogheda*	Barry Bryne
1977	*Drogheda*	Barry Bryne
1979	*Charisma*	Vic Locke
1981	*Gailforce*	Roger Goodlet
1983	*Mandalay*	Nigel Stevens
1985	*Rapid Transit*	Charlie Smith
1987	*Charlie*	Jaron Leet
1989	*Bimblegumbie*	Keith Jacobs
1991	* *Rothmans*	Lawrie Smith
1993	*X-Rated*	Rick & Ingie Strompf
1995	*Bimblegumbie*	Keith Jacobs
1997	*Ffree Fire*	Sam Chan
1999	*Jelik*	Frank Pong

Above *ZEPHYRUS IV* AT THE START OF THE 2000 CAPE TO RIO RACE, SPONSORED BY CELLPHONE NETWORK COMPANY, MTN. *ZEPHYRUS IV* SMASHED THE RECORD SET BY *MORNING GLORY* BY TWO DAYS.

TRANSPACIFIC (LINE HONOURS)

YEAR	ENTRIES	BOAT	OWNER/SKIPPER	ELAPSED TIME
1906	3	*Lurline*	H H Sinclair	12 days 9 hrs 59 mins
1908	4	*Lurline*	H H Sinclair	13 days 21 hrs 31 mins
1910	3	*Hawaii*	syndicate	14 days 3 hrs 23 mins
1912	4	*Lurline*	A E Davis	13 days 17 hrs 3 mins
1923	4	*Mariner*	L A Norris	11 days 14 hrs 46 mins
1926	6	*Invader*	Don M Lee	12 days 2 hrs 48 mins 3 secs
1928	6	*Talayha*	L Lippman	13 days 4 hrs 58 mins 30 secs
1930	4	*Enchantress*	Morgan Adams	12 days 13 hrs 22 mins 52 secs
1932	2	*Fayth*	William S McNutt	14 days 14 hrs 33 mins
1934	12	*Vileehi*	H T Horton	13 days 3 hrs 42 mins 26 secs
1936	22	*Dorade*	James Flood	13 days 7 hrs 20 mins 4 secs
1939	26	*Contender*	Richard R Loynes	14 days 7 hrs 50 mins
1941	7	*Stella Maris II*	Dr A Steele	13 days 21 hrs 3 mins 55 secs
1947	34	*Chubasco*	W L Stewart Jr	12 days 15 hrs 51 mins 18 secs
1949	24	*Morning Star*	Richard S Rheem	10 days 10 hrs 13 mins 9 secs
1951	27	*Morning Star*	Richard S Rheem	10 days 16 hrs 44 mins 33 secs
1953	32	*Goodwill*	R E Larrabee	11 days 2 hrs 17 mins 24 secs
1955	53	*Morning Star*	Richard S Rheem	9 days 15 hrs 5 mins 10 secs*
1957	34	*Barlovento*	Frank Hooykaas	11 days 13 hrs 2 mins 44 secs
1959	41	*Goodwill*	Ralph Larrabee	10 days 12 hrs 16 mins 15 secs
1961	41	*Sirius II*	Howard F Ahmanson	10 days 10 hrs 38 mins 35 secs
1963	32	*Ticonderoga*	Robert Johnson	11 days 16 hrs 46 mins 33 secs
1965	55	*Ticonderoga*	Robert Johnson	9 days 13 hrs 51 mins 2 secs
1967	71	*Stormvogel*	Kees Bruynzeel	11 days 14 hrs 10 mins 56 secs
1969	72	*Blackfin*	Kenneth DeMeuse	9 days 10 hrs 21 mins
1971	69	*Windward Passage*	Mark Johnson	9 days 9 hrs 6 mins 48 secs
1973	60	*Ragtime*	Ragtime Syndicate	10 days 14 hrs 40 secs
1975	65	*Ragtime*	White/Pasquini	9 days 23 hrs 54 mins 51 secs
1977	69	*Merlin*	Bill Lee	8 days 11 hrs 1 min 45 secs
1979	80	*Drifter*	Harry Moloschco	11 days 18 hrs 1 min 4 secs
1981	74	*Merlin*	Nick Frazee	8 days 11 hrs 2 mins 31 secs
1983	66	*Charley*	Nolan K Bushnell	9 days 1 hr 53 mins 48 secs
1985	64	*Swiftsure III*	Nick/Robert Frazee	10 days 19 hrs 21 mins 47 secs
1987	55	*Merlin*	Donn Campion	8 days 12 hrs 40 secs
1989	49	*Silver Bullet*	John DeLaura	8 days 12 hrs 50 mins 35 secs
1991	42	*Chance*	Robert McNulty	9 days 21 hrs 59 mins 35 secs
1993	42	*Silver Bullet*	John DeLaura	9 days 9 hrs 11 mins 17 secs
1995	38	*Cheval 95*	Hal Ward	9 days 1 hr 32 mins 20 secs
1997	38	*Pyewacket II*	Roy Disney	7 days 15 hrs 24 mins 40 secs
1999	34	* *Pyewacket III*	Roy Disney	7 days 11 hrs 41 mins 27 secs

CAPE TO RIO (LINE HONOURS & HANDICAP)

YEAR	BOAT	SKIPPER	ELAPSED TIME
1971	*Ocean Spirit*	Robin Knox-Johnston	23 days 18 hrs 40 mins 47 secs
(Handicap)	*Albatross II*	John Goodwin	
1973	*Stormy*	Kees Bruynzeel	21 days 12 hrs
(Handicap)	*Stormy*	Kees Bruynzeel	
1976	*Ondine*	Huey Long	17 days 5 hrs 35 mins 20 secs
(Handicap)	*Chica Tica*	C di Mottola Balestra	
1993	*Broomstick*	Hanno Teuteberg	15 days 3 hrs 10 mins
(Handicap)	*Morning Glory*	Hasso Plattner	
1996	*Morning Glory*	Hasso Plattner	14 days 14 hrs 52 mins
(Handicap)	*Renfreight*	Norge Kennedy	
2000	* *Zephyrus IV*	Robert McNeil	12 days 16 hrs 49 mins 41 secs
(Handicap)	*Zephyrus IV*	Robert McNeil	

AUCKLAND–FIJI (LINE HONOURS)

YEAR	BOAT	ELAPSED TIME
1956	*Wanderer*	11 days 12 hrs 26 mins
1966	*Roulette*	9 days 12 hrs 50 mins
1969	*Kahurangi*	7 days 14 hrs 51 mins
1973	*Ta'aroa*	5 days 12 hrs 52 mins
1977	*Anticipation*	5 days 23 hrs 39 mins
1979	*Anticipation*	9 days 8 hrs 8 mins
1981	*Ta'aroa*	6 days 17 hrs 50 mins
1983	*Urban Cowboy*	7 days 18 hrs 4 mins
1985	*Urban Cowboy*	5 days 8 hrs 53 mins
1987	*Satellite Spy*	5 days 19 hrs 22 mins
1989	*Future Shock*	4 days 14 hrs 42 mins
1991	*Longfellow*	5 days 16 hrs 58 mins
1993	*Ice Fire*	7 days 22 hrs 21 mins
1995	*Antaeus*	4 days 19 hrs 31 mins
1997	*Hydroflow*	5 days 12 hrs 5 mins 22 secs
1998	* *Antaeus*	4 days 8 hrs 53 mins 14 secs
1999	*Wild Thing*	6 days 17 hrs 26 mins 26 secs

Note: 1956–1995 race start from Fiji; 1997 onwards race start from Denarau

MINI-TRANSAT (Line honours)

Year	Boat	Skipper
1977	*Petit Dauphin*	Daniel Gillard
1979	*American Express*	Norton Smith
1981	*Iles du Ponant*	Jacques Peignon
1983	*Voiles Cudennec*	Stéphane Poughon
1985	*Aquitaine*	Yves Parlier
1987	*Exa*	Gilles Chiorri
1989	*Thom Pouss*	Philippe Vicariot
1991	*GTM Enterprise*	Damien Grimont
1993	*Amnesty International*	Thierry Dubois
1995	*Omapi-Saint Brevin*	Yvan Bourgnon
1997	*Karen Liquid*	Sébastien Magnen
1999	*Voile Magazine Jeanneau*	Sébastien Magnen

VOLVO [WHITBREAD] (Handicap)

Year	Boat	Skipper	Elapsed time
1973/74	*Sayula II*	Ramón Carlín	152 days 9 hrs
1977/78	*Flyer*	Cornelis van Rietschoten	136 days 5 hrs 28 mins 48 secs
1981/82	*Flyer*	Cornelis van Rietschoten	120 days 6 hrs 34 mins 14 secs
1985/86	*L'Esprit d'Equipe*	Lionel Pean	132 days 0 hrs 15 mins 19 secs
1989/90	*Steinlager II*	Peter Blake	128 days 9 hrs 40 mins 30 secs
1993/94	*New Zealand Endeavour*	Grant Dalton	120 days 5 hrs 9 mins 23 secs
1997/98	* *EF Language*	Paul Cayard	117 days 7 hrs 39 mins 1 sec

Note: 1993/94 and 1997/98 results reflect Line Honours

AROUND ALONE [BOC CHALLENGE] (Line honours)

Year	Class 1	Class 2
1982/83	Philippe Jeantot (France)	Yuko Tada (Japan)
1986/87	Philippe Jeantot (France)	Mike Plant (USA)
1991/92	Christophe Auguin (France)	Yves Dupasquier (France)
1994/95	Christophe Auguin (France)	David Adams (Australia)
1998/99	Giovanni Soldini (Italy)	J P Mouligné (Franco-American)

BT CHALLENGE (Line honours)

Year	Boat	Skipper	Elapsed time
1992/93	* *Nuclear Electric*	John Chittenden	151 days 11 hrs 49 mins 11 secs
1996/97	*Group 4 Securitas*	Mike Golding	161 days 5 hrs 25 mins 18 secs

VENDÉE GLOBE CHALLENGE (Line honours)

Year	Boat	Skipper	Elapsed time
1989/90	*Ecureuil d'Aquitaine*	Titouan Lamazou	109 days 8 hrs 48 mins 50 secs
1991/92	*Bagages Superior*	Alain Gautier	110 days
1996/97	* *Géodis*	Christophe Auguin	105 days 20 hrs 31 mins 23 secs

JULES VERNE TROPHY (Fastest elapsed time)

Year	Boat	Skipper	Elapsed time
1993	*Commodore Explorer*	Bruno Peyron, Cam Lewis	79 days 6 hrs 15 mins 56 secs
1994	*Enza New Zealand*	Robin Knox-Johnston, Peter Blake	74 days 22 hrs 17 mins
1997	* *Sport-Elec*	Olivier de Kersauson	71 days 14 hrs 18 mins

Top TEAM ILLBRUCK TRAINING ON BOARD A SECOND-GENERATION WHITBREAD 60 IN PREPARATION FOR THE 2001 VOLVO ROUND THE WORLD RACE.

Centre *RHÔNE-POULENC*, COMPETING IN THE 1993 BT CHALLENGE, BEATS TO WINDWARD THROUGH THE ATLANTIC OCEAN'S ROUGH, ICY SEAS EN ROUTE TO CAPE TOWN DURING LEG THREE OF THE RACE.

Bottom *ENZA* TRAILING WAVES IN THE ENGLISH CHANNEL AS SHE APPROACHES THE FINISH OF THE JULES VERNE TROPHY IN 1994, AFTER AN EPIC ROUND THE WORLD JOURNEY OF UNDER 75 DAYS.

Top THE TEAM OF *PRADA* IN ITS USUAL POSITION – FOLLOWING TEAM NEW ZEALAND – DURING THE FINALS OF THE 2000 AMERICA'S CUP, WHICH WAS RESOUNDINGLY WON BY THE NEW ZEALANDERS.

Centre AN IMAGE REPRESENTING TECHNOLOGY AND YACHT DESIGN BEING PUSHED TO THE LIMIT AS *YOUNG AMERICA* SPLITS IN TWO DURING THE AMERICA'S CUP EVENT OF 2000.

Bottom *VENTURE A COMPETITION* TAKING PART IN THE 1999 ADMIRAL'S CUP – IN THIS TRICKY TACTICAL REGATTA, PRECISE NAVIGATION IS A KEY TO SUCCESS.

AMERICA'S CUP

Year	Winning team	Team defeated
1851	*America* USA	5 British Boats UK
1870	*Magic* USA	*Cambria* UK
1871	*Columbia/Sappho* USA	*Livonia* UK
1876	*Madeline* USA	*Countess of Dufferin* Canada
1881	*Mischief* USA	*Atalanta* Canada
1885	*Puritan* USA	*Genesta* UK
1886	*Mayflower* USA	*Galatea* UK
1887	*Volunteer* USA	*Thistle* Scotland
1893	*Vigilant* USA	*Valkyrie II* UK
1895	*Defender* USA	*Valkyrie III* UK
1899	*Columbia* USA	*Shamrock* UK
1901	*Columbia* USA	*Shamrock II* UK
1903	*Reliance* USA	*Shamrock III* UK
1920	*Resolute* USA	*Shamrock IV* UK
1930	*Enterprise* USA	*Shamrock V* UK
1934	*Rainbow* USA	*Endeavour* UK
1937	*Ranger* USA	*Endeavour II* UK
1958	*Columbia* USA	*Sceptre* UK
1962	*Weatherly* USA	*Gretel* Australia
1964	*Constellation* USA	*Sovereign* Australia
1967	*Intrepid* USA	*Dame Pattie* Australia
1970	*Intrepid* USA	*Gretel II* Australia
1974	*Courageous* USA	*Southern Cross* Australia
1977	*Courageous* USA	*Australia* Australia
1980	*Freedom* USA	*Australia* Australia
1983	*Australia II* Australia	*Liberty* USA
1987	*Stars & Stripes* USA	*Kookaburra II* Australia
1988	*Stars & Stripes* USA	*New Zealand* New Zealand
1992	*America³* USA	*Il Moro di Venezia* Italy
1995	*Team New Zealand* New Zealand	*Stars & Stripes* USA
2000	*Team New Zealand* New Zealand	*Prada-Luna Rossa* Italy

ADMIRAL'S CUP (Best team result based on handicap)

Year	Boats	Country	No. of Nations
1957	*Myth of Malham, Uomie, Jocasta*	UK	2
1959	*Griffin II, Ramod, Myth of Malham*	UK	3
1961	*Windrose, Figaro, Cyane*	USA	5
1963	*Clarion of Wight, Outlaw, Noryema*	UK	6
1965	*Quiver IV, Noryema IV, Firebrand*	UK	8
1967	*Mercedes III, Balandra, Caprice of Huon*	Australia	12
1969	*Red Rooster, Carina, Palawan*	USA	11
1971	*Prospect of Whitby, Morning Cloud, Cervates IV*	UK	17
1973	*Saudade, Rubin, Carina III*	Germany	16
1975	*Noryema X, Yeoman XX, Battlecry*	UK	19
1977	*Moonshine, Yeoman XX, Marionette*	UK	19
1979	*Police Car, Impetuous, Ragamuffin*	Australia	19
1981	*Victory of Burnham, Yeoman XXIII, Dragon*	UK	16
1983	*Sabina, Pinta, Outsider*	Germany	15
1985	*Outsider, Rubin G VIII, Diva*	Germany	18
1987	*Propaganda, Goldcorp, Kiwi*	New Zealand	14
1989	*Jamarella, Juno IV, Indulgence VII*	UK	14
1991	*Corum Saphir, Corum Rubis, Corum Diamant*	France	8
1993	*Pinta, Rubin XII, Container*	Germany	8
1995	*Capricorno, Brava Q8, Mumm a Mia*	Italy	8
1997	*Flash Gordon 3, MK Café, Jameson*	USA	7
1999	*Mean Machine, Trust Computers, Innovision 7*	Netherlands	9

INDEX

Page numbers in italics represent photographs

'I spent New Year's Eve with 200 Aussie sailors.' — WRITTEN ON ISABELLE AUTISSIER'S T-SHIRT AFTER HER NEW YEAR'S RESCUE AT SEA BY THE AUSTRALIAN NAVY IN *1994/95.*

ACKNOWLEDGEMENTS

THE AUTHORS WOULD LIKE to thank the following people for their contributions to this book: Mike Urwin, Kate Langley, Sarah Bustamante and Lindstrom Beatty Communications, Masumi Yamaoka, Dave Foord, Catherine Léourier, Rich Roberts, George Bauer, Rob Sharp, Craig Middleton, Paul Middleton, Tracey Rhodes, Mark Bartlett for all his help on the Auckland–Russell Coastal Classic, Vic Locke and Kelly Gilkison from Royal Hong Kong Yacht Club for information on the San Fernando Race, designer Dudley Dix for his invaluable input on yacht design as well as Guy Ribadeau, Bill Lee and the offices of Farr Yacht Design and Van der Stadt Design for permitting us to reproduce their yacht design-profiles.

The publishers would like to thank Joyce Talbot for her patience, advice and verification of facts on the New Zealand-based races, and Geoff Meek of North Sails for taking the time to appraise our historical race results.

PHOTOGRAPHIC CREDITS

Key: DPPI = Agence DPPI; KOS = KOS Picture Source; SN = Stock Newport; TL = Touchline.

DPPI/Billy Black 132 (centre); **DPPI/Daniel Forster** 150 (bottom), 158 (top and centre); **DPPI/P Garenne** 130 (bottom left); **DPPI/Jean-Marie Liot** 27, 28 (bottom left), 29, 30 (top), 31, 65 (top right); **DPPI/Franco Pace** 18; **DPPI/Benoit Stichelbaut** 69, 73 (right); **DPPI/Henri Thibault** 64, 130 (top right and bottom right); **DPPI/Jacques Vapillon** 70 (top), 115 (top), 122 (centre); **Anthony Steward** 12, 13; **Argus** 88; **Billy Black** endpapers, 43 (bottom left and right), 79 (top), 110 (centre), 114 (bottom left), 160; **Cedric Robertson** 86, 87, 89, 90 (bottom), 91 (bottom), 156; **Christel Clear** 124 (bottom), 142 (bottom); **Garmt de Vries Collection** 130 (top left); **Goss Challenges Ltd** 9; **Ivor Wilkins** 51, 111, 131, 139 (bottom), 140 (top), 144 (bottom); **Jon Nash Photography** 117 (centre and bottom); **Karina Wang** 46 (bottom), 48–49, 49; **KOS** 4–5, 11 (top left), 21 (bottom and centre), 22 (right), 37, 65 (top left and bottom), 106, 107 (top), 109 (right), 116, 118 (bottom), 120, 134 (top), 136–137, 139 (centre), 143 (top), 144 (top and 2nd from bottom), 146, 147, 148, 149 (top), 158 (bottom); **KOS/Carlo Borlenghi** 14 (bottom right), 22 (left), 102, 110 (bottom), 132 (bottom), 135 (top), 140 (bottom), 142 (top); **KOS/Roger Garwood** 35 (bottom); **KOS/Bob Grieser** 60–61; **KOS/ Heinrich Hecht** 149 (bottom); **KOS/Marc Lavaud** 14 (bottom left); **KOS/Gilles Martin-Raget** 11 (top centre), 21 (top), 66 (top, centre, bottom), 67, 123, 127 (left), 151 (bottom left), 158 (bottom), **KOS/Merit Crew** 105 (top row, right); **KOS/G-J Norman** 68, 132 (top); **KOS/Eric North** 24 (top right), 107 (top right); **K Soehata** 81, 82–83, 84, 85; **KOS/Henri Thibault** 26, 30 (bottom); 70 (bottom left), 71 (left), 72–73, 124 (top), 125 (top), 126 (left); **KOS/Jacques Vapillon** cover spine, 114 (bottom centre), 122 (top and bottom), 126 (right), 127 (right); **Mike Hunter** 52, 53 (top and bottom right); **Neil Rusch** 90 (top); **Onne van der Wal** 38, 39, 43 (top left and right), 105 (bottom row, right), 133, 134 (bottom); **Pixie Thomas** 58 (top); **PPL** 10 (top), 14 (top), 24 (top left and bottom), 33, 34 (centre), 35 (top and centre), 42, 83 (top), 144 (2nd from top), 153 (top), 155; **PPL/Jack Alterman** 113 (left); **PPL/Richard Bennett** 34 (bottom left); **PPL/Peter Bentley** 129 (centre), 138; **PPL/Gis Bermuda** 41; **PPL/Chichester Archive** 10 (bottom); **PPL/Peter Danby** 108 (top right); **PPL/Paul Egan** 157 (centre); **PPL/Bob Fisher** full title, 83 (bottom), 107 (bottom left), 141 (top row, centre and centre row [all]); **PPL/Robert D Hagan** 115 (bottom); **PPL/Rob Haine** 121 (bottom left); **PPL/Heath** 117 (top); **PPL/Jono Knight** front cover, 32; **PPL/Jamie Lawson-Johnston** 16–17, 20, 112, 139 (top), 141 (bottom row, right), 143 (bottom); **PPL/Ian Mainsbridge** 34 (right); **PPL/Jon Nash** 6–7, 11 (top right), 70 (bottom right), 98–99, 105 (top row, centre), 121 (top and bottom right); **PPL/Skip Novak** 104 (centre and bottom), 105 (centre row, left and centre); **PPL/Mark Pepper** 63, 79 (centre), 108 (left), 118 (top), 119, 129 (bottom), 157 (bottom); **PPL/Barry Pickthall** 40, 56, 57, 58 (bottom), 59, 62, 104 (top), 107 (centre, top), 141 (top row, left and right, and bottom row, left); **PPL/RAAF** 125 (bottom left); **PPL/Nick Rains** 141 (bottom row, centre); **PPL/Cedric Robertson** 91 (top); **PPL/Pierre Saboulin** 66 (right), 128, 129 (top); **PPL/Philippe Schiller** 103 (top and centre), 105 (bottom row, left); **PPL/Eric Simonson** 135 (bottom); **PPL/Onne van der Wal** 107 (bottom); **PPL/Phil Wade** 105 (centre row, right); **PPL/West Australia** 125 (bottom right); **Roger de la Harpe/Africa Imagery** back cover; **SN** 105 (bottom row, centre); **SN/Carlo Borlenghi** half title, 103 (bottom), 105 (top row, left), 108 (bottom right), 109 (top left and bottom), 113 (right); **SN/Skip Novak** 80, **SN/Onne van der Wal** 110 (top), 114 (top and bottom right); **Terry Fong** 50, 53 (bottom left and centre), 54, 55 (top and centre), 92, 93, 94, 95; **Thierry Martinez** 8–9, 19, 23, 25, 28 (top), 34 (top), 36–37, 71 (right), 96–97, 145, 150–151 (top row), 151 (right), 152, 153 (bottom), 157 (top); **TL** 55 (bottom); **TL/Stephen Munday** 79 (bottom); **Walter Cooper** 44, 45, 46 (top), 47, 48 (top left); **Yoichi Yabe/KAZI** 74, 75, 76, 77, 78.

Philip Zepter
watches
PlayStation
PlayStation